D1369924

THE SCARECROW AUTHOR BIBLIOGRAPHIES

FLOYD DELL:

an annotated bibliography of secondary sources, 1910-1981

by
JUDITH NIERMAN

Scarecrow Author Bibliographies, No. 69

The Scarecrow Press, Inc.
Metuchen, N.J., & London
1984

Library of Congress Cataloging in Publication Data

Nierman, Judith.
   Floyd Dell : an annotated bibliography of secondary
sources, 1910-1981.

   (Scarecrow author bibliographies ; no. 69)
   Includes index.
   1. Dell, Floyd, 1887-1969--Bibliography.
I. Title.   II. Series.
Z8225.15.N54   1984   [PS3507.E49]   016.818'5209   84-13852
ISBN 0-8108-1718-7

This book is dedicated to

ELLIOT, EMILY, BILL

for help material, immaterial, nonmaterial.

CONTENTS

ACKNOWLEDGMENTS

For assistance in my research I wish to thank the following libraries and their staffs: The University Library, the University of California, Berkeley, California; the Library of Congress, Washington, D.C.; the Theodore McKeldin Library, the University of Maryland, College Park, Maryland; the Montgomery County Public Library, Rockville, Maryland; and the Berkeley Public Library, Berkeley, California.

I also wish to recognize the help of numerous libraries in all parts of the country which responded to interlibrary loan requests or to petitions for photocopies. Coming at a critical time, both the encouragement and advice of Dr. Jackson R. Bryer of the University of Maryland were greatly appreciated.

INTRODUCTION

"A valiant gentleness, a robust sensitiveness,
a faun at the barricades!"

With this description Sinclair Lewis characterized Floyd Dell in 1921,
seven months after the publication of his enormously successful first
novel, Moon-Calf (no. 240,* p. 245). The words were apt because they
portrayed the dichotomies in Dell's character. He was a man devoted
to socialism and "the revolution," who could focus his powerful abilities as a conversationalist on the intricacies of socialist theory. At
the same time he was a utopian, an intellectual, a romantic visionary,
a dreamer living in the realms of poetry and ideas. His radical reputation was fueled not only by his adherence to socialism but also by
his rebellion against established mores relating to social and sexual
behavior and to marriage. An iconoclast capable of shocking behavior,
he was at the same time gentle, kind, and deeply interested in matters relating to marriage, family life, love, and children. Dell was
a man who could labor earnestly in editorial positions on the Friday
Literary Review, The New Review, the Masses, the Liberator, and
the New Masses and still author Broadway plays, become a financial
success, and write for Parents' Magazine.

Floyd Dell, the romantic revolutionary, socialist, feminist, journalist, editor, radical, literary critic, novelist, Freudian, playwright,
and spokesman for his generation, was born in Barry, Illinois, on June
18, 1887. He lived in a series of small midwestern towns where his
father eked out a marginal living. The last child of middle-aged parents, the boy was shy and introverted, a habitué of the public library. He began writing poetry and was converted to socialism as
a youth. After high school he worked as a reporter on a newspaper in Davenport, Iowa. Among his friends and supporters were the
local writers George Cram Cook, Susan Glaspell, and Arthur Davison
Ficke.

In 1909, like so many others of his era, Dell left the village
for the opportunities of Chicago. Once in Chicago, he secured employment with the Chicago Evening Post. Although the oft-repeated
anecdote about Dell and another man sharing one job and splitting one
salary is not true (nos. 107 & 256), it serves as a reminder of the
contrast between Dell's unknown and humble status upon his arrival

---

*Numbers in this Introduction refer to items in the Bibliography.

in Chicago and his later position as a central participant in the Chicago Renaissance. After Francis Hackett left the Post, Dell became literary editor of the newspaper's Friday Literary Review section. In this position he established a standard of critical excellence and created a model for literary supplements. Many would have agreed that Dell developed the Friday Literary Review into America's best literary criticism (no. 22). Unabashed in praising new and unconventional work, his enthusiasm for contemporary literature led him to introduce new writers to Chicago. Dell and his first wife, Margery Currey, whom he married while living in Chicago, instituted an informal salon for writers which was frequented by Sherwood Anderson, Theodore Dreiser, Margaret Anderson, and others who later became well known. Margaret Anderson remembered that Margery helped her socially shy husband by relieving "him of all social responsibilities and present[ing] him as an impersonal being whose only function in life was to talk" (no. 637, p. 37). Dell and Currey practiced his radical beliefs on marriage by continuing in individual careers and by maintaining separate residences and lives. At the same time that he was gaining a reputation as a brilliant editor and conversationalist, he also became known as an unconventional, and some say "disagreeable" (no. 305, p. 65), man. The story was told that Dell was once a guest in the home of George Burman Foster, a noted theological scholar at the University of Chicago. Another guest, a painter of sentimental landscapes, gave a fatuous talk on "art." When the artist finished and invited questions, Dell responded politely by inquiring, "'What is the difference between art and apple butter?'" His disrespect established Dell "as rude, insulting, egotistic, unprincipled, and dangerous (no. 305, pp. 66, 68). But, as "The Literary Spotlight" pointed out, "it is probably true that his intention was not so much to shock the bourgeoisie as to let the bourgeoisie know that its ideas profoundly shocked him" (no. 305, p. 68).

Changes in the Post's editorial policy and the failure of his marriage precipitated his move to New York in 1913. There he abandoned the high Byronic collar and black stock he affected in Chicago and instead allowed his proletarian spirit to show in his fireman's and sailor's blue flannel shirt (no. 913, p. 147). He settled in Greenwich Village and became a member of the Liberal Club and an organizing force behind the famed Provincetown Players. The anecdote told by Phyllis Duganne to Edmund Wilson of Dell chasing a laughing Edna St. Vincent Millay out of the Provincetown Playhouse, her long hair flowing, epitomized the gay but serious spirit of the Greenwich Village of the times (no. 1066, p. 56). Into this spirit Dell entered without reservation. He wrote plays for the Liberal Club and the Provincetown Players, organized costume parties, and became managing editor of the Masses, a publication devoted to art and radical socialism. In 1917 he and others associated with the Masses were tried by the federal government for sedition. It was charged that they obstructed recruiting and enlistment in the armed forces of the United States by means of articles and art in the Masses. Dell welcomed the opportunity of expounding his views before the judge and jury. His cross-examination by the prosecutor "had the air of a Socratic dialogue" (no. 929, p. 37). Two trials rallied the artistic and radical community of New York, but did not result in a conviction. Although in April 1917 Dell had written " 'Conscientious objector against this war!' " across his draft card (no. 929, p. 36), he later served honorably, but briefly, in the United States Army.

While living in Greenwich Village, Dell became one of the country's first advocates and popularizers of Freudian psychoanalysis. After undergoing the experience himself with the analyst Dr. Samuel A. Tannenbaum, he resolved deep-seated conflicts in his personality. He was then able to make a strong commitment to a monogamous relationship, and in 1919 he married again. His bride was B. Marie Gage, a socialist and pacificist from California. They were married until his death. He was also able to overcome the inability to complete the novel on which he had been working for a number of years. After analysis he finished Moon-Calf (1920) in a few months. It was published in the same year as Main Street and This Side of Paradise and competed with those two novels for critical attention. Autobiographical and introspective, it remains his best known piece of fiction.

From 1920 to 1934 Dell published eleven novels dealing with his personal development, love, marriage, family life, and feminism. At the same time he was writing important nonfictional works. From his home in Croton-on-Hudson, Dell, during much of this period, was to young people a role model of the literate, urbane, socialistic rebel. Mike Gold (no. 491) and Llewellyn Powys (no. 382) conceded his unique position as teacher. Joseph Freeman cited his "genius for friendship with younger people" (no. 782, p. 247) and went on to say that "in life he was father confessor to dozens of moon-calves to whom he opened his house, gave time and energy, literary and material help, to whom he talked with that profusion of ideas, that wealth of information, that brilliance for which he was famous in the prewar Village." While making his living as a novelist, Dell continued working for the socialist/communist publications the Liberator and the New Masses. A changing emphasis in his personal life together with conflicts with the editors brought about his resignation from the editorial staff of the New Masses in 1929. His departure was particularly bitter. His socialist comrades felt that his novels, his financial success, and his adherence to a monogamous, bourgeois marriage branded him a poseur. V.F. Calverton accused him of giving up his economics for "sex-playboying" in his novels (no. 480). Mike Gold charged that he had become a greedy capitalist in dress suits (no. 623).

After 1929 Dell withdrew from politics and economics and concentrated on writing. In spite of the Depression, he co-authored a second Broadway play, "Cloudy with Showers" (1931). The first, "Little Accident," had been produced in 1928. Although his novels were increasingly less well received, his autobiography, Homecoming (1933), was praised. His career as a creative writer ended with The Golden Spike (1934). In 1935 he became a salaried employee of the Works Progress Administration in the Federal Writers Project and later wrote speeches for John L. Lewis and Eleanor Roosevelt. He retired from government service in 1947 and died at his home in Bethesda, Maryland, on July 23, 1969.

On the eve of the appearance of Moon-Calf Floyd Dell was a familiar figure. According to John Hart, "By the early 1920's Dell was already well-known in intellectual circles not only in Chicago and New York but also in the nation and in Europe. As editor and reviewer he had, in one way or another, come in contact with the leading writers and thinkers of his time" (no. 1030, p. 108). His Chicago repute and the publication in 1913 of the feminist Women as World Builders placed Dell firmly and publicly with the social liberals. His activities as editor of The New Review, the Masses, and the Liberator reinforced his standing as a rebel and a socialist. During the Masses trial, his name became widely known as a socialist and liberal. Though Dell was a familiar personage, it was his radical, not his visionary, utopian nature, which was recognized. His reputation encompassed only the rebellious side of his character.

The varied contemporary critical reception of Moon-Calf was greatly influenced by Dell's existing reputation. Needless to say, liberals were shocked and dismayed that the book was not revolutionary in form and content. It thwarted their expectations of Dell. Writing in the Liberator, Arturo Giovannitti was astounded at the "unbelievable egotism" (no. 137), the personal revelations highly improper for a revolutionary. Instead of socialist dogma and avant-garde form, what they found was the treatment in fiction of the development of Dell's personality from birth to his departure for Chicago. The organizing factor was his relationships with girls and women. Although the novel also treated his conversion to socialism, his activities for the party, and his scorn for bourgeois life and property, the emphasis was on his emerging artistic and moon-calf character, not on the rebellious aspect of his personality.

Other reviewers, less entangled in liberal expectations, bestowed high praise. The novel received lavish commendation from Dell's friend from his Iowa days, Harry Hansen. For him, Moon-Calf was "the clearest and most promising note struck in American literature in our day and generation" (no. 146). Heywood Broun declared, "'Drop whatever you are doing and read Floyd Dell's Moon-Calf. Yes, Main Street can wait'" (no. 123). Fanny Butcher labeled it "impressive" (no. 130). Carl Van Doren said it approached "a classic roundness and grace" (no. 164). The Liberator, trying at last to promote one of its own, called it "one of the permanently fine novels of our period" (no. 283).

Many reviewers considered the specifics of genre, the treatment of sexual matters, and character portrayal. Trying to place

Moon-Calf in a genre resulted in chaos. Some defined it as a work of realism (nos. 105 & 205) or romance (no. 254); others as part of the Midwest literature of revolt (no. 329), and as part of no modern school of writing (no. 129). Commentators expounded on Dell's reticence (no. 125) or frankness (nos. 118 & 168) in sexual matters. Although Heywood Broun found Moon-Calf "perfectly clear and straightforward" (no. 123), efforts to clarify the character portrayal of the hero produced confusion. It was not obvious to every critic that Felix Fay was Dell's persona. H.L. Mencken (no. 247) and Booklist (no. 168) made valid observations when the former noted that Felix was aesthetic, not political, and the latter defined the method of character portrayal as that of "narrated episodes rather than detailed analysis." No critic made a scholarly or penetrating effort to elucidate and comment upon the novel's theme or construction.

The Briary-Bush, Moon-Calf's sequel, appeared late in 1921. This novel was also autobiographical and treated Felix Fay from his arrival in Chicago, through the development of his career and his marriage to Rose-Ann Prentiss, to his reconciliation with his wife. In this book Felix was the idealistic intellectual trying several life-styles and putting into practice his theories about living. The lifestyle that received the majority of authorial attention was the married life. Felix and Rose-Ann lived out their liberal notions, but found that without old-fashioned individual commitment and love they were dissatisfied. The practical reality of their ideas was unhappiness. Felix discovered that his masculine freedom was a state in which he had nothing of value to lose. Again, Dell focused on the moon-calfish, dreaming side of his own character, not on his rebellious nature. Although he wrestled with advanced sociological ideas, he did not dwell on political or economic causative forces.

Like Moon-Calf, The Briary-Bush frustrated those who expected pure revolution from Dell. Dorothea Mann in the Boston Evening Transcript voiced with "special interest" the fact that a man such as Dell would condemn the excessive freedom of modern marriage (no. 243). Still, the novel's critical reception ranged from extravagant praise to disappointment in Dell's performance. Harry Hansen called it "the most important novel of marriage between two persons of literary and artistic impulses that has ever been written in the United States" (no. 235). In contrast, Mary Colum found it "a very feeble performance" (no. 286). Carl Van Doren highly praised The Briary-Bush. "Taken by itself, it seems to me to hover over the dark waters of the unconscious on the surest, lightest wings an American novel has ever used" (no. 297). But John Peale Bishop asserted that it failed because, instead of treating the theme of marriage versus free love with ironic detachment, Dell established "a mood of sentimental reminiscences" (no. 206). There were inevitable comparisons to Moon-Calf. The Briary-Bush was seen as better, displaying a "firmer handling, a more sharply defined purpose, a keener grasp of character" (no. 243). But the New York Times Book Review and Magazine claimed it "rather missed the charm" of its predecessor (no. 203). The disappointment it

engendered was, perhaps, the reason that the question of Dell's ability and place as a writer became such a topic of interest so early in
his career. This concern also provoked disagreement. Dell was credited with producing a "serious book" (no. 243) and with having the
ability to be an "original and creative talent" (no. 231). Yet Edmund
Pearson stated that in spite of what young intellectuals claimed, Dell
was not a major writer (no. 254). The potential which some critics
acknowledged may have been not only Dell's genuine talent as a novelist but also partly the ability to conform to his pre-Moon-Calf reputation in matters of fiction as well as personal behavior.

Dell's third novel, the non-autobiographical Janet March, was
published in 1923. This novel took a feminist standpoint and treated
it from the individual perspective of the character Janet. The main
emphasis was not feminism in its political or economic implications. Just
as the theme was not unadulterated social revolution, likewise the form
was not avant-garde. Although it was banned in Boston, Janet March
received less critical attention than Dell's first two novels. Grant Overton's review praised the novel for being well written. "As a chroni-
cler of contemporary manners and as a social historian, Mr. Dell is
possibly the best writer who has given us a novel" (no. 341). But
character portrayal was criticized for lacking plausibility (nos. 307
& 323). The heroine was described as representative, not individual,
and thus neither real nor believable (no. 323). Dell was scored for
his frank treatment of changing sexual mores (nos. 317, 326, & 347).
The contrast between banal style and revolutionary theory was noted
(no. 323). The New York Times Book Review called the style "pedestrian and worse" and went on to predict that the novel was the
turning point in Dell's career. "If the author cannot overcome his
juvenilities he will never reach the heights to which the intermingled
evidences of maturity justify him in aspiring" (no. 307). Although
Upton Sinclair saw Dell as "one of the ablest literary minds of our
time" (no. 347), the prevalent sense was one of disappointment in
Dell's performance as a novelist.

In 1925 Dell published two novels, This Mad Ideal and Runaway,
which firmly cast him in the role of a writer who did not live up to
early promise. The heroine of This Mad Ideal was a feminist moon-
calf, Judith Valentine, who refused to compromise her ideals by accept-
ing marriage. The novel elicited differing critical responses. It was
vigorously approved as equal to Moon-Calf (no. 395), as Dell's best
since Moon-Calf (no. 427), and as one of the season's outstanding
novels (no. 428). One review cited an improved, crisp, dynamic, less
literary style (no. 421), but others noted a "colorless" (no. 390) style
lacking in realistic detail (no. 400). The plausibility of the heroine
was argued (nos. 390 & 432). Some reviewers remarked on Dell's reworking of old material (nos. 432 & 437). There was the familiar sense
of unfulfilled authorial ability. If Dell could not move beyond the subject
matter of youth, predicted Louis Kronenberger, he would remain a
minor novelist (no. 432).

Runaway told the story of Michael Shenstone, a man who abandoned his family to escape dullness and returned seventeen years later to reacquaint himself with his daughter and gain acceptance by conventional townsfolk. It likewise occasioned varied reviews. Critics tried to place the work in Dell's canon and to assess his development as an artist. Runaway was called mature (nos. 413, 415, & 416) and Dell's best (no. 416). According to the Boston Evening Transcript, Dell here made a "radical change" in trying to move beyond the pessimism and eccentricity of the post-war period but had not produced his best work (no. 439). William Langfeld and Harrison Smith wrote perceptive reviews focusing on the novel. Langfeld charged Dell with aiming for popularity, which he predicted Dell would achieve, but with disappointing the reader artistically by abandoning his honest protest, spontaneity, and dissent (no. 433). In the New York Herald Tribune Books Smith claimed that Runaway was decidedly inferior to Dell's first two novels because of poor character depiction and "the hypocritical suggestiveness which is the stock in trade of the editors of women's magazines" (no. 442).

An Old Man's Folly (1926) received even fewer reviews than Runaway. Dell's sixth novel, it related the tale of Nathaniel Windle, an elderly man who vicariously experienced his own lost youth and the radical life through two young rebels. Like most of Dell's novels, it fictionalized events from his own life. The first part of the book was praised for its characterization of Windle, but it was felt that the characters in general were lifeless, the plot a vehicle for radical ideas. The story was a trivial one, never making "any of those disturbing revelations that exalt or terrify, stripping reality bare for the startled eye" (no. 501). Still, the questions of Dell's ability as a novelist and his known radicalism continued to vex critics. Some commentators suggested that Dell had abandoned radicalism and rebellion for the bourgeois life (nos. 473 & 517). The New York Times Book Review felt that the novel was "unworthy of a man like Floyd Dell" (no. 469). Before it was too late, the author should try to regain the excellence foreshadowed by his first novel. Yet John Farrar held that An Old Man's Folly "shows him a novelist of proportions which have never before been fulfilled" (no. 490).

The volume of critical response remained steady with the appearance of An Unmarried Father in 1927. This novel treated the sociologically advanced ideas of the absence of inherent maternal instincts and of paternal parenthood outside conventional marriage. Ernest S. Bates in the Saturday Review of Literature claimed that it was "the most spontaneous, the most readable, and perhaps, the best of Mr. Dell's works" (no. 537). But still the belief that Dell had not realized his potential was firmly expressed. Arthur Herman in the New York Evening Post stated that the "colorlessness of style and aridity of characterization" did not match Dell's capabilities (no. 553).

Dell's work as a novelist extended through four more books,

Souvenir (1929), Love Without Money (1931), Diana Stair (1932), and
The Golden Spike (1934). Not one was well received. Souvenir, the
account of Felix Fay and the son from his marriage to Rose-Ann,
sparked little interest. Love Without Money initiated mainly negative
comments. According to The New Yorker, while his early style was
"beguiling," Dell now had "remarkably little of any substance to say"
(no. 689). From this nadir of acceptance, Dell's career as a novelist never recovered. Diana Stair and The Golden Spike received rel-
atively little contemporary critical attention. Diana Stair--at 280,000
words Dell's longest novel--dealt with a feminist and abolitionist in
pre-Civil War times. The Golden Spike carried on Dell's frequent
theme of marriage in the person of Diana's granddaughter. Yet in
spite of his critics, Dell had not lost his allure for all. Lorine Pruette in the New York Herald Tribune Books described the end of Diana Stair as "brilliant story telling" (no. 717), and Basil Davenport
in the Saturday Review of Literature called The Golden Spike "a full,
rich book" (no. 756). However, after 1934 Dell published no more
novels.

Writing in 1932, V.F. Calverton cited Dell's loss of influence
in the radical community because of his continued production of sentimental novels (no. 708). To the end, Dell the novelist was viewed,
not only by radicals but by many commentators, in light of his early
radical reputation and his continuing association with radical publications. Based on his pre-Moon-Calf reputation, the expectations of
critics were frustrated by his novels. They recognized his talent as
a writer, in many cases circumscribed it by their perceptions of it,
and interpreted it according to their bafflement. Confusion was augmented when Dell produced weak novels and did not seem to grow in
his creative abilities. Also, no division was comprehended between
Dell the revolutionary and Dell the moon-calf. A dichotomy in Dell's
character and his writings was not allowed. Indeed, it was seen as
hypocrisy at worst and lack of talent at best and was not recognized
as a legitimate aspect of his work or personality. Irrespective of short
or mundane commentary, no investigation of Dell's work was accomplished
and no studied interpretation was attempted independent of the effort
to fit his writing into the mold of his radical critics' expectations and
his reputation.

While Floyd Dell carried on an active career as a novelist, he
simultaneously produced many other kinds of writings. His several
books of nonfiction social commentary began with Women as World Builders (1913), a collection of short biographies of notable feminists. This
volume helped establish Dell's reputation as a liberal, a feminist, and
"a skirmisher of the left wing" (no. 34). It was praised by most and
viewed as "an earnest of better things" (no. 21). Dell's next book
of social observation was Were You Ever a Child? (1919), a discussion
of the educational system. Here he argued that schools should teach
children to live in the real world. The book was notable for its form
in which a narrator participated in dialogue with a child, an artist,
a philosopher, an immigrant, and others. Critics praised his prose

style and his ability to develop in the reader an interest in education. But since the book was a popularization of ideas already current, it was charged that he did not make a "profound contribution" (no. 75). Looking at Life (1924), a collection of essays on contemporary American life and literature, expressed sociological concerns but was not, on the whole, political in tone. It provoked numerous reviews. As a popular as well as a serious writer, Dell was praised for his observations and approach to life. The Dial commended the "elfish, pucklike quality" of the essays (no. 361). Still, others saw Looking at Life as a dated representation of the socialism of the previous generation (nos. 365 & 376). Frank C. Davison asserted that Dell's outlook was limited and lacked "that final, post-graduate amoral viewpoint" (no. 369).

Intellectual Vagabondage: An Apology for the Intelligentsia (1926) was Dell's most discussed, and perhaps most lasting, book of social commentary. Part sociological criticism and part autobiography, it originally appeared in the Liberator as a series of articles. Part One of the book, "Literature and the Machine Age," was a historical survey of the role played by the intelligentsia, that is, by the rebels against convention. Part Two, "A Spiritual Autobiography of My Own Generation in Its Literary and Social Aspects," was an account of the ideas that influenced the thought of Dell's contemporaries. The book was not uniformly received by critics. Those who praised it commended its style, its "fluid grace and constant charm" (no. 448). In fact, according to the New York Times Book Review, "the facility with which the subject of the book is handled overshadows all else" (no. 455). Dell's ideas and thought were applauded as "remarkably penetrating" (no. 465), "full of pith and provocation" (no. 486). Dell here was "informative and amiably, urbanely profound" (no. 448). Still, some argued that Dell's ideas were dated, incorrect, or inadequate. Although Ernest Boyd questioned whether Dell could speak for the younger generation (no. 475), others agreed upon Dell's role as interpreter of and spokesman for his own generation of writers. Thirty years after its publication, Intellectual Vagabondage was recognized as "one of the important early works interpreting literature from a social and economic standpoint" (no. 913, p. 229).

Love in the Machine Age: A Psychological Study of the Transition from Patriarchal Society (1930) was Dell's final volume of social commentary. Here he united his interests in sociology, psychology, anthropology, youth, and marriage. In this volume his social vision was still revolutionary but not in accord with predominant socialist ideas. He argued that the patriarchal organization of society had fostered subservience, dependence, oppression, and an immature level of sexual development. Resulting from the Industrial Revolution, the Machine Age has allowed young men and women to become independent, self-supporting, and thus adult at an earlier age. The Machine Age has again brought together marriage and romantic love, concepts separated by patriarchalism. There was little agreement among critics as to his book's merit. Malcolm Cowley ridiculed Dell's views (no.

654), while Francis Snow labeled the book "sickening" and "futile" (no. 668). Max Eastman thought it lifeless and detached from reality (no. 759). Irwin Edman praised Dell's synthesis of psychiatry, social science, history, and morals (no. 655). Writing in The Annals of the American Academy of Political and Social Science, William White "cannot think of another book on mental hygiene which is its equal" (no. 669).

In 1926 Dell published a collection of miscellaneous compositions, Love in Greenwich Village. The volume included eight short stories, four poems, and a two-part sketch of the history of the rise and fall of Greenwich Village. Reviewers generally agreed that Dell conveyed the authentic spirit and image of the pre-World War I Greenwich Village. Though not a profound study, the book was entertaining and nostalgic. Other reviewers saw the book as evidence that Dell was indeed a rebel who had fallen away from rebellion and who was living the middle-class life. Some interpreted this favorably. In the Saturday Review of Literature, an anonymous critic stated that Dell's ego was "mellowing" and that he was preparing for the future (no. 464). His liberal critics, represented by V.F. Calverton, charged him with "inadequacy and failure." "He seems to be on the path by which, in America, our literary radicals reach ineffectuality, sterility, and a place in Who's Who" (no. 480). Nevertheless, Love in Greenwich Village established Dell for many as the "logical historian" of the Village (no. 507).

Dell's career also included work as book editor, biographer, and playwright. Of the five books he edited, Wilfrid Scawen Blunt's Poems (1923) and Robert Burton's The Anatomy of Melancholy (1927), co-edited with Paul Jordan-Smith, were the most reviewed. Working six years, Dell and Jordan-Smith translated all the Latin in Burton's book. Mark Van Doren (no. 603) and others praised the quality of the translation. Fifty years later the Dell/Jordan-Smith edition was still being cited (nos. 1077 & 1091). Blunt's volume received mostly favorable reviews commending Dell's judgment in selection. Dell's work as a biographer was limited to Upton Sinclair; A Study in Social Protest (1927). This book was received with the overwhelming sense that Dell's treatment of Sinclair was uncritical and was unconvincing of his merit. Some of Dell's Greenwich Village plays were collected in King Arthur's Socks and Other Village Plays (1922), a volume which Dell in his Prefatory Note called a "not-too-solemn memorial" to a dead "intellectual play-time." Yet some critics scolded him for the lack of intellectual seriousness (nos. 277, 280, & 282). Ludwig Lewisohn saw the plays as an important part of the little theater movement (no. 334). Together with Thomas Mitchell, Dell wrote the Broadway plays "Little Accident" (1928) based on An Unmarried Father and "Cloudy with Showers" (1931). "Little Accident" was viewed with favor by most and was a financial success. "Cloudy with Showers" was praised with reservations, but failed financially.

About Dell's autobiography Homecoming (1933) there was unanimity of opinion that the book's importance lay in Dell's portraits of his contemporaries and their times. Its significance was founded in what Dell saw, not in "what he was and is" (no. 729). Homecoming solidified Dell's role as the "Symbol of a Period" (no. 730), and if it did not fully represent the final passing of that period, it certainly marked the near end of Dell's public career as a creative writer and thinker and the decline of his reputation. After this book his literary output was meager and his reputation faded.

At the age of forty-eight, after a prolific career as a creative writer, Floyd Dell turned to a salaried government position. Although he may have continued to write, with the exception of an occasional magazine article he no longer published. It is no doubt a matter of wonder that Dell's life took such a turn. Why he chose this path has not been fully investigated. Perhaps it is simply indicative of the dichotomies in his personality. Certainly the Depression made it difficult if not impossible to make a living as a writer. And Dell, a man committed to marriage and family life, had a family of three to support. G. Thomas Tanselle and John Hart were the only ones to treat this problem in any other than a cursory manner. Tanselle saw economic necessity as the reason Dell turned to government work. He did not return to fiction "because his governmental duties came to occupy a special place in his life" (no. 913, p. 437). Indeed, Dell's move to Washington, D.C., was a final step in his lifelong search for stability. Hart, noting Dell's financial distress, his health problems, and his waning influence, concluded that he took the position in Washington in order to earn a living (no. 1030, p. 164). Still, the reason Dell selected the year 1935 to give up his struggle to make his way as a creative writer invites further inquiry.

From the early 1920's, Dell's contemporaries tried to establish his place in literature. He was classified as part of the Midwest revolt, a realist, a social revolutionary, a representative figure of the twenties, and an authority on the "younger generation." An early sense of Dell's unfulfilled promise as a writer existed side by side with the acknowledgment of his great writing talent. Yet after his autobiography and his final novel in 1934 and up until the late 1950's, Dell's critical reputation was mainly in eclipse. He was seen as a writer and rebel who had failed to achieve lasting success. Those few critics who wrote about him limited their comments to short remarks and spoke of him in the past tense, although he lived until 1969. Partial exceptions to the fade-out of critical attention were Harlan Hatcher's Creating the Modern American Novel (no. 775) and Joseph Freeman's An American Testament (no. 782). Hatcher's was one of the first assessments of Dell not limited to brief remarks. He noted Dell's accomplishments, commented on each novel, and concluded that Dell, not having grown since Moon-Calf, was a minor novelist. Freeman's memoir was important for placing Dell in the revolutionary, literary, and socialist milieu of the first third of the century. He evaluated Dell as a leading writer of the twenties. Freeman's book sparked commentary by Horace Gregory conceding Dell's central place in radical journalism (no. 783).

Beginning in the late 1950's and represented by G. Thomas Tanselle's dissertation "Faun at the Barricades; The Life and Work of Floyd Dell" (no. 913), there has been a growing wave of interest in Dell studies. Tanselle not only chronicled and interpreted Dell's life and writings, he also contributed an extensive, unannotated bibliography of works by and about Dell which provided scholars with a tool for studying Dell. Other works giving a serious, general treatment of Dell's career included Richard O. Horberg's dissertation "To the Twentieth Century and Back; A Round Trip with Floyd Dell" (no. 999) in which he contended that a study of Dell helped elucidate the social, political, and literary movements of America before and after World War I. John E. Hart's important Floyd Dell (no. 1030) was a major contribution to Dell studies. It analyzed Dell's life and work and was one of the few sources to deal with his life after 1934. It included a short annotated bibliography of works about Dell and an abbreviated list of primary sources.

Besides general treatments of Dell, a number of articles and longer works dealt with specific aspects of his career. John T. Smith's dissertation "Feminism in the Novels of Floyd Dell" (no. 1019) examined Dell's feminist outlook. Martha Anne Cheney's dissertation "Millay in the Village" (no. 1031) devoted a chapter to Dell's association with Edna St. Vincent Millay. G. Thomas Tanselle contributed several articles dealing with Dell's relationships with other writers. John Hart studied Dell as an intellectual vagabond (no. 940). A letter from Dell was the occasion for John T. Flanagan to discuss Dell's life and achievements and to speculate on why his impact as a creative writer was "weakened" (no. 1044). The Psychoanalytic Review presented Leslie Fishbein's "Floyd Dell: The Impact of Freud and Marx on a Radical Mind" (no. 1073) in which he discussed Dell's understanding of Marx and Freud and his inability to provide a synthesis of the two. Later, Fishbein surveyed the impact of Freudianism on Greenwich Village using Dell as an example (no. 1097). Thomas N. Walters contended that Dell's personal movement from radicalism to conservatism was a typically American evolution (no. 1092).

Dell's multifaceted accomplishments are beginning to be more widely recognized, a prelude to their more intensive study by scholars. One aspect of his work which has received attention, his literary criticism, is seen as fundamental to the development of Marxist criticism. Bernard Smith in Forces in American Criticism; A Study in the History of American Literary Thought named Dell as a founder of a school of modern American literary criticism. He "raised socialist criticism to a plane that would entitle him to be called the true precursor of Marxist critical writing in America" (no. 803). More recently, James Gilbert's Writers and Partisans: A History of Literary Radicalism in America dealt with Dell's sociological criticism and its relationship to communism (no. 1001). David R. Peck's dissertation "The Development of an American Marxist Literary Criticism: The Monthly New Masses" credited Dell's sociological criticism with providing a foundation for Marxist criticism (no. 1005).

Indeed, Dell's status is that of a central figure of his era. His life was entwined with many of the literary and social trends of his time. Not only is he treated in the memoirs of many prominent people whom he knew and helped, but his own memoirs cite numerous important people and events of the times. As Hart pointed out, Dell's "memories and observations are ... the source materials of an era" (no. 1030, p. 171). A number of sources name Dell as a central personage in Chicago's bohemia, and his place as the historian and representative male figure of pre-war Greenwich Village is secure. His achievement as a popularizer of Freudian psychoanalysis and as a pioneer in the use of Freud in literature has been cited. In addition, his accomplishments as novelist, social critic, editor of the Friday Literary Review, Masses editor, advocate of frankness in sexual matters, and his important place among radicals and socialists provide justification for Joseph Freeman's view of Floyd Dell as the modern universal man (no. 782).

ABOUT THE BIBLIOGRAPHY

The principle guiding selection of items for this bibliography was inclusiveness. When seen together, even minor references indicate trends of opinion about Dell. The consecutively numbered entries are grouped chronologically by year of publication and then listed alphabetically by author. Full-length studies (books) are separated from shorter writings under those years in which both types appeared. Page numbers include the entire article or section under a particular title. Page numbers in brackets are those on which Dell is actually mentioned.

The intent of the annotations is to make known the contents of the entry through means of a brief description, summary, or quotation. Entries marked by an asterisk (*) were not examined. The annotation includes whatever information was available about the citation as well as its source. A designation of "unlocatable" indicates that the accuracy of the original citation is in question. Entries are limited to those in the English language.

PARTIAL LIST OF PRIMARY WORKS

NOVELS

Moon-Calf; A Novel. New York: A.A. Knopf, 1920.

_____. New York: A.A. Knopf, 1921.

_____. American Century Series. New York: Sagamore Press,
1957.

The Briary-Bush; A Novel. New York: A.A. Knopf, 1921.

Janet March; A Novel. New York: A.A. Knopf, 1923.

_____. Revised edition. New York: George H. Doran, 1927.

This Mad Ideal; A Novel. New York: A.A. Knopf, 1925.

Runaway; A Novel. New York: George H. Doran, 1925.

An Old Man's Folly; A Novel. New York: George H. Doran, 1926.

An Unmarried Father; A Novel. New York: George H. Doran, 1927.

Souvenir; A Novel. Garden City, N.Y.: Doubleday, Doran, 1929.

Love Without Money. New York: Farrar and Rinehart, 1931.

Diana Stair. New York: Farrar and Rinehart, 1932.

The Golden Spike. New York: Farrar and Rinehart, 1934.

SHORT STORIES AND POEMS

Love in Greenwich Village. New York: George H. Doran, 1926.

_____. Freeport, N.Y.: Books for Libraries Press, 1970.

NONFICTION

Women as World Builders; Studies in Modern Feminism.   Chicago:
Forbes, 1913.

_____. Pioneers of the Woman's Movement series. Westport, Conn.: Hyperion Press, 1976.

Were You Ever a Child? New York: A.A. Knopf, 1919.

_____. New York: A.A. Knopf, 1921.

Looking at Life. New York: A.A. Knopf, 1924.

Intellectual Vagabondage; An Apology for the Intelligentsia. New York: George H. Doran, 1926.

The Outline of Marriage. Pamphlets on Birth Control, no. 12. New York: The American Birth Control League, 1926.

Love in the Machine Age; A Psychological Study of the Transition from Patriarchal Society. New York: Farrar and Rinehart, 1930.

_____. Octagon Books. New York: Farrar, Straus, 1973.

_____. Boston: Telegraph Books, 1981.

PLAYS

"King Arthur's Socks," in The Provincetown Plays. First Series. New York: F. Shay, 1916.

The Angel Intrudes; A Play in One Act as Played by the Provincetown Players. New York: E. Arens, 1918.

Sweet and Twenty; A Comedy in One Act. Stewart Kidd Modern Plays. Edited by F. Shay. Cincinnati: Stewart Kidd, 1921.

King Arthur's Socks and Other Village Plays. New York: A.A. Knopf, 1922.

_____. One-Act Plays in Reprint series. Great Neck, N.Y.: Core Collection Books, 1977.

"Little Accident." With Thomas Mitchell. 1928.

"Cloudy with Showers." With Thomas Mitchell. 1931.

BIOGRAPHY

Upton Sinclair; A Study in Social Protest. The Murray Hill Biographies series. New York: George H. Doran, 1927.

_____. Long Beach, Cal.: Upton Sinclair, 1927.

_____. New York: AMS Press, 1970.

_____. New York: AMS Press, 1983.

AUTOBIOGRAPHY

Homecoming; An Autobiography. New York: Farrar and Rinehart, 1933.

_____. Port Washington, N.Y.: Kennikat Press, 1969.

EDITED WORKS

Blunt, Wilfrid Scawen. Poems by Wilfrid Scawen Blunt. Edited by Floyd Dell. New York: A.A. Knopf, 1923.

Herrick, Robert. Poems of Robert Herrick. Edited with an introduction by Floyd Dell. Little Blue Book, no. 701. Edited by E. Haldeman-Julius. Girard, Kan.: Haldeman-Julius, 1924.

Blake, William. Poems and Prose of William Blake. Edited with an introduction by Floyd Dell. Little Blue Book, no. 677. Edited by E. Haldeman-Julius. Girard, Kan.: Haldeman-Julius, 1925.

Burton, Robert. The Anatomy of Melancholy. Edited by Floyd Dell and Paul Jordan-Smith. New York: Farrar and Rinehart, 1927.

_____. New York: Tudor, 1948.

Reed, John. Daughter of the Revolution, and Other Stories. Edited with an introduction by Floyd Dell. New York: Vanguard Press, 1927.

_____. Short Story Index Reprint Series. Salem, N.H.: Arno, no date (LC 75-134975).

THE BIBLIOGRAPHY

1910

1 COOK, GEORGE SHAW. Letter to the Editor. Chicago Evening
Post (14 January), Friday Literary Review sec., p. 4.
   Comments on Dell's unsigned review of Georgine Milmine's
The Life of Mary Baker G. Eddy in the January 7 Friday Literary Review. Corrects errors made by Milmine which might
be interpreted as being those of the reviewer. Dell has committed no error.

1911

2* HENDERSON, CLARA. Letter to the Editor. Chicago Evening
Post (29 December), Friday Literary Review sec., p. 5.
   Cited in no. 913, p. 510. Said to be a comment on Dell's
editorial "The Quality of Woman" in the Friday Literary Review
of 15 December. This section is not on the microfilm copy of
the Chicago Evening Post owned by the Illinois State Historical Society.

1912

3 ANON. "Floyd Dell Talks of Cook's Book." Davenport Daily
Times (16 April), p. 9.
   Reports Dell's talk before the Davenport S.I.A. club. He
reviewed George Cram Cook's book Chasm. Long quotations
from Dell on book's place in contemporary literature and the
Christian, socialist, and Nietzschean outlooks on life. See
no. 8 for pseudonym.

4* BEIFELD, JAMES. Letter to the Editor. Chicago Evening Post
(19 July), Friday Literary Review sec., p. 4.
   Cited in no. 913, p. 521. Not available from the Center for
Research Libraries, Chicago, Illinois; Northwestern University,
Evanston, Illinois; the Illinois State Historical Society; or the
Chicago Historical Society. Tanselle says this is a comment on
Dell's letter to the editor "A Flagrant Case" in the July 12
Friday Literary Review.

---

*Asterisks indicate items not examined.

5* BONE, ANTOINETTE. Letter to the Editor. Chicago Evening
Post (19 July), Friday Literary Review sec., p. 4.
   Cited in no. 913, p. 521. Not available from libraries named
in entry above. Tanselle says this is a comment on Dell's letter to the editor "A Flagrant Case" in the July 12 Friday Literary Review sec., p. 4.

6 LLONA, V.M. "The Case of Anatole France." Chicago Evening Post
(22 November), Friday Literary Review sec., p. 8.
   Letter to the editor. Comment on Dell's review "Anatole
France" in the Friday Literary Review of November 15, 1912.
Concerns France's At the Sign of the Reine Pédauque. Does
not mention Dell by name. Points out his confusion of Madame
de Staël with Mme. Roland. Questions his interpretation of
France's style. Notes Dell's poor French.

7* LLONA, V.M. Letter to the Editor. Chicago Evening Post (29
November), Friday Literary Review sec., p. 4.
   Cited in no. 913, p. 520. Tanselle says this is a comment
on Dell's review of At the Sign of the Reine Pédauque, "Ana-
tole France," in the November 15, 1912 Friday Literary Review.
Not available from the libraries named in no. 4.

8 THE ONLOOKER. "Floyd Dell Talks of Cook's Book." Davenport Daily Times (16 April), p. 9.
   This is a pseudonym. See no. 3.

1913

9 ANDERSON, MARGARET C. Letter to the Editor. Chicago
Evening Post (7 February), Friday Literary Review sec.,
p. 8.
   Comment on Dell's "Of O. Henry" in the Friday Literary Review (24 January 1913), p. 1. This is a review of Henry's
Rolling Stones. Anderson defends Henry against claim that
he lacked style and failed to write novels.

10 ANON. Review of Women as World Builders. New York Globe
and Commercial Advertiser (12 April), p. 8.
   Lists women studied by Dell in this book. Dell's thesis is
that "women are the born fighters of the race."

11 ANON. "The Feminist Movement." Boston Evening Transcript
(16 April), p. 25.
   Review of Women as World Builders woven with review of
Women and To-Morrow by W.L. George. The two are "a vital
and unusual discussion of the woman question." Identifies
Dell as "a Chicago writer of critical note" and gives long quote
from book. "The two books together form a clear, precise,
and since a man passes judgment, a convincing manual of feminism."

12 ANON. Review of Women as World Builders. The Athenaeum,
    1 (26 April), 465.
        Short. The sketches of ten women are too short to serve
    as biographies. The attempt to explain the principles of fem-
    inism does not go beyond what those already acquainted with
    and favorable to the movement know. Others would not be
    converted to feminism by reading this work.

13 ANON. Review of Women as World Builders. New York Times
    Review of Books (4 May), p. 266.
        Brief. Describes contents. The book "is provocative of
    thought and well worth the reading of any one who wants to
    have his ideas on this subject well raked over and stirred up."

14 ANON. Review of Women as World Builders. New York Sun
    (17 May), p. 8.
        Brief. The women treated in the book have little in com-
    mon except their notoriety and their sex. The book is not
    informative.

15 ANON. Review of Women as World Builders. The American Re-
    view of Reviews, 47 (June), 760.
        Short. Restates Dell's thesis. Names some of the women
    considered.

16 ANON. "Something Personal." The Smart Set, 40 (June), 159-
    60 [159].
        Quotes the New York Globe's comment on the publication of
    Dell's story "Jessica Screams" in the April 1913 Smart Set.
    Disapproves of the story. Globe article could not be located.

17 ANON. Review of Women as World Builders. Annals of the Amer-
    can Academy of Political and Social Science, 48 (July), 261.
        Short description. Names women discussed and notes that
    all are worker types.

18 ANON. Review of Women as World Builders. The Chautauquan,
    71 (2 August), 204-205.
        Mainly composed of quotations. Lists women discussed.
    The volume is "full of suggestion," although Dell's basic ex-
    planation of the reason for the women's movement is open to
    question. Still, he has greater esteem for women than might
    be imagined from his view of them as satisfying man's ideas
    of what they ought to be.

19 ANON. Review of Women as World Builders. The Dial, 55 (16
    September), 215.
        Cites Dell's method of pairing women under discussion.
    Relates the book to the English pamphlet tradition. Dell
    views the feminist movement "from a standpoint new to Amer-
    ican discussion."

20 ANON. "Literary Editors." Chicago Evening Post (3 October),
Friday Literary Review sec., p. 14.
Editorial commenting on Francis Hackett's and Dell's depar-
ture from the staff of the Friday Literary Review. Notes
Dell's "intelligence and enthusiasm" and the "courage and
vivacity" with which he wrote about contemporary literature.

21 CHENERY, WILLIAM LUDLOW. Review of Women as World Builders. Chicago Evening Post (11 April), Friday Literary Review sec., p. 2.
Criticizes Dell for advocating battle rather than conciliation
as the means to women's suffrage. Dell, a Shavian, does not
understand that those who ignore society's sexual mores will
suffer. "If into his colors the author has not ground his soul,
he has facilely turned out with a craftsman's skill this volume,
an earnest of better things, a boon full of service for the
present."

22 COOK, GEORGE CRAM. "New York Letter." Chicago Evening
Post (31 October), Friday Literary Review sec., p. 17.
Briefly reports a debate between Paula Jacobi and Dell on
feminine militancy which Dell defended. Notes that the Globe
refers to Dell having developed the Friday Literary Review
into America's best literary criticism. Globe article cannot be
located.

23 COOK, GEORGE CRAM. "New York Letter." Chicago Evening
Post (28 November), Friday Literary Review sec., p. 17.
Briefly mentions production of Dell's "St. George in Greenwich Village" at the opening of the Liberal Club's new head-
quarters. Brief description of its reception.

24 H[APGOOD], N[ORMAN]. "Two Kinds of Mothers." Harper's
Weekly, 58 (20 September), 15.
Article on the idealization of motherhood. Mentions "an ex-
tremely good book on the feminist movement" and quotes from
Women as World Builders.

25 H[APGOOD], N[ORMAN]. "Women as World Builders." Harper's
Weekly, 58 (20 September), 25.
Review. Cites the readable quality and fairness of Women
as World Builders. Discusses women's place in society and
looks at the nature of women as projected by the personalities discussed in Dell's book. "He has written much in a
small space, and written with pleasantness and depth."

26 HERVEY, JOHN L. Letter to the Editor. Chicago Evening Post
(31 January), Friday Literary Review sec., p. 8.
Does not name Dell but comments on his review of O. Henry's
Rolling Stones titled "O. Henry" (Friday Literary Review [24
January], p. 1). Uses the review to discourse at length on
Henry James and Hawthorne.

27 PEATTIE, ELIA W. Review of <u>Women as World Builders</u>. <u>Chi-cago Tribune</u> (19 April), p. 9.
    Restates Dell's thesis. He writes "brilliantly." "An exhil-arating book, daring of youth, and as heartening to the women actors in this new, vivid drama of unknown documents as the applause of many hands in a darkened theater."

28 WING, DEWITT C. "Youth's Books." <u>Chicago Evening Post</u> (16 May), <u>Friday Literary Review</u> sec., p. 9.
    Letter to the editor commenting on <u>Women as World Builders</u>. Its central idea is far from the truth. Author is displeased with the negative critical response and attributes it to the general antagonism between the young and the old. Most of the article discourses on the attitude of the aged toward young people.

1914

29 ANON. "Magazine Notes." <u>Chicago Evening Post</u> (16 January), <u>Friday Literary Review</u> sec., p. 8.
    Short section on the <u>Masses</u> notes that Dell is now managing editor and has written much of the text of the January issue. Mentions several articles.

30 ANON. "Announcement." <u>The New Review</u>, 2 (May), 257-58 [257].
    Dell's name listed among the editors of this publication. The article discusses the editorial policy of the publication.

31 BAX, E. BELFORT. "Socialism and Feminism." <u>The New Re-view</u>, 2 (November), 654-56.
    Highly critical comment on "Socialism and Feminism," Dell's June 1914 article in <u>The New Review</u>. Finds Dell's defense of feminism excessive.

32 COOK, GEORGE CRAM. "New York Letter." <u>Chicago Evening Post</u> (16 January), <u>Friday Literary Review</u> sec., p. 9.
    Brief mention of suggestion to collect Dell's critical writing from the <u>Friday Literary Review</u> and elsewhere into a book on literary interpretation.

33 COOK, GEORGE CRAM. "New York Letter." <u>Chicago Evening Post</u> (23 January), <u>Friday Literary Review</u> sec., no page number.
    Brief mention of Dell helping Max Eastman edit the <u>Free-woman</u>, a feminist magazine. Sequentially this article is on page 9.

34 COOK, GEORGE CRAM. "New York Letter." <u>Chicago Evening Post</u> (6 February), <u>Friday Literary Review</u> sec., p. 8.
    Reports plans for feminist mass meetings at Cooper Square

sponsored by People's Institute. Dell, one of the speakers, is identified as "a skirmisher of the left wing."

35 COOK, GEORGE CRAM. "New York Letter." Chicago Evening Post (27 February), Friday Literary Review sec., p.9.
     Brief mention of Dell scheduled to speak on revolutionary feminism in fact and fancy at the Socialist Press Club.

36 COOK, GEORGE CRAM. "New York Letter." Chicago Evening Post (29 May), Friday Literary Review sec., p.9.
     Part of the article deals with James Oppenheim having written "patternless" poetry after being psychoanalyzed. Briefly mentions that Dell, after having read Oppenheim's work, was so moved that he too wrote some poems in this style.

37 COOK, GEORGE CRAM. "New York Letter." Chicago Evening Post (5 June), Friday Literary Review sec., p. 8.
     Discusses The New Review, a socialist publication. Names Dell as a member of editorial board.

38 COOK, GEORGE CRAM. "New York Letter." Chicago Evening Post (10 July), Friday Literary Review sec., p. 9.
     Article on summer residences of New York literary figures. Names Dell, says he spent the last week end in Provincetown, Mass. Says he wants to edit the Masses from there for a month.

39* MARSHALL, MARGUERITE MOOERS. Review of Women as World Builders. New York Evening World (9 January), p. 3.
     Cited in no. 913, p. 522. This article could not be located.

1915

40 ANON. "'Everybody' Is Doing Something." New York Sun (5 December), sec. 5, p. 6.
     Short article on Greenwich Village includes several photos of locale and personalities. Picture of Dell identifies him as editor of the Masses.

41 COOK, GEORGE CRAM. "New York Letter." Chicago Evening Post (22 January), Friday Literary Review sec., p. 10.
     Part of this article deals with brief essays published in the New York Tribune by authors on why they lived in Greenwich Village. Commentary on Max Eastman's contribution includes a brief mention of Dell and a humorous quote predicting Eastman's future.

42 COOK, GEORGE CRAM. "New York Letter." Chicago Evening Post (29 January), Friday Literary Review sec., p. 8.
     Brief mention of Dell being part of a group which included

Dreiser. Reports their discussion of Village morality with a woman from the Midwest.

43 COOK, GEORGE CRAM. "New York Letter." <u>Chicago Evening Post</u> (12 February), <u>Friday Literary Review</u> sec., p. 8.
Deals with the Liberal Club's discussion of means of financing little theaters, the Washington Square Players, and a proposed Chicago Liberal Club. Briefly mentions that Dell's "The Rim of the World" will be produced by the Liberal Club in conjunction with an Arabian Nights costume ball at Webster Hall.

44 SANDERS, EMMA V. "More on Feminism." <u>The New Review</u>, 3 (April), 219-20.
Letter to the editor. Comments on Dell's ideas in his article "Socialism and Feminism" in the June 1914 <u>New Review</u>. Feminists do not want to give up legal protection unique to women, but they do want legal equality with men.

<u>1917</u>

45 ANON. "Socialists to Test the Espionage Act." <u>New York Times</u> (10 July), p. 7.
Discusses problems radical publications, in particular the <u>Masses</u>, have with the Espionage Act. Dell, identified as managing editor, is reported to have claimed that the August issue will not be put through the mail to avoid punishment. Dell insists there is nothing in the issue to interfere with conscription.

46 ANON. "Seditious Editors Now Fear Prison." <u>New York Times</u> (4 November), sec. 1, p. 17.
Briefly names Dell as an "officer" of the <u>Masses</u>. This article deals with the possible indictment of the editors after the <u>Masses</u> was barred from the mail.

47 ANON. "Indicts the Masses and 7 of Its Staff." <u>New York Times</u> (20 November), p. 4.
Outlines the indictment against the magazine and seven individuals. Dell is accused of writing an article, "Conscientious Objectors." Identifies him as the former literary editor of a Chicago newspaper who is now managing editor and book reviewer for the <u>Masses</u>.

48 ANON. "Reed, Agitator, in Russia." <u>New York Times</u> (22 November), p. 4.
Centers on radical nature of John Reed and on pleas of others indicted in <u>Masses</u> case. Says Dell and others were arraigned and pleaded not guilty to conspiracy. Dell held for $500 bond.

49 ANON. "The Masses Staff Under Arrest." The Survey, 39
    (24 November), 207.
    Details the charges against the staff members of the Masses.
    Lists amounts of bail.

50 CHAPIN, ANNA ALICE. Greenwich Village. New York: Dodd,
    Mead, pp. 285, 286, 287.
    Gossipy history of Greenwich Village from pre-Revolutionary
    times to modern days. Names Dell as editor of the Masses
    and describes the publication. Quotes Dell on the early days
    of the Masses. Quotes Dell's description of the Liberal Club.

51 MORRIS, LLOYD R. The Young Idea; An Anthology of Opinion
    Concerning the Spirit and Aims of Contemporary American
    Literature. New York: Duffield, pp. xvii, 145, 147.
    Dell's response to Morris' request for his opinion of contem-
    porary American literature is grouped with those of Benjamin
    DeCasseres, Donald Marquis, and John Curtis Underwood.
    These four men are called "the pessimists" because they find
    nothing important in the literature upon which they comment.

52* SCHWARTZ, SOPHIA. Comment on Dell Essay. Slate, 1 (April),
    93.
    Cited in no. 913, p. 539. Says this comments on Dell's
    "The Sacred Sisterhood." Slate: A Magazine for Teachers Who
    Are Not Dead; And for Their Friends, 1 (January 1917), 8-9.
    This issue of Slate could not be located. It may be in the
    New York Public Library. The cost of a search was prohib-
    itive.

1918

53 ANON. "Malone Joins Hillquit." New York Times (11 April),
    p. 15.
    Briefly names Dell, managing editor of the Masses, as being
    under indictment for criminal conspiracy.

54 ANON. "Staff of Masses on Trial Today." New York Times
    (15 April), p. 10.
    Names defendants, including Dell, and indicates charges
    against them.

55 ANON. "Hard to Get Jury for 'Masses' Trial." New York Times
    (16 April), p. 8.
    Names Dell as defendant. Quotes long conversation among
    Morris Hillquit, jurors, and Judge Learned Hand on pacifism.

56 ANON. "Creel May Testify in the Masses Trial." New York
    Times (24 April), p. 9.
    Announces that government censor may testify. Misspells

Dell's name in subtitle ("Dill"). Names him as one of day's principal witnesses. Quotes Dell's testimony on purpose of certain editorials written by him and on his conscientious objector status.

57 ANON. "Creel Denies He OK'd Masses Pledge." New York Times (25 April), p. 13.
Recounts testimony of public censor in Masses trial. Names Dell as co-defendant. Notes he helped establish The Liberator.

58 ANON. "Fate of Eastman in the Jury's Hands." New York Times (26 April), p. 20.
Quotes from Malone's and Hillquit's summarizing speeches in the Masses trial. Names Dell co-defendant and contributor to the Masses.

59 ANON. "Orders Masses Jurors to Continue Work." New York Times (27 April), p. 24.
Names Dell. Notes jury's temporary deadlock in Masses trial.

60 ANON. "Judge Dismisses the Masses Jury." New York Times (28 April), p. 5.
Deadlocked jury is dismissed. Names jurors and defendants.

61 ANON. "The Masses Case." The Liberator, 1 (June), 5-6 [6].
Outlines the case against the Masses editors and defends them. Dell mentioned briefly by name as having put together the magazine in the summer.

62 ANON. "Army Ousts Masses Editor." New York Times (17 July), p. 8.
Short. Dell is released from the military because he is under Federal indictment. He had "waived exemption from military duty."

63 ANON. "Snapshots of People Who Count: Floyd Dell." Pearson's Magazine, 40 (December), 73.
Gives author's idea of Dell's self-description as detached, timid, devoted to art. But the popular impression differs and is supported by a poem by Arthur Davison Ficke. Claims Dell denies being a literary critic. Says he sees his short stories as his best work.

64 BARNES, EARL B. "A Tribute." The Liberator, 1 (June), 18.
Poem celebrating the Masses editors who were on trial. Barnes was prosecuting attorney. Describes Dell as "a trained journalist, a writer of / Exquisite English, / Keenly ironical, bitingly sarcastic."

65 EASTMAN, MAX. "Speeches of Max Eastman and Morris Hillquit at the Masses Dinner, May 9." The Liberator, 1 (June), 19-20.
    Eastman defends himself and questions government actions against citizens. Briefly mentions Dell's wish to make known publicly his views on the war if he is to go to jail for them.

66 HILLQUIT, MORRIS. "Speeches of Max Eastman and Morris Hillquit at the Masses Dinner, May 9." The Liberator, 1 (June), 21.
    Defense attorney in Masses trial discusses new Espionage Law. Briefly mentions Dell, saying he had known him only slightly before the trial. Praises the defendants. Cites need to preserve freedom of speech.

67 JOHNSON, JAMES WELDON. "Negro Poetry--A Reply." The Liberator, 1 (April), 40-41, 43.
    Letter to the editor in response to Dell's review of Johnson's Fifty Years and Other Poems in the March 1918 Liberator. Johnson takes issue with Dell's wishing he had taken inspiration from Negro spirituals and used Negro speech and phraseology. Johnson argues that his poems express his deepest feelings and these could not be expressed had he confined himself to dialect.

68 LINDSAY, NICHOLAS VACHEL. "From Vachel Lindsay." The Liberator, 1 (May), 47.
    Letter to Dell commenting on Dell's inaccuracy in a review of The Chinese Nightingale in The Liberator (April 1918). Thanks Dell for encouraging him in writings in the Chicago Evening Post. See no. 69.

69 MONROE, HARRIET. "From Harriet Monroe." The Liberator, 1 (June), 41.
    Letter to Dell commenting on Vachel Lindsay's letter of May 1918. Says Dell discovered Lindsay's poetry and made Monroe aware of his existence. See no. 68.

70 REED, JOHN. "About the Second Masses Trial." The Liberator, 1 (December), 36-38 [36].
    Discusses the political nature of the Masses trial. Briefly mentions Dell's defense of conscientious objectors.

71 ROBINSON, BOARDMAN. Sketch of Floyd Dell. The Liberator, 1 (June), 13.
    Robinson's visual interpretation of Dell.

72 U[NTERMEYER], L[OUIS]. "Three Best." The Liberator, 1 (April), 43.
    Cites Dell's list (Liberator of March 1918) of the three most important literary events of the year.

1919

73 ANON. Review of Were You Ever a Child? The Dial, 67 (15
    November), 464.
    Brief description of contents. Lists what Dell attacks and
what he advocates. "The author's studied audacity and his
pleasing conversational prose should be sufficiently stimulating to awaken reflection in the minds of those who have never
been forced by experience to examine the debris of what has
been called an education."

74 ARENS, EGMONT. The Little Book of Greenwich Village; A
    Handbook of Information Concerning New York's Bohemia with
    Which Is Incorporated a Map and Directory. New York: Eg-
    mont Arens at the "Sign of the Flying Stag," Washington
    Square Book Shop, pp. 3, 15, 21, 23.
    This small book is a witty interpretation of Greenwich Vil-
lage. Thanks Dell for quotes from his Liberator writings.
Identifies Dell among Who's Who in the Village as part of "The
Old Masses Crowd."

75 BUTCHER, FANNY. Review of Were You Ever a Child? Chi-
    cago Sunday Tribune (30 November), sec. 7, p. 5.
    The book is "wholly delightful" but makes "no profound
contribution" to education. It succeeds in proving that education need not be written about in a boring style. The book
appeals to all. Describes Dell's personality as childlike in its
naiveté, curiosity, and interest in creating beauty.

76 MALONEY, WILLIAM J. Letter to Floyd Dell. The Liberator,
    2 (March), 34.
    Praises Dell's review of Francis Hackett's Ireland: A Study
in Nationalism in the February 1919 Liberator. It is "the
most stimulating article on Ireland I have ever seen in the
American press."

77 P., K. "To F.D." The Liberator, 2 (February), 50.
    Poem addressed to Dell by poet whose work has many times
been rejected for publication by Dell. Playful.

1920

78 [ADAMS, FRANKLIN P.] "The Conning Tower." .New York
    Tribune (13 November), p. 10.
    Reports Adams' activities for November 11, 1920. Says he
finished reading Moon-Calf, "a fine book," "earnest" and
"well wrote" [sic].

79* ANON. Comment on Moon-Calf. Community Service, Inc.,
    Bulletin, No. 389.
    Cited in no. 913, p. 549. Cannot identify or locate.

80   ANON. Listing of <u>The Angel Intrudes</u>. <u>Monthly Bulletin of</u>
     <u>the Carnegie Library of Pittsburgh</u>, 25 (January), 38.
       Includes the play in list of works acquired by the library.
     This is the Arens 1918 edition in the "Flying Stag Plays for
     the Little Theatre" series.

81   ANON. Review of <u>Were You Ever a Child?</u> <u>The Booklist</u>, 16
     (January), 113.
       Briefly describes contents. "Nothing new but written in a
     way to appeal to many people who ordinarily would not read
     books about education."

82   ANON. Review of <u>Were You Ever a Child?</u> <u>The Liberator</u>, 3
     (January), 45.
       Advertisement supplied by publisher. Outlines thesis.
     Notes Dell's "customary brilliancy of style and thought."

83   ANON. Review of <u>Moon-Calf</u>. <u>The Liberator</u>, 3 (November),
     30.
       Advertisement supplied by publisher. Describes hero.
     It "is without question the most important and interesting
     novel by an American that has come to us."

84   ANON. Review of <u>Moon-Calf</u>. <u>Metropolitan</u>, 52 (November),
     67.
       Brief. "It is told with an artistic restraint that somehow
     does not bring out Mr. Dell's full set of powers, but it is a
     noteworthy book for all that, written sincerely and simply."
     <u>The Liberator</u> of December 1920 attributes this article to
     Clarence Day (no. 132).

85   ANON. Review of <u>Moon-Calf</u>. <u>Publishers' Weekly</u>, 98 (6 Novem-
     ber), 79.
       Blurb supplied by publisher. Describes Felix and the nov-
     el's setting.

86   ANON. Untitled Comment on Dell Essay. <u>New York Evening</u>
     <u>Post Literary Review</u> (13 November), p. 8.
       Comments on Dell's essay "Psychoanalysis and Recent Fic-
     tion" in <u>Psyche and Eros</u>, 1 (20 July), 39-49. Mainly a long
     quotation from essay. Brief comment says he has "interest-
     ing things" to say.

87   ANON. "Floyd Dell's <u>Moon Calf</u> Veracious Western Picture."
     <u>Newark Evening News</u> (17 November), p. 8.
       Review of <u>Moon-Calf</u>. Tells plot. Concentrates on com-
     menting on Felix. Dell's aim is to show the development of
     "one of our literati." Felix's character is "likable and plau-
     sible." "It is, perhaps, because of the success of the presen-
     tation of that [Midwest] background that Mr. Dell's laurels
     as a novelist will ultimately be granted."

88 ANON. Commentary on Moon-Calf and Photo of Dell. New York
     Tribune (21 November), sec. 7, p. 9.
          Large photo of Dell. Moon-Calf is set in the Midwest. Fe-
     lix Fay is "one of the younger generation who revolts against
     the code and ideals of pioneer parents."

89 ANON. "Some Fiction of the Current Hour." New York World
     (21 November), editorial section, p. 4E.
          Review of Moon-Calf. Relates plot. The style is that of
     "the carry-on." "It is not a story for the bromidic reader.
     On the other hand, it offers no lure to the rapids of radical-
     ism." Looks to a sequel.

90 ANON. "Author Credits Psychoanalysis." New York Globe and
     Commercial Advertiser (27 November), p. 2.
          Reports interview with Dell on subject of psychoanalysis
     and its relationship to creativity. Lengthy quote and para-
     phrase of Dell. He is identified as an editor of The Libera-
     tor, the author of Moon-Calf, "a man well known in the field
     of letters."

91 ANON. Biography of Dell. Boston Herald (27 November), p. 5.
     Brief.

92 ANON. "Domestication of Moon-Calves." New York Sun (27
     November), p. 7.
          Brief review. Compares Dell's solution for his moon-calf
     to Maugham's in "The Moon and Sixpence." Fay experiences
     a Darwinian adaptation to society.

93 ANON. "In Bookland." New York Call (28 November), maga-
     zine section, p. 11.
          Includes short comment on Moon-Calf. The novel is very
     popular. After six years of struggling with it, Dell wrote
     the book in seven months.

94 ANON. "Modern Fortune-Telling." New York Globe and Com-
     mercial Advertiser (29 November), p. 12.
          Comments on psychoanalysis as a new method which is not
     outside the natural order and is not yet fully integrated into
     society as a commonplace. Half the article relates Dell's diffi-
     culty in writing Moon-Calf until he was psychoanalyzed.
     Speculates that the analyst did not tell Dell anything he did
     not already suspect. See no. 155 for reprint. See Charles
     Grant Miller, no. 154.

95 ANON. Review of Moon-Calf. Canadian Bookman, 2 (Decem-
     ber), 97.
          Identifies Dell as a person of "originality" and "a critic of
     repute." "His first novel is a noteworthy example of Amer-
     ican workmanship in a genre which has hitherto been much

better practiced in Europe--the intimate biographical record of youth." Questions the importance of the genre. Praises Dell's frank portrayal of relations between the sexes.

96 ANON. Reivew of Moon-Calf. Current Opinion, 69 (December), 882.
      Short. It is "a study of the evolution of a dreamer." Describes Felix Fay.

97 ANON. Review of Moon-Calf. Indianapolis Star (4 December), p. 12.
      Short. Tells plot in terms of love versus career. Recognizes it as autobiographical. "It is a well-written exposition of a real idea, and not clogged with too great a supply of detail."

98* ANON. Comment on Moon-Calf. St. Paul News (5 December).
      Cited in no. 913, p. 549. Not available from the Minnesota Historical Society or the St. Paul Public Library.

99 ANON. "An Epigram on Moon-Calf." New York Tribune (5 December), sec. 7, p. 9.
      Brief statement. Dell's novel shows "the other side of This Side of Paradise, that is, the poor boy's side."

100* ANON. Review of Moon-Calf. Detroit Free Press (5 December).
      Unlocatable. Cited in no. 913, p. 547. There is no review of Moon-Calf on this date.

101* ANON. Review of Moon-Calf. Rochester Herald (5 December).
      Cited in no. 913, p. 547. Reference not verified. Available at great cost from the Rochester Public Library.

102 ANON. Review of Moon-Calf. St. Louis Globe-Democrat (11 December), p. 9.
      Describes Felix and relates plot. Concentrates on Felix-Joyce relationship. Felix is unheroic and inconsequential. The depiction of several minor characters is praised. Looks for sequel.

103 ANON. "Strong Notes of Realism from Our New Novelists." Daily Brooklyn Eagle (11 December), holiday book number. p. 2.
      Review of Moon-Calf. Long relating of plot. It is a distinguished first novel. Looks for better work to follow. "Here is an authentic voice from the prairies, a spokesman for the nonreading, unbookish millions.... His message should be valuable."

104 ANON. Review of Moon-Calf. Hartford Daily Courant (12 December), sec. 5, p. 6X.

Briefly tells plot. Praises poetry included in the biography of Felix. Finds sincerity, beauty of style, and an accurate portrayal of the "deadly, horrible" dreariness of the small midwestern town.

105 ANON. Review of Moon-Calf. New York Times Book Review and Magazine (12 December), p. 20.
High praise for Dell's first novel. Character portrayal is outstanding. Felix's childhood and boyhood are the "heights of character delineation." Cites Dell's work as that of the successful realist. Believes Knopf, the publisher, has praised the novel excessively.

106 ANON. "Floyd Dell Speaks at Civitas Club." Brooklyn Daily Times (16 December), p. 9.
Long quotations from Dell's speech before a Brooklyn women's club. Speech based on article in Atlantic Monthly on wild young people. Claims Dell has been referred to as wild.

107 ANON. "Author Gossip." The Publishers' Weekly, 98 (18 December), 1845.
Part of this section contains an anecdote about Dell. Claims Leigh Reilly, managing editor of the Chicago Evening Post, split one salary between two applicants for the same job, one of whom was Dell. See no. 162.

108 ANON. Review of Moon-Calf. New London [Conn.] Day (20 December), p. 6.
"A rambling, semi-autobiographical narrative in which the hero is noted only for his bookish characteristics, in which the studies of the poverty of slovenly people are too intimately, purposelessly crude to be anything but repulsive, in which the climactic theme is an exposition of the theories of free-love, is hardly to be considered as a literary achievement."

109* ANON. "Felix Fay, Moon Calf." Boston Traveller (22 December).
Cited in no. 913, p. 548. Reference not verified. Available at great cost from the Boston Public Library. This is a review.

110 ANON. "Favorites of the Week." Baltimore News (24 December), p. 11.
Moon-Calf listed number two behind Main Street on list of best sellers.

111 ANON. "Books Most in Demand." Philadelphia Public Ledger (25 December), p. 9.
Lists books most frequently requested the past week at the Philadelphia Library. Moon-Calf is listed number four in fiction category.

112 ANON. "The Year's Literature." Indianapolis News (25 December), p. 6.
  Includes Moon-Calf in list of outstanding books of 1920 not mentioned by William Lyon Phelps in an article for the Yale Alumni Weekly, "The Glorious Year A.D. 1920."

113 ANON. "Books." Huntington [W.Va.] Herald-Dispatch (26 December), p. 17.
  Review of Moon-Calf. Compares development of modern Russian literature to the Midwest revolt that is taking place in America. Dell is part of this revolt against "middle-class Philistinism." Short biography. Brief comparison of Moon-Calf to Main Street. Moon-Calf "implies" and shows "underlying forces." Main Street depicts the surface. It "displays." The focus in Moon-Calf is the "'love interest.'" Names female characters. "For a 'first' novel Moon-Calf is unusually good."

114 ANON. "College Girls Do Not Scorn to Read, Librarians Say." New York Herald (30 December), p. 20.
  Moon-Calf included in list of books most requested at the New York Public Library.

115* B., C. Review of Moon-Calf. Baltimore Sun (11 December). Cited in no. 913, p. 547. Unlocatable.

116 BENCHLEY, ROBERT C. "Books and Other Things." New York World (13 December), p. 12.
  Review of Moon-Calf. Reviewer is weary of realistic Midwestern novels. "Moon-Calf seems to combine the pictorial quality of Main Street with the much deeper poetical values of Poor White, and should therefore, I suppose, be rated as a better book than either of them. But I can't bring myself to do it." The language used by the characters, the knowledge of Nietzsche presupposed of villagers, and the dialogue are not realistic. Reprinted in no. 117.

117 BENCHLEY, ROBERT C. "Books and Other Things." Cincinnati Commercial Tribune (20 December), p. 6.
  Reprinted from no. 116.

118 BOYNTON, H.W. "Midland Realism." The Weekly Review, 3 (22 December), 623.
  One-third of this article is a review of Moon-Calf. It is "a more considerable book" than Main Street which is also reviewed here. Praises the "ease and restraint" with which the story is told. Brief outline of Felix's struggles. Half the review denounces the seduction and desertion of the character Joyce as an inadequate representation of reality and as misleading to youth.

119 BROUN, HEYWOOD. "Books." New York Tribune (27 October),
    p. 10.
      Broun briefly mentions Dell's name before turning his entire
    column over to him to comment on Lewis' Main Street.

120 BROUN, HEYWOOD. "Books." New York Tribune (10 Novem-
    ber), p. 10.
      Brief comment on Moon-Calf. "The chapter called 'What Is
    Known as Egotism' seems to us an extraordinary piece of
    work." Thinks the novel will be "something to shout for."
    Reprinted in no. 127.

121 BROUN, HEYWOOD. "Books." New York Tribune (12 Novem-
    ber), p. 10.
      The column largely quotes Dell's comparison of Main Street
    to Moon-Calf and his statement on the nature of "moon-
    calfishness." Two introductory paragraphs by Broun com-
    ment on young novelists' concern with pointing out America's
    ills. Compares Sinclair Lewis and Dell on their attitudes to
    American life. See no. 158. Quoted in no. 128.

122 BROUN, HEYWOOD. "Books." New York Tribune (17 Novem-
    ber), p. 10.
      Suggests Moon-Calf as a Christmas gift. Notes that Dell
    was born in 1887.

123 BROUN, HEYWOOD. "Books." New York Tribune (19 Novem-
    ber), p. 10.
      Review of Moon-Calf. "Drop whatever you are doing and
    read Floyd Dell's Moon-Calf. Yes, Main Street can wait."
    Notes the apparent emergence of a new spirit in American
    literature. Finds the novel "perfectly clear and straight-
    forward." It is not too heavy with Freudian implications.
    The early chapters dealing with Felix's boyhood represent
    the book at its best. "No writer of our day has gone so
    fully or so deeply into the heart of a child." Long quote
    from novel.

124 BROUN, HEYWOOD. "Books." New York Tribune (26 Novem-
    ber), p. 10.
      Brief mention of Moon-Calf. Finds Edith Wharton's The
    Age of Innocence, Sinclair Lewis' Main Street, and Moon-
    Calf similar in that they all treat the idealist's conflict with
    his surroundings.

125 BROUN, HEYWOOD. "Books." New York Tribune (29 Novem-
    ber), p. 10.
      Short comment on Dell's reticence to deal more explicitly
    with sexual relationships in Moon-Calf. But notes censor-
    ship problems for more direct authors.

126 BROUN, HEYWOOD. "Books." New York Tribune (13 December), p. 8.
　　　Review of Sherwood Anderson's Poor White. States impression that Anderson "is trying to outdo Gopher Prairie, of Sinclair Lewis, and Port Royal, of Floyd Dell."

127 BROUN, HEYWOOD. "Broun's Bookish Chatter." Baltimore News (13 November), p. 7.
　　　Reprinted from no. 120.

128 BROUN, HEYWOOD. "Broun's Bookish Chatter." Baltimore News (20 November), p. 7.
　　　Quotes but does not reprint no. 121. Quotes long statement by Dell comparing Moon-Calf to Main Street and This Side of Paradise. Broun places Dell's work in the genre of "questioning literature," that which questions America's values. Surprised that, as a liberal, he is not more vehement.

129 BURKE, KENNETH. "Felix Kills His Author." New York Evening Post Literary Review (31 December), p. 3.
　　　Review of Moon-Calf. In treating the Endymion motif, Dell falls victim to his hero's mediocrity. Although selected parts represent good writing, the book is generally lacking in composition. The words are "dull and unpenetrative" and the form illuminates nothing. "One is lost in a meandering of incident which has been given no significance by any concerted impulse, any synthetic grasp of the subject, any consistent overtone or generality." Reviews modern schools of writing and concludes that Dell belongs to none of them. See no. 241 for comment on this review.

130 BUTCHER, FANNY. Review of Moon-Calf. Chicago Sunday Tribune (7 November), sec. 1, p. 9.
　　　Praises the Midwest as inspiration for the novel. Felix is convincing. The novel is autobiographical. " 'Moon-Calf' is a fine, free, honest, sincerely beautiful piece of work, young ... [,] unsophisticated in the ways of ordinary tricks of the novel trade, but ... convincing and impressive." Dell and F. Hackett made the Friday Literary Review "the most distinguished literary supplement in America."

131 DAWSON, N.P. Review of Moon-Calf. New York Globe and Commercial Advertiser (20 November), pp. 8, 11.
　　　The book is disappointing because it does not reflect the author's social philosophy. Moon-Calf is not interesting and for the most part is not written like a novel but like an autobiography. Compares Moon-Calf to This Side of Paradise, Main Street, and to Sherwood Anderson's unnamed novel. Compares settings of novels and states by what means they missed writing "the great American novel."

132 [DAY, CLARENCE.] Review of Moon-Calf. Metropolitan, 52
(November), 67.
See No. 84.

133 DIGBY, KENELM. "The Literary Lobby." New York Evening
Post Literary Review (13 November), p. 24.
Briefly mentions that Dell worked as a farmhand in Buf-
falo, Iowa. He helped George Cram Cook raise cantaloupes.

134 DUZER, WINIFRED VAN. "Self Discovery Aid to Success."
Washington Herald (4 December), p. 8.
Reports interview with Dell on subjects of psychoanalysis
and Moon-Calf. Several extended quotes from Dell. Brief
list of his accomplishments. Notes great popularity of Moon-
Calf. Comments on how novel was written and its relationship to Dell's psychoanalytic experience. Dell is temperamental in appearance. Reprinted with title change in nos.
223 and 224.

135 EASTMAN, MAX. "Education Made Happy." The Liberator,
3 (February), 41-42.
Review of Were You Ever a Child? Defends book against
Paul Jordan-Smith's charge that it presents nothing new.
The book is unique because it asks questions. Also, it
proposes teaching children about "love." Freudian ideas
have caused Dell to become too conservative in his approach
to "love." Dell is "a skilful artist, a lucid philosopher and
an efficient workman" who is self-educated.

136 GARLAND, ROBERT. Review of Moon-Calf. Baltimore News
(27 November), p. 7.
Describes Felix Fay. Praises the view of the American
Midwest. "'Moon-Calf' is the surprise novel of the year."
A "fine achievement," it places Dell "for once and all among
the few Americans who are to be seriously considered in the
field of fiction."

137 GIOVANNITTI, ARTURO. "Felix Fay." The Liberator, 3 (December), 26, 28, 31.
Review of Moon-Calf. Long review occasionally bordering
on the ironic if not the sarcastic. Finds Felix Fay dull and
unrealistic as a character. Dell's self-revelation shows "unbelievable egotism."

138 GRANICH, IRWIN. "Floyd Dell Revealed in 'Moon Calf.'"
New York Call (5 December), magazine sec., p. 10.
Review. Dell has spent years thinking about this autobiographical novel. He describes the native-born American
revolutionary. The hero is an original addition to the "thinly
populated gallery of American figures who have been brushed

by the revolution." Praises the depiction of Midwest life.
Dell has done a service for American revolutionary fiction.
The novel is "a sort of declaration of the young American
intellectual for the first time in fiction."

139   H., F.   Review of Moon-Calf. The New Republic, 25 (8 De-
      cember), 49.
            Final judgment is reserved until the sequel appears. It
      is not, however, "a distinguished novel." The book is not
      creative. It lacks the rebelliousness expected from Dell.
      Much of the plot is retold with quotes. Dell is charged with
      sentimentality. See no. 141.

140   H., M.J.   Review of Moon-Calf. The Woman Citizen, 5 (4 De-
      cember), p. 750.
            Tells plot. Contrasts Felix with boy heroes of Booth Tar-
      kington. The title is inappropriate because it does not urge
      the reader to take Felix seriously. Dell is aloof with a "trago-
      comic point of view." "This lack of egotism is, in the annals
      of autobiography, an achievement as great as the art of the
      book."

141   H[ACKETT], F[RANCIS].   Review of Moon-Calf. The New
      Republic, 25 (8 December), 49.
            This article is attributed to Hackett by Tanselle in no.
      913, p. 547. See no. 139.

142   H[AMBRIDGE], G[OVE]. "Sound Workmanship." The World
      Tomorrow, 3 (December), 381.
            Review of Moon-Calf. In spite of what the reader expects
      from a professional propagandist, Dell's novel has "a long-
      drawn mellowness" and a "warm human quality."

143   HANSEN, HARRY. Advertisement for Moon-Calf. The Libera-
      tor, 3 (December), p. 29.
            Placed by Knopf. Quotes from no. 146.

144   HANSEN, HARRY. "A British Poet on Ireland." Chicago Daily
      News (8 December), p. 12.
            This long article contains brief, favorable comments on
      Moon-Calf. This novel as well as Main Street and Poor
      White is not influenced by European standards. Each is
      thoroughly American. "Our most cherished possession is a
      first edition copy of 'Moon Calf' [sic], the novel that we
      expect to see forge to the front as the most remarkable lit-
      erary accomplishment of the year."

145   H[ANSEN, HARRY]. "The First Review." Chicago Daily News
      (29 December), p. 12.
            Says that the Chicago Daily News printed the first review
      of Moon-Calf. This review is now available in pamphlet

form. Reports the critical and popular success of the
novel.

146 HANSEN, HARRY. "His First Novel--and Fame." Chicago
Daily News (27 October), p. 12.
    Review of Moon-Calf. "A great character: Felix Fay.
A great book: Moon-Calf. And an author, full-fledged,
assured by this one book of a permanent place in the literature of America: Floyd Dell." This is the first characterization of the moon-calf personality, the beginning of the
"American intellectual radical," Gives own remembrances of
Dell in Davenport. Dell's style is free of tricks and manner-
isms. Moon-Calf "is the clearest and most promising note
struck in American literature in our day and generation."
Quoted in no. 143.

147 HOPKINS, MARY ALDEN. "A Boy Who Dreamed." The Publishers' Weekly, 98 (18 December), 1885.
    Review of Moon-Calf. Describes Felix, the hero. "This
is a psychological analysis of the development of Felix's personality." The book is written by and for the thinking man.

148 JONES, LLEWELLYN. Advertisement for Moon-Calf. The
Liberator, 3 (December), p. 29.
    Placed by Knopf. Quotes a review by Jones in the Chi-
cago Evening Post. "'A power of organizing the most deli-
cate material of life without distorting it that definitely puts
Mr. Dell well to the fore among our few serious novelists.'"
See no. 149.

149 JONES, LLEWELLYN. "First Novel Real Achievement." Chicago Evening Post (29 October), Friday Literary Review
sec., p. 13.
    Review of Moon-Calf. Defends Dell against his personal
unpopularity in Chicago. Briefly notes influence of H.G.
Wells on Moon-Calf. Briefly tells plot. The novel is a
"spiritual autobiography." Praises insight, incisive humor,
and organization. This review is quoted in no. 148.

150 L., W.D. Review of Were You Ever a Child? The Survey,
43 (13 March), 752.
    Dell has manifested a true interest in education. Although
he expounds no new theories, his ideas are unfamiliar to the
general public. The subject of education is made interesting. "To have written a book of this sort that is at once
sound and captivating is no mean achievement."

151 LINDIN, CARL ERIC. Letter to the Editor. The Liberator,
3 (May), 49.
    Briefly praises Dell's article "A Psycho-Analytic Confes-
sion" in the April 1920 Liberator. The letter mainly focuses
on Carl Larsson, Swedish painter.

152 M., D.L. "The Moon Calf." Boston Evening Transcript (1
December), part 4, p. 11.
Review. General discussion of a writer's attitude toward
a first novel. Cites "sureness and an impression of truth
which very many first novels lack." Concentrates on family's
desire for Felix Fay's education. Dell's treatment of Felix
Fay is convincing, natural, and sympathetic.

153 MACQUEEN, JOSEPH. Review of Moon-Calf. Portland Sunday
Oregonian (19 December), sec. 5, p. 3.
Very brief. Gives brief plot summary. It is "an attrac-
tive novel."

154 [MILLER, CHARLES GRANT]. "Modern Fortune-Telling."
New York Globe and Commercial Advertiser (29 November),
p. 12.
Editorial on psychoanalysis. Though it is now a fad, in
time it will become a useful tool for treating mental disorder.
Dell, author of Moon-Calf, was psychoanalyzed to facilitate
his writing. But the analyst did not tell Dell anything
about himself that he did not already know. This article
is reprinted in no. 155. The author's name does not appear here. The article is attributed to him in no. 913, p.
549.

155 MILLER, CHARLES GRANT. "Modern Fortune-Telling." Syra-
cuse Journal (9 December), p. 8.
Reprinted from no. 154.

156 MINOT, JOHN CLAIR. Review of Moon-Calf. Boston Herald
(4 December), p. 6.
Briefly describes Felix's character. He is of a type appearing more frequently in American fiction. "The story
is as vigorous and unconventional in style as in theme.
Plainly Floyd Dell is no more a bromide than his young hero
is."

157 MORLEY, CHRISTOPHER. "The Bowling Green." New York
Evening Post (13 December), p. 6.
Includes humorous story on bookstore customer's confusion
of Ethel Dell with Floyd Dell. Bookseller calls Moon-Calf
"'very meritorious.'"

158 P., W.H. "Books." New York Tribune (17 November), p.
10.
Heywood Broun quotes extensively from W.H.P. in this
his column. W.H.P. comments on Dell's opinion of November 12, 1920. See no. 121. Compares Carrie of Main Street
as reformer to Felix of Moon-Calf as idealist. Comments on
status of women in response to Dell's ideas.

159 PEATTIE, ELIA W. "The New Education." Chicago Tribune
(31 January), p. 13.
Review of Were You Ever a Child? Announces Dell's ap-
pointment to the Association for the Advancement of Progressive Education, formed by Charles W. Eliot. States the book's
thesis. "At moments he is exhilarating; at others he appears
... to be absurd. But at least he is not hackneyed, though
he does to an extent follow trails which have already been
blazed if not much trodden."

160 R., Q. "A Literary Letter." Boston Christian Science Monitor (8 December), p. 14.
Includes short comment on Moon-Calf. Says the novel has
sold out at local bookstores due to a favorable review in the
New York Tribune by Heywood Broun.

161 REDMAN, BEN RAY. Review of Moon-Calf. Bronxville Review
(4 December), p. 13.
Expresses great surprise at the lack of propaganda in a
novel by an associate editor of The Liberator. The truth is
that the author of this "masterpiece of fiction" is "more of
an artist than a revolutionary." Felix is autobiographical,
but Dell is detached from his character. The hero is "a real
and vital individual." Moon-Calf is enjoyable as well as "pro-
vocative of serious consideration."

162 REILLY, LEIGH. "Too Small to Divide." The Publishers' Weekly, 99 (18 December), 28.
Letter to the editor correcting errors in fact in no. 107.

163 TOOHEY, JOHN PETER. Comment on Moon-Calf. New York
Tribune (25 December), p. 6.
Doggerel written after reading Main Street, Miss Lulu Bett,
Poor White, and Moon-Calf. Expresses author's preference
for city life. Appears in the column "The Conning Tower."

164 V[AN] D[OREN], C[ARL]. "Moon-Calf on the Mississippi."
The Nation, 111 (8 December), 670, 672.
Review of Moon-Calf. Theme and style are perfectly suited.
There is no sentimentality. At first Felix's world appears
insubstantial. It is contrasted with the milieu of Main Street.
Milieu made concrete by endless evidence. "Moon-Calf has
equal erudition, but has absorbed it, has worked it into the
narrative, and hints at its wealth without revealing it." Dell
is closer than Lewis to "a classic roundness and grace."
Highly praises the characterization of the older men and the
episode between Felix and Rose.

165 W., R.H. "Moon Calf a Perfect Novel." Springfield (MA)
Union (5 December), p. 5.

Review of Moon-Calf. Tells plot. Dell portrays Felix with "a master's pen, the pen of genius." The main character is believable. Praises Dell for showing Felix in several phases of chronological development as opposed to Booth Tarkington who deals only in adolescence. Felix's character is "consistent" and the novel as a whole is "perfect."

166 WILLIAMS, SIDNEY. "A Moving Story of Proud Youth." Philadelphia North American (27 November), p. 15.
Short review of Moon-Calf. Describes Felix and tells plot. "Mr. Dell has made a substantial contribution to the literature of life."

1921

167 A[DAMS], F[RANKLIN] P. "The Conning Tower." New York Tribune (8 November), p. 12.
Reports Adams' activities for November 6, 1921. He began reading The Briary-Bush "which promises fine things."

168 ANON. Review of Moon-Calf. The Booklist, 17 (January), 157.
Short recounting of plot. "A subtle character study accomplished by narrated episodes rather than detailed analyses." Notes possible readers' moral objection.

169 ANON. Review of Moon-Calf. The Dial, 70 (January), 106.
Short. The novel "has the importance of showing how serious and how well-composed an American novel can be without losing caste. It is an effective compromise, in manner, between the school of observation and the school of technique."

170 ANON. Review of Moon-Calf. Edited by Mary Katharine Reely. Wisconsin Library Bulletin, 17 (January), 20-21.
Short. This first novel is "remarkable for its sympathetic treatment" of a bookish young boy. Notes author's "insight" in handling character of hero. Brief statement on phases of his maturation.

171 ANON. "Books in Demand at Local Libraries." Philadelphia Public Ledger (1 January), p. 9.
In list of fiction books most requested at the Philadelphia Library the past week, Moon-Calf is number five.

172 ANON. "Floyd Dell Looking West." Good Morning, 3 (1 January), 16.
Satirical, humorous comment on how Moon-Calf came to be written. "To put it bluntly, Moon-Calf is a suppressed

desire, dug from its subterranean lair by the psychic spade
of a Freudian."

173 ANON. "Books and Authors." New York Times Book Review
and Magazine (2 January), p. 25.
A brief part of this long article comments on Dell. Notes
that Were You Ever a Child? is being translated into Russian
and will be distributed in the Soviet Union. Notes that Dell
is working on The Briary-Bush. Says Alfred A. Knopf,
publisher of Moon-Calf, responded to December 12, 1920, review of the novel by saying he did not publish Willa Cather
or Joseph Hergesheimer.

174 ANON. "Economics in Fiction." Detroit Evening News (6 January), p. 4.
Examines attitudes of socialists in light of Dell's Moon-Calf.
Relates incident in novel. Concludes that socialists and capi-
talists are both working, though through different means,
for the same goal. Notes that Moon-Calf and Main Street "are
competing with each other as literary sensations."

175 ANON. "Afterthoughts." New York Sun (8 January), p. 9.
Brief comment on source for term "moon-calf." It is not
Thomas Carlyle, but Shakespeare's The Tempest.

176 ANON. "Books and Authors." New York Times Book Review
and Magazine (9 January), p. 29.
Anecdote on Dell being hired at the Chicago Evening Post.
Identifies him as the author of Moon-Calf.

177 ANON. "Radical's Book Sermon Against Radicalism." Oakland
Tribune (9 January), p. W-4.
Review of Moon-Calf. Long description of Felix's character. No comment on autobiographical connection with
author. The novel is "a preachment against taking the
radical too seriously." Dell is a "skillful writer of book
reviews, radical of sorts and one of the editors of the
Liberator."

178 ANON. "Books Most in Demand." Philadelphia Public Ledger
(15 January), p. 15.
In list of fiction books most requested at the Philadelphia
Library the past week, Moon-Calf is number four.

179 ANON. "'Moon-Calf.'" San Francisco Bulletin (15 January),
p. 13.
Review. Praises novel. Compares early chapters to
Jack London's experience as a boy. Finds "charm" in Felix's maturation. "It is not the great American novel--it
is less than great and might have been written in any

country--but it is a peculiarly convincing study of a youth as real as he is unusual." Identifies Dell as a literary critic.

180 ANON. Review of Moon-Calf. Washington [D.C.] Herald (15 January), p. 6.
Dell is the first to analyze the moon-calf character. Praises "simple," "charming" style and the portrayal of the small town.

181 ANON. Statement on Moon-Calf. Chicago Evening Post (21 January), Friday Literary Review sec., p. 9.
Briefly names Moon-Calf as best seller in its fifth edition.

182* ANON. Washington [D.C.] Times (21 January).
Unlocatable. Cited in no. 913, p. 602.

183* ANON. Comment on Were You Ever a Child? Saturday Night (22 January).
Cited in no. 913, p. 558. Not available from the University of California at Los Angeles library, the University of Southern California library, the Los Angeles Public Library, the Los Angeles County Public Library, or the Library of Congress.

184 ANON. "Favorites of the Week." Baltimore News (22 January), p. 9.
Lists Moon-Calf as number six in order of popularity in the category of fiction.

185 ANON. "Books." Rochester Herald (23 Jnuary), p. 7.
Includes brief paragraph telling how Dell and another man were hired simultaneously by the Chicago Evening Post.

186 ANON. "Books and Their Authors." Huntington (W.Va.) Herald-Dispatch (23 January), sec. 3, p.[3].
Repeats the story of how Dell and another man split the salary of one job when first hired by Leigh Reilly of the Chicago Evening Post.

187* ANON. Comment on Were You Ever a Child? Toronto Sunday World (23 January).
Cited in no. 913, p. 543. Not available from the National Library of Canada.

188 ANON. Review of Moon-Calf. Jacksonville Sunday Times-Union (23 January), p. 7.
Included among reviews of books received by the Jacksonville Free Public LIbrary. Describes character of Felix. Briefly tells plot. "Readers of good fiction" will enjoy it.

189 ANON. "Rose Pastor Stokes Appears in a Play." St. Louis
     Post Dispatch (27 January), p. 10.
        Report of Stokes, a socialist and radical, playing the lead
     in "King Arthur's Socks." The performance was in the
     Manhattan Lyceum for tailors and their families. Focuses
     on Stokes. She calls the play "a foolish little bit of comedy
     of the bourgeoisie." Gives synopsis of plot. Calls play
     "a mild sex drama."

190 ANON. "Books Most in Demand." Philadelphia Public Ledger
     (29 January), p. 15.
        In list of fiction books most requested at the Mercantile
     Library the past week, Moon-Calf is number three.

191* ANON. Moon-Calf a Best Seller. Baltimore Sun (29 January).
     Cited in no. 913, p. 549. Unlocatable.

192 ANON. "The Gossip Shop." The Bookman, 52 (February),
     569-576 [574].
        Announces a sequel to Moon-Calf. Says Dell is a novel-
     ist and editor of The Liberator. He is "slight, a little shy"
     and has a "fine sense of humor." Quotes Dell on F. Scott
     Fitzgerald and the younger generation.

193* ANON. Review of Moon-Calf. Cumberland [Md.] News (4
     February).
        Cited in no. 913, p. 548. Not available from the Allegany
     County Library. The publisher has no microfilm and no copy
     machine.

194 ANON. "Favorites of the Week." Baltimore News (5 Febru-
     ary), p. 7.
        Moon-Calf listed number four in fiction.

195 ANON. "'Blind.'" New York Call (6 February), magazine
     sec., p. 10.
        Review of Ernest Poole's novel Blind. Compares it to
     Moon-Calf and other novels. Moon-Calf "deals with a
     thwarted little semi-artistic nobody of a man." Miss Lulu
     Bett is better than Moon-Calf or Main Street.

196 ANON. Review of Moon-Calf. Monthly Bulletin of the Car-
     negie Library of Pittsburgh, 26 (March), 118.
        Brief. "A study of the development of the mind and
     character of a boy from childhood to manhood, showing the
     effects of various radical theories in which he becomes suc-
     cessively interested."

197 ANON. "Tense and Vivid Little Dramas." New York Sun
     (28 May), p. 6.

Review of The Provincetown Plays edited by George Cram
Cook and Frank Shay. Talks about the contribution made
by the Provincetown Players. Lists "The Angel Intrudes,"
"a comedy by Floyd Dell" as part of contents.

198 ANON. Comment on Were You Ever a Child? Publishers'
Weekly, 99 (1 June), p. 27.
Announces a Russian translation by Lunacharasky. The
book will be published by the Soviet Government of Russia.

199 ANON. "Floyd Dell, Author, Drops In." Chicago Daily News
(22 June), p. 12.
Announces Dell's visit in Chicago on his way to Davenport, Iowa, and to California. Notes that he is the author
of Moon-Calf and the soon-to-be published The Briary-Bush.
Includes photo of Dell and his wife.

200 ANON. "Books Popular in May." Library Journal, 46 (July),
607.
Moon-Calf listed among six fiction books most popular in
public libraries in May 1921.

201 ANON. Review of The Briary-Bush. The Liberator, 4 (November), 31.
Advertisement by publisher. Describes plot which is
centered on modern marriage.

202 ANON. "Some Well Known Authors." New York Tribune
(2 November), Graphic Section, pp. 8-9 [8].
Photo of Dell trying to milk a cow while his father looks
on. Caption identifies Dell as author of The Briary-Bush.

203 ANON. "The Year in Books." New York Times Book Review
and Magazine (27 November), pp. 1, 22, 25 [22].
Brief mentions. Uses Moon-Calf as example of good first
novel. The Briary-Bush "rather missed the charm" of its
predecessor.

204 ANON. Review of The Briary-Bush. The Open Shelf (December), 99.
Brief plot summary. The novel is " 'talky' but absorbing."

205 BENCHLEY, ROBERT C. "Heroes of Realism." The Bookman,
52 (February), 559-60.
Review of Moon-Calf and Sherwood Anderson's Poor White.
Some comparison. Moon-Calf is in the genre of "realistic
reporting" but departs from form to introduce a hero outside the ordinary. The "vein of poetry" running through
Moon-Calf does not allow Dell to create an ordinary hero.
The sense of incompleteness imparted by the novel derives
from the promise of a sequel.

206 BISHOP, JOHN PEALE. Review of The Briary-Bush. Vanity
     Fair, 17 (November), 10.
         Recounts the plot. The theme of free love versus mar-
     riage is out of date although the novel might have been a
     success if Dell had treated it with detachment. Instead of
     writing a satire or a tragedy, Dell presents the novel "in a
     mood of sentimental reminiscence. This is unfortunate, but
     perhaps inevitable."

207 BISHOP, JOHN PEALE. "Three Brilliant Young Novelists, No
     One of Whom Is Over Twenty-five." Vanity Fair, 16 (Octo-
     ber), 8-9 [8].
         The novelists are Fitzgerald, Dos Passos, and S.V. Benét.
     Dell, however, is mentioned on the first page as a post-
     war novelist who has revolted "against the silliness and com-
     placency of commercialized literature."

208 BLACK, JOHN. "The Moon-Calf Tries Marriage." New York
     Herald Magazine and Books (13 November), p. 11.
         Review of The Briary-Bush. This book is not as satisfy-
     ing as Moon-Calf. It lacks the beauty, intensity, and whim-
     sicality present in its predecessor. Dell is an "old school
     novelist, among the very first in the country." His dia-
     logues and "amours" are Victorian and his world view omits
     the baser aspects of life. His characters escape complacency
     only through his artistry. Praises the narrative and the
     characters' "mental analyses." "The book is important and
     compelling, alike for its excellent diction, its keen analysis
     and its vivid report of the midwestern mind. It may not be
     dismissed."

209 BOYD, THOMAS ALEXANDER. "Moon Calf." St. Paul Daily
     News (30 January), Society sec., p. 6.
         Review. Tells plot at length. Characterization of Felix
     praised. "There's not a dull moment in the book nor a dull
     word."

210 BROUN, HEYWOOD. "Books." New York Tribune (19 Janu-
     ary), p. 10.
         Includes long quote from Dell on the number of sequels
     to Moon-Calf. Shows that he already had Janet March in
     mind. Reprinted in no. 211.

211* BROUN, HEYWOOD. Albany Knickerbocker Press (20 January).
         Cited in no. 913, p. 549. Said to be a reprint of no.
     210. Not available from the Albany Public Library. There
     is no microfilm source.

212 BROUN, HEYWOOD. "It Seems to Me." New York World
     (19 November), p. 11.
         Comment on episode in The Briary-Bush concerning a

kiss which is given extreme importance. Notes that Dell
writes "Yale-Harvard game" instead of "Harvard-Yale game."

213 BROUN, HEYWOOD. "It Seems to Me." New York World (15
December), p. 15.
Includes letter from Dell on subject of children's books.
Brief comments on letter and on episode in The Briary-Bush.
Dislikes hiatuses in narrative.

214 BURTON, RICHARD. "Plays, Past and Present." New York
Evening Post Literary Review (28 May), p. 3.
Includes review of The Provincetown Plays edited by
George Cram Cook and Frank Shay. Comments on individual
plays. "And as for Floyd Dell's 'The Angel Intrudes,' when
once the initial query of taste is disposed of, it can be commended for its funniness."

215 BUTCHER, FANNY. Comment on Were You Ever a Child?
Chicago Sunday Tribune (30 January), sec. 2, p. 7.
Says the book will be published in translation by the
Soviet government of Russia. It is "serious and brilliant."
Its humor and paradox make it effective. Placed beside
Moon-Calf, it "proves what a really broad thinker Floyd
Dell is and what a skilled writer."

216 BUTCHER, FANNY. List of Best Library Circulators.
Chicago Sunday Tribune (23 January), sec. 2, p. 7.
Moon-Calf is number one on the list.

217 BUTCHER, FANNY. List of Best Library Circulators.
Chicago Sunday Tribune (30 January), sec. 2, p. 7.
Moon-Calf is number three on the list.

218 BUTCHER, FANNY. List of Best Library Circulators.
Chicago Sunday Tribune (6 February), sec. 2, p. 7.
Moon-Calf is number one on the list.

219 BUTCHER, FANNY. Review of The Briary-Bush. Chicago
Sunday Tribune (20 November), sec. 8. p. 1.
Long quotation. The Chicago scene is realistic, but the
book is not a roman à clef. The characters are transformed
by art from whatever real counterparts there may have been.
The book is "a much finer piece of work than 'The Moon
Calf,' as fine a novel as has ever been written about mar-
riage, and as true."

220 CARY, LUCIAN. "The Problem of the Sensitive Soul." The
Freeman, 2 (5 January), 403.
Review of Moon-Calf. "Mr. Dell's first novel, in short,
shows us that a well-equipped intelligence and a new perception have been brought to bear on the particular in-

stance of the sensitive soul, the particular instance that lies
at the heart of all our questioning and that the endless circle of sensitive souls and terrifying American towns is broken
at last."

221* CLARK, ALFRED S. Review of Moon-Calf. Boston Globe (6
January).
Cited in no. 913, p. 548. Unlocatable.

222 DAWSON, N.P. Comment on The Briary-Bush. New York
Globe and Commercial Advertiser (9 November), p. 16.
Quotes part of episode of Rose-Ann's snow bath. Notes
it is not in the mode of the "new realism."

223* DUZER, WINIFRED VAN. "Author in Mental Deadlock Seeks
Aid of Mind Doctor; Writes Most Popular Book." Charleston
[S.C.] American (3 January), p. 7.
Cited in no. 913, p. 549. Reprinted from no. 134.
Microfilm from University of South Carolina is illegible.
Only title, author, date, and page can be verified. Ar-
ticle is two columns wide, each eight inches long.

224 DUZER, WINIFRED VAN. "Author Tells of Emotional Deadlock." Richmond [Va.] Times-Dispatch (2 January), p. 5.
Reprinted with title change from no. 134.

225 ELIOT, RUTH. "Happy Realism." The Publishers' Weekly,
100 (15 October), 1350.
Review of The Briary-Bush. Mainly reviews the plot
and Felix's progress in life. Some of the book is "irrele-
vant and inconsequential" because it mirrors real life. "It
is a refreshing, sunny story, well-told and altogether delightful."

226 FEIPEL, LOUIS N. "The Fiction of 1920--A Library Survey."
The Library Journal, 46 (15 September), 749-54 [753].
Survey of inclusion of new fiction titles of 1920 in representative American public libraries. Lists fifteen libraries which have acquired Moon-Calf.

227 FIELD, LOUISE MAUNSELL. Review of The Briary-Bush.
New York Times Book Review and Magazine (27 November),
p. 28.
Notes two themes of the novel. One is the conflict of
the dreamer with reality and the other is the theme of
"useless, unjustified fears." Notes view of marriage expressed in book. While the novel would have profited
from editing, it is "well written, sometimes very well
written."

228* FITZGERALD, F. SCOTT. "The Credo of F. Scott Fitz-

gerald." St. Paul Daily News (20 February), feature sec.,
p. 8.
> Cited in no. 1032 and read there. Reprinted in no. 229.
Cannot determine if no. 229 is with or without omissions.
Annotation appears there since it is the earliest version
actually examined. Reprinted with omissions in nos. 1032
and 1094.

229 FITZGERALD, F. SCOTT. "The Credo of F. Scott Fitzgerald." Chicago Daily News (9 March), p. 12.
> Letter to Thomas A. Boyd, literary editor of the St. Paul
Daily News. Complains about current vogue of authors writing about their lives as young men. Moon-Calf, written
"without distinction of style," "reaches the depth of banality."

230 FITZGERALD, F. SCOTT. "Three Soldiers." St. Paul Daily
News (25 September), feature sec., p. 6.
> Review of John Dos Passos' novel. Briefly mentions Dell
as a member of H.G. "Wells' faithful but aenemic platoon"
of imitators. Reprinted in no. 1034.

231 FOLLETT, WILSON. "The Truth About Realism." New York
Evening Post Literary Review (26 November), pp. 199-200.
> Review of The Briary-Bush provides occasion for attack-
ing realism in novels. Realism assumes the perfectability
of man and works for a social goal. The author is likely
to remain unremembered. Although Dell is writing in the
realistic strictly biographical mode, he reveals himself to
be "a potentially original and creative talent, capable of attacking difficult problems and achieving beauty on arduous
terms." This potential is shown by his not making Fay's
success credible, by not quoting from Fay's writing, and
by imposing order in the form of the comic to Fay's adventures. See nos. 285 and 288.

232 G., R. Review of Moon-Calf. San Francisco Argonaut (1
January), p. 8.
> Highly critical of Dell's treatment of character, setting,
and diction. The hero should be presented humorously
instead of with the "appalling solemnity," of this "monoto-
nous chronicle of ... ordinary egotism." The Midwest is
shown as a garish land of socialistic, "animalistic, unin-
teresting people." The diction is anachronistic. Deplores
the introspective nature of the psychological novel.

233 GROPPER. "'I Like Trouble'--F.D." The Liberator, 4
(October), 26.
> Cartoon featuring Dell behind a desk with floor littered
with papers and key to the city hanging on the wall.

234 HACKETT, FRANCIS. Review of The Briary-Bush. The New
     Republic, 29 (14 December), 78-79.
          Finds the source of the novel in H.G. Wells and in Howell's
     Hazard of New Fortunes. The book's atmosphere is literary,
     divorced from outer reality. The psychology of the charac-
     ters is poor in that Dell attempts to make Rose-Ann detached
     when in reality Felix is the cold, egocentric, inward-looking
     personage. Dell does not seem aware that he is treating
     "mediocre personalities" lacking in depth of feeling. "The
     solid realities of The Briary-Bush are confined to Felix Fay's
     notions and interests, which are commonplace. If the world
     is to be penumbral to Felix's dreams, his dreams should be
     more dazzling."

235 HANSEN, HARRY. "Approaching Mastery." Chicago Daily
     News (9 November), p. 12.
          Review of The Briary-Bush. It "is the most important
     novel of marriage between two persons of literary and artis-
     tic impulses that has ever been written in the United States."
     It is so successful in portraying emotions and feelings that
     it is beyond comparison. Dell's artistic powers have grown.
     Praises his style and restraint. Dell is the only current
     American novelist who is as good as established English nov-
     elists. Praises characterization of Rose-Ann and minor char-
     acters. Quoted in no. 290.

236 HANSEN, HARRY. "Hot Weather Book Gossip." Chicago Daily
     News (22 July), p. 12.
          Includes brief announcement of Dell's presence in Chicago.
     He has many friends there. He has "traveled far since he
     left Chicago--and the best part of his pilgrimage still lies
     ahead."

237 HANSEN, HARRY. "Russia and the Little Apple." Chicago
     Daily News (12 January), p. 12.
          Includes brief mention of Moon-Calf. Enos Mills praised
     it highly to Hansen.

238 HANSEN, HARRY. "The Truth About 1920." Chicago Daily
     News (5 January), p. 12.
          Brief comment on Moon-Calf. It is one novel which is
     not "debauched by the conventional happy ending." In-
     cludes photo of Dell. Identifies him as "a New York critic."

239 HANSEN, HARRY. "The Truth About 1921." Chicago Daily
     News (28 December), p. 12.
          Review of books published in 1921. The year 1920 was
     marked by Moon-Calf, a novel which contains fine writing.
     The Briary-Bush of 1921 will enhance Dell's reputation.
     "This is proved by the fact that, although Moon-Calf was

sneered at by some eastern critics, the recent book has
been given careful and scholarly attention everywhere."

240 LEWIS, SINCLAIR. "Floyd Dell." The Bookman, 53 (May),
     245.
        One of a series of literary portraits. Coins phrase
     "faun at the barricades" to refer to Dell. Brief comments
     on Moon-Calf and Were You Ever a Child? Emphasizes the
     contrast between Dell's knowledgeable Marxianism and his
     "graceful genius for loafing" and enjoying life.

241 LINDSAY, DONALD. "Dell's 'Moon-Calf.'" New York Eve-
     ning Post Literary Review (15 January), p. 14.
        Letter to the editor in response to Kenneth Burke's re-
     view of Moon-Calf. See no. 129. Burke's article does not
     illuminate the novel. By quoting fragments and suggesting
     critical opinions, Burke makes a "Socialistic sneer" at the
     novel. The author attacks Burke's ideas on composition.
     Praises Dell's vivid minor characters and his "refreshing
     subtleties."

242 LINN, JAMES WEBER. "This, That an' th' Other Book."
     Chicago Herald and Examiner (17 January), p. 6.
        Review of Moon-Calf. Since the novel is autobiographi-
     cal, Dell may be a one-book author. The book is "a chron-
     icle of history of emotions, developed by incident. Yet
     the handling of the various incidents is masterly." Focuses
     on the influence of reading and women on Felix. Men play
     no real part in his development.

243 MANN, DOROTHEA LAWRANCE. "The Rise of a Chicago
     Journalist." Boston Evening Transcript (10 December),
     part 4, p. 8.
        Review of The Briary-Bush. Cites verisimilitude of Felix's
     journalistic experience. But the main theme is his marriage.
     Discusses the nature of the bond between Felix and Rose-
     Ann. It is of "special interest" that Dell, a young man and
     a radical, can condemn the excessive freedom of modern-
     style marriage. The Briary-Bush is a better novel than
     Moon-Calf. It has "a firmer handling, a more sharply de-
     fined purpose, a keener grasp of character. It is a serious
     book and a real accomplishment."

244 MARSHALL, MARGUERITE MOOERS. "Floyd Dell, Novelist,
     Author of Modern Marriage Novels, Now Believes Old-
     Fashioned Marriages Best." New York Evening World (27
     December), p. 3.
        Reports interview with Dell on subject of marriage. Finds
     his ideas very conservative and conventional. Contrasts
     Dell's ideas today with his ideas five years ago. Includes

eight photos of Dell. Dell called the "author of brilliant novels."

245 MENCKEN, H[ENRY] L. "The American Novel." Voices, 5 (February), 46-47.
Highly critical of literary criticism emanating from American universities. Books that challenge socially acceptable mores are ignored. Dell's work is "good" but not "remarkable." It does not reflect his liberal attitudes and is therefore praised by the literary establishment. Moon-Calf is a "quite decorous story--well planned and extremely well written, but still perfectly respectable." Mencken predicts that the second novel in Dell's planned trilogy will shock the critics. This article also comments on S. Lewis, E. Wharton, T. Dreiser, and W. Cather.

246 MENCKEN, H[ENRY] L. Review of Moon-Calf. The Atlanta Journal (30 January), Sunday Magazine sec., p. 10.
Solely a quotation from no. 247.

247 MENCKEN, H[ENRY] L. Review of Moon-Calf. The Smart Set, 64 (February), 141.
Praises novel highly. Is not propagandistic. Hero is not political, but is an esthetic character. Dell delineates his character so as to individualize him. Dell "contrives to make him seem important." The love affair "is the high point in a novel marked throughout by very competent writing." The novel is "thoroughly entertaining and the entertainment that it offers is of a civilized order." Quoted in no. 246.

248 MENCKEN, H[ENRY] L. "A Soul's Adventures." The Smart Set, 64 (March), 141-42.
Commentary on Moon-Calf and Main Street. Although some argue that the appearance of these novels is a sign of revitalization in American literature, the excitement over them is mainly uncritical. Novels equally as good have appeared for several years. Moon-Calf has been praised because, as a socialist novel, it is largely noninflammatory, "free from both sexual Bolshevism and political fornication."

249 NOCK, ALBERT JAY. "A Study in Literary Temper." The Freeman, 2 (26 January), 464-67 [464, 465].
This article is addressed to a group of young American writers including Dell. Praises their ability and sincerity. Discusses a short story by Gogol and commends to the Americans his writing style, disinterestedness, and the fact that he likes people.

250* OSBORN, E.W. "Felix Fay, the Moon-Calf, Gravely Turns

to Folly." New York World (13 December).
Unlocatable. Cited in no. 913, p. 553.

251 P., E. Review of Moon-Calf. The Dial, 70 (January), 106.
Short. "The author has surprised his enemies by not
writing à thèse and delighted his friends by a masquerade,
but Moon-Calf, as it stands, has the importance of showing how serious and how well-composed an American novel
can be without losing caste. It is an effective compromise,
in manner, between the school of observation and the school
of technique."

252 P., R. "Rose-Ann Takes a Snow-bath the Morning After Her
Marriage." Chicago Daily News (28 December), p. 12.
Poem based on incident in The Briary-Bush. Used by
Alfred Knopf as advertisement for the novel.

253* PAGE, BRETTE. Comment on King Arthur's Socks. Roch-
ester Herald (6 February).
Cited in no. 913, p. 556. Available from the Rochester
Public Library.

254 PEARSON, EDMUND LESTER. Review of The Briary-Bush.
The Independent and the Weekly Review, 107 (3 December),
237.
Jocular treatment of the improbability of anyone rolling
in the snow in midwinter as the heroine does. Brief serious commentary. Sees Dell as "a writer of romances," not
a realist or a revolutionist. "He is not one of the major
prophets, as you might think if you listened to the excited
young intellectuals." Praises his dialogue.

255 R., Q. "A Literary Letter." Boston Christian Science
Monitor (12 January), p. 12.
Includes commentary on Moon-Calf. It is a study of a
poet adjusting to midwestern life. Contrasts Edith Wharton
and Xingu with Dell and Moon-Calf. The latter is "a realistic analysis of a youth, sincere and talented, who is eager
for culture, and yet avoids the word." Dell represents a
young generation of Americans with no debt to New England
literary tradition. He writes about the Midwest "with vigor
and with feeling."

256 REILLY, LEIGH. Letter to the Editor. Publishers' Weekly,
99 (1 January), p. 28.
Comments on story that Dell and another split a salary
while employed by the Chicago Evening Post. Reilly was
managing editor of the Post.

257 ROGERS, ELSIE CLAY. Review of Moon-Calf. South Bend
News-Times (30 January), sec. 2, p. 7.

<u>Moon-Calf</u> is better than the average Midwest novel. Tells plot. Includes long quotation. While Felix is "average," "we can thank Floyd Dell for putting so many emotions in an objective light."

258 S., E.S. Review of <u>Moon-Calf</u>. <u>The Atlantic Monthly</u>, 127 (March), Bookshelf Section, 12.
Compares the novel to <u>Main Street</u> and <u>Miss Lulu Bett</u>. Because Dell's work is autobiographical, he attempts more than Lewis or Gale and thus risks a greater failure. Though the book succeeds on occasion, it does not create enough reader sympathy for Felix. Dell tends to sentimentalize his hero. "Mr. Dell has another difficulty: he is always trying to be a descendant of Howells and the realists as well as an heir of Rolland." He does not eliminate or evoke enough to combine the two genres. But by using his creativity, Dell may yet produce a mature character.

259 SAWYER, ETHEL R. "The Literary Periscope." Portland <u>Sunday Oregonian</u> (16 January), sec. 5, p. 5.
Includes short comment on <u>Moon-Calf</u>. Quotes unidentified review on Felix's ability to mold reality based on his imagination. Sawyer sees this as example of how psychoanalysis is becoming applied science.

260 SINCLAIR, UPTON. "Out of Kansas." <u>The Liberator</u>, 4 (March), 28, 30, 32 [32].
Review of <u>Dust</u> by Mr. and Mrs. Emanuel Haldeman-Julius. Brief reference to Dell, a socialist from Greenwich Village. "<u>Moon-Calf</u> has shown us how an artist's soul can be keen and strong, and at the same time sensitive and tender."

261 STEARNS, HAROLD "America and the Young Intellectual." <u>The Bookman</u>, 53 (March), 42-48 [44, 45].
Speculates that Dell and others do not need the advice of critics. The genius does not step out of his society but reflects it. Written in response to no. 249.

262* STOCKBRIDGE, FRANK PARKER. <u>The Bookman</u>, 53 (July).
Unlocatable. Cited in no. 200.

263 WOLF, ROBERT. Review of <u>Three Soldiers</u>. <u>The Liberator</u>, 4 (November), 32-33 [33].
Brief mention of Dell's opinion on why men like the army. His psychoanalytic description is "'homosexual irresponsibility.'"

1922

264 ANON. "Dell, Floyd." <u>Who's Who in America</u>. Edited by

Albert Nelson Marquis. Vol. 12. Chicago: A.N. Marquis, 899.
Brief biography and list of jobs and writings.

265 ANON. "A Moon-Calf Bawls for More Rope." The [Richmond, Va.] Reviewer, Vol. 2 (January), 227-28.
Edited by Hunter Stagg. Ironic and critical review of The Briary-Bush. The book is a "comparative failure" as a sequel. Dell has forgotten that Felix's charm lay in his ordinariness and has come to perceive him as extraordinary. Also, compared with Moon-Calf, the characters are "too lightweight" to sustain interest throughout. Simply as a story, the book is in the vein of G.A. Henty and Horatio Alger. "That the character of Felix Fay never carries the conviction of [Dell's] talent is a detail which only the petty will allow to interfere with their enjoyment of what is, when you learn where to skip, as refreshing a tale as Brave and Bold, or The Young Bank Messenger."

266 ANON. Review of The Briary-Bush. The Booklist, 18 (January), 121.
Brief recounting of plot. Story is "leisurely, intimate, affectionate."

267 ANON. Review of The Briary-Bush. The Dial, 72 (January), 104.
Brief. Counsels Dell to read Henry James. Says the novel "fulfills the promise of chaos and failure which was by no means the most obvious thing in The Moon Calf."

268 ANON. Review of The Briary-Bush. Monthly Bulletin of the Carnegie Library of Pittsburgh, 27 (Feburary), 54.
Brief. "The attempt of two intensely modern young people to solve the marriage problem in a modern way. A sequel to Moon-Calf."

269 ANON. "The Gossip Shop." The Bookman, 55 (March), 87-96 [90, 92].
Short mention of author having met Dell followed by quote of "gossip" provided by Dell. Ends by describing Dell's bookplate.

270 ANON. "Liberator News." The Liberator, 5 (March), 26-27.
Two brief mentions of Dell. Notes his debate on marriage with Mike Gold and his presence on the board of directors of The Liberator.

271 ANON. "A Reviewer's Notebook." The Freeman, 5 (26 April), 166-67.
Long commentary on The New Republic's supplement "The Novel of Tomorrow." Very briefly names Dell and quotes

his idea on the purpose of the novel as stated in the supplement.

272 ANON. Review of The Briary-Bush. The Bookman, 55 (May), 294.
   Included in long list of recent fiction. Very brief summary of plot. Book is especially recommended.

273 ANON. Review of Moon-Calf. London Times Literary Supplement, 21 (25 May), 341.
   Compares Dell's attitudes to milieu and social distinction to those of the English reader. The hero takes himself seriously, but he is not a bore as a character.

274 ANON. "A Trans-Atlantic Highbrow." London Times (26 May), p. 16.
   Short review of Moon-Calf. Felix is distinguished by his contentment with intellectual rather than physical rebellion. "There is a quiet humour in the treatment which keeps Felix interesting in spite of himself."

275 ANON. "The Gossip Shop." The Bookman, 56 (September), 119-28 [126].
   Brief mention of Dell's birthday party and his work on a new novel. Mentions also the presence of his son.

276 ANON. "Some Changes." The Liberator, 5 (October), 30.
   Short announcement that Dell, "one of America's leading literary critics," will resume his position as an editor of The Liberator.

277 ANON. Review of King Arthur's Socks and Other Village Plays. Boston Evening Transcript (15 November), "The Christmas Bookstalls Section," p. 7.
   Short general description of plays. Their satire is "rather silly." "Mr. Dell's future intellectual programme, with less time out for play, will no doubt show more impressively what that programme or intellect has to offer."

278 ANON. Review of King Arthur's Socks and Other Village Plays. The Bookman, 56 (December), 478.
   Brief. Notes that most of the plays "have been produced in obscure little theatres."

279 ANON. "Eight Americans." The Bookman, 56 (December), no page number.
   In the front of this issue is a photo of Dell by Nickolas Muray. Also a reproduction of his signature. Brief sentence identifying him. "A critic turned novelist, he achieved immediate recognition with his 'Moon-Calf' and its sequel 'Briary-Bush.'"

280 ANON. Review of King Arthur's Socks and Other Village
    Plays. New York Evening Post Literary Review (9 Decem-
    ber), p. 300.
       Harshly critical. Dell is not original in his treatment of
    modern concerns. Characterization is poor and thus the
    sketches are failures as dramatic entertainment. "This is
    not what one expects of a man said to possess an active and
    astringent mind with a radical trend."

281 ANON. Review of The Briary-Bush. London Times Literary
    Supplement, Vol. 21 (21 December), 859.
       Discusses modern conversation and dilemmas in the novel.
    Title is symbolic of the lives of the main characters. "Mr.
    Dell has an able, attractive style, and he is not without
    imagination. If only one could believe that he had written
    'The Briary-Bush' with his tongue in his cheek, as a satire
    on the modern psychological novel! But it is informed, in
    every line, with the earnestness of a young author who
    feels that it is time somebody looked into these questions
    of love and marriage."

282 BARNES, DJUNA. "Floyd Dell as Playwright." New York
    Tribune (12 November), sec. 5, p. 10v.
       Review of King Arthur's Socks. Borders on sarcasm.
    Recalls conversation with Dell on Dostoevsky. Finds Dell
    overly influenced by B. Shaw and A. France. Dell has
    always been a romantic. Praises one episode in Moon-Calf
    as "a lovely thing done well." The plays in King Arthur's
    Socks do not attempt to be serious. "This everlasting light-
    ness that might better be heavy, this so-called whimsy, this
    frolicking and butting into space, may be all very nice for
    space, but I wish all intellectual America's attention were not
    going out-field."

283 BROUN, HEYWOOD. "The Briary-Bush." The Liberator, 5
    (January), 29.
       Review of The Briary-Bush. Compares it to Moon-Calf.
    The latter is "one of the permanently fine novels of our
    period." Felix there is presented more clearly than in the
    sequel. The Briary-Bush presents physical setting more
    vividly than Moon-Calf. But the reviewer wishes Dell had
    developed Felix's relationship to the newspaper for which
    he works. Final paragraph mutilated in copy available.

284 BUTCHER, FANNY. Review of King Arthur's Socks. Chi-
    cago Sunday Tribune (26 November), sec. 7, p. 25.
       Short. Describes contents. The plays are "casual bits
    of literature."

285 CARY, LUCIEN. "Realism?" New York Evening Post Liter-
    ary Review (11 February), p. 422.

Letter to the editor. Comments on Wilson Follet's review of The Briary-Bush (no. 231) and Dell's reply. Claims both men are in error when they interpret The Briary-Bush as a realistic novel. It is an "engaging romance."

286 COLUM, MARY M. "Certificated, Mostly." The Freeman, 5 (26 April), 162-64.
Reviews of The Briary-Bush, The Beautiful and Damned by Fitzgerald, and Rahab by Waldo Frank woven together. Dell's book is "a very feeble performance" compared to the other two works. The central character is boring and cannot sustain or justify the length of the novel.

287 DAWSON, N P. "Books in Particular." New York Globe and Commercial Advertiser (11 January), p. 18.
Comment on The Briary-Bush based on letter received from Dell. Rose-Ann's snow bath is "one of the new story's few exciting features." Quotes Dell's letter, including his definition of realism.

288 HADY, J.L. "On Mr. Follett's Criticism." New York Evening Post Literary Review (14 January), p. 358.
Letter to the editor about Follett's "The Truth About Realism" (no. 231). His criticism of Dell is unfair because his comments pertain to the general concept of realism, not to Dell's concrete example. "The only valid philosophical criticism to be brought against Mr. Dell is that in a concrete instance he has failed to achieve that complete synthesis which is the aspiration of the aesthetic and social conscience --an ideal which the idealistic critic has failed even to envisage."

289 HANSEN, HARRY. "Hergesheimer's 'Cytheria.'" Chicago Daily News (11 January), p. 12.
Briefly mentions long note received announcing birth of Dell's son Anthony.

290 HANSEN, HARRY. Review of The Briary-Bush. The Atlantic Monthly, 129 (January), Bookshelf sec., p. 9.
Quoted from no. 235.

291 MANLY, JOHN MATTHEWS, and EDITH RICKERT. Contemporary American Literature: Bibliographies and Study Outlines. New York: Harcourt, Brace, pp. 41, 171, 172, 177.
Brief biography and bibliography of Dell's works and of works about him. Includes his name in several lists of authors. Revised edition, no. 626.

292 MENCKEN, H[ENRY] L. Review of The Briary-Bush. The Smart Set, 67 (January), 141.
Short. The novel does not equal Moon-Calf. It lacks

the "careful observation and brilliant detail." The story is
simply the dull analysis of a poor marriage between two un-
interesting characters. The book is like a rewritten act of
"A Doll's House."

293 P., R. "A poem based on Floyd Dell's novel The Briary-Bush."
New York Times Book Review and Magazine (5 February),
p. 18.
Advertisement for Knopf publication. Consists of three
stanzas. The first is Rose-Ann speaking to Felix on the
subject of love. The second is Felix addressing Rose-Ann.
In the third Floyd Dell describes their love and defines
its inevitable end.

294 RASCOE, BURTON. "A Bookman's Daybook." New York Tribune Magazine and Books (31 December), p. 20.
Short section on Dell and Francis Hackett and their contributions to literary Chicago through positions on the Chicago Evening Post. Credits them with introducing many
modern authors to Chicago readers. "They wrote with a
gusto, without pedantry or academic unction. They wrote
about literature in terms of Chicago." They were the first
to interest readers in modern literature beyond that represented by the older genteel tradition. "They were radical,
exuberant, cocksure, aggressive, intolerant, young, and
not very well educated; but they were alive, intelligent,
eager."

295 REID, FORREST. Review of Moon-Calf. The Nation and
Athenaeum, 31 (8 July), 510, 512.
Moon-Calf is "better" than Anderson's Winesburg, Ohio
with which it is compared. Finds "beauty," "poetry," and
"spiritual charm" in Dell's book. Praises the portrayal of
Felix's childhood which Reid does not find to be autobiographical. The book lacks "unity of tone" because of the
clash between Felix's childhood and his maturing. There is
"a clashing of moods, and the transitions are too rapid."

296 TOWNSEND, R.D. Review of The Briary-Bush. The Outlook,
130 (4 January), 33.
Dell lacks an ironic overview of his characters. He is not
always aware that his personages are not tragic but comic.
"The young idiots themselves, with the connivance of the
author, are so solemnly portentous about the egotistic in-
volutions of Felix's desire to be above any human shackles,
to bathe in beauty and revel in liberty, that the reader has
to smile quietly and cautiously." Praises characterization of
two minor personages and the glimpses of Chicago life.

297 VAN DOREN, CARL. Review of The Briary-Bush. The Nation, 114 (4 January), 19.

Praises the novel highly. "Taken by itself, it seems to
me to hover over the dark waters of the unconscious on the
surest, lightest wings an American novel has ever used."
The external surface of the novel is muted, confused, lacking in emphasis. Underneath the monotone is a revelation
of character and strong impulses. There is a battle between the unconscious and rebellious reason. Praises Dell's
style, his insight, and his lyricism.

298 WALPOLE, HUGH. "An Open Letter to H.L. Mencken." The
Bookman, 55 (May), 225-28 [225, 226].
Attacks Mencken's presumptions about English criticism
and English reception of American novels. Dell mentioned
as one of a group of new, "brilliant" novelists. Moon-Calf
is distinctly American, not English. The language of Moon-
Calf is difficult for an Englishman to understand.

1923

299 AIKMAN, DUNCAN. "Floyd Dell's Novel of Modern Girl's Development in Love Has Electric Touch of Life." El Paso
Times (25 November), p. 33.
Review of Janet March. Tells plot. Discusses differences
between analytical and life-creative novelists, both of whom
are seriously interested in character. Dell belongs to the
latter. "It is doubtful if any American novel of the year
gives a more buoyant sense of living it through with its
characters than Janet March." Dell achieves the effect of
making the reader participate in the action by using "alive
words" and "by a sympathy, an understanding, a study of
his characters that leaves no detail of their circumstances
and psychology unexplained." Dell makes a "brilliant selection of what is artistically relevant."

300 ANON. "Floyd Dell." The Bookman, 56 (January), 648.
Dell is included in a series of descriptions of writers of
contemporary fiction whose work is serious and good. These
are F.S. Fitzgerald, Z. Gale, W. Cather, and S. Anderson.
Includes a brief biography and commentary. "He is progress-
ing with steady determination toward a firm place in the front
ranks of American writing."

301 ANON. "The Gossip Shop." The Bookman, 56 (January),
663.
Describes a dinner given by P.E.N., an international
literary society. Dell was in attendance. Notes his conversation with Kate Douglas Wiggin (Mrs. Riggs) on the subject of being shocked by printed material.

302 ANON. Review of King Arthur's Socks and Other Village

Plays. The Booklist, 19 (January), 114.
Brief. Lists contents. Quotes Dell's description of the
volume.

303 ANON. Review of King Arthur's Socks and Other Village
Plays. Monthly Bulletin of the Carnegie Library of Pitts-
burgh, 28 (January), 28.
Lists plays included. Brief.

304 ANON. "New York's Bohemia." Springfield Republican (4
January), 6.
Review of King Arthur's Socks. "For the most part these
are blithe, smart, amusing episodes" of love in New York's
bohemia. Brief comment on individual plays.

305 ANON. "The Literary Spotlight; XVII: Floyd Dell." The
Bookman, 57 (March), 65-71.
Portrait of Dell by a person who claims to know him.
Concentrates on his life in Chicago. Discusses the differences in him before and after psychoanalysis. Brief commentary on his works. Credits him with initiating "the
contemporary little theatre movement in New York." Reprinted in no. 1020.

306 ANON. Review of Wilfrid Blunt's Poems. The Freeman, 7
(28 March), 70-71.
Brief mention of Dell's editorial wisdom in selecting the
poems included here.

307 ANON. Review of Janet March. New York Times Book Review (14 October), 8.
The heroine's character is not believable. The initial
history of her family is not an integral part of the novel.
The book is naive, but at the same time it contains pro-
fundities. "Mr. Dell's style is pedestrian, and worse."
The novel may be the turning point in Dell's career. "If
the author cannot overcome his juvenilities he will never
reach the heights to which the intermingled evidences of
maturity justify him in aspiring."

308* ANON. St. Paul News (4 November).
Not available. Cited in no. 913, p. 558.

309* ANON. Review of Janet March. Red Wing (Minn.) Republican (23 November).
Cited in no. 913, p. 558. The Red Wing Public Library
could not find this review in either the daily or the weekly
Red Wing Republican on this date. Reprinted in no. 310.

310 ANON. Review of Janet March. Edited by Grant Overton.
New Orleans States (25 November), sec. 2, no page number.

Briefly tells plot. As a heroine, Janet does not move the
reader. Her unconventional behavior fails to shock. "The
book is very honest, very well-written, and seems to be
more of a study than a genuinely felt or moving story."
According to no. 913, this is reprinted from no. 309.

311 ANON. "Weekly Book Review." Olean [N.Y.] Evening Times
(26 November), p. 9.
Includes review of Janet March. Criticizes novel for excessive length. Style is "complicated and repetitious" in
order to examine problems of youthful behavior. "Dell
stands as the apostle of realism."

312 ANON. Review of Janet March. The Bookman, 58 (December), 453.
Brief. "Perhaps the most modern of all modern heroines
moves disturbingly through this competent but amazing novel."

313 ANON. Review of Janet March. St. Louis Post-Dispatch
(1 December), p. 9.
Long retelling of plot. Believes Dell begins a new novel
when, after lengthy section on Janet, he begins to give
history of Roger. Notes incongruency between Dell's liberal life-style and the conventional ending. "Thus does
Puritanism make Philistines of us all."

314 BECHHOFER, C.E. The Literary Renaissance in America.
London: William Heinemann, pp. 128, 133.
Pseudonym. See Roberts, Carl Eric Bechhofer, no. 344.

315 BENET, WILLIAM ROSE. Review of Wilfrid Scawen Blunt's
Poems. New York Evening Post Literary Review (12 May),
p. 680.
Short. Only mentions Dell as having selected the poems
with the author's approval.

316 CHEW, SAMUEL C. "Blunt's Poems." The Nation, 116 (30
May), 636.
Review of Poems by Wilfrid Scawen Blunt. Praises Dell's
selection of poems to be included. "The selection could
hardly be bettered."

317 C[LOVER], S[AM] T. Review of Janet March. Saturday
Night (10 November), p. 16.
Extended relation of plot. Janet is not an attractive
character because she "is only a few removes from a cour-
tesan." Dell is criticized for his attitude to sexual morality.

318 DAY, DOROTHY. "'Girls and Boys Come Out to Play.'"
The Liberator, 6 (November), 30-31.

Review of Janet March. Written as a letter to Dell, Day's supervisor for her reviews in the Masses. Mainly describes Janet. Contrasts her straightforward action with Felix Fay's introspection. Long quotes from the novel.

319 DEAN, JAMES W. "Character Told by His Works." Danville (Va.) Bee (11 December), p. 14.
Commentary on Dell's story "Phantom Adventure" in December 1923 Century. Tells plot. The story illustrates Dean's belief that fiction expresses the author's character. Dell is shown to be "a practical dreamer," "an unequivocable romanticist." "He perceives the function of the fiction writer to be that of bringing romance into communion with romance." Discusses other writers in similar context. Reprinted in nos. 320, 321, and 322.

320* DEAN, J[AMES] W. Comment on a Dell Short Story. Huntington [W.Va.] Advertiser (16 December).
Cited in no. 913 as a reprint of no. 319. Not available at the West Virginia Department of Archives and History, the Cabell County Public Library, or the Huntington Public Library.

321 DEAN, JAMES W. "Character of an Author Told by His Works." Saginaw Daily News (11 December), p. 5.
Reprinted with title change from no. 319.

322 DEAN, JAMES W. "They Reveal Themselves in Their Short Stories." Lynchburg [Va.] News (16 December), sec. 2, pp. 2, 3 [2].
Reprinted with title change from no. 319.

323 DUNBAR, OLIVIA HOWARD. "That Younger Generation." The World Tomorrow, 6 (December), 379.
Review of Janet March. Dell does not succeed in portraying the heroine both realistically and with "sufficient substance." She is representative and therefore undistinguished. Her only attribute which is explored in detail is her sexual development. The reviewer remarks a contrast betwen revolutionary theory and banal manner. The novel lacks "magic and humor and passion."

324 EMMART, A.D. "The Limitations of American Magazines." The Modern Quarterly, 1 (July), 18-30 [22, 23].
A section of this article reviews The Liberator as a radical magazine. Dell is mentioned as part of nucleus of writers that could do important work, but does not. Dell does not connect art with social revolution. The magazine itself fails to give a comprehensive view of the basis of socialism. See North, Richel for pseudonym, no. 340.

325 F[ARRAR], J[OHN]. Mention of Wilfrid Scawen Blunt's Collected Poems. The Bookman, 57 (April), 230.
Dell's edition of Blunt's poetry is one sign of encouragement in the current season's poetry books.

326 F[ARRAR], J[OHN]. Review of Janet March. The Bookman, 58 (December), 459.
The book is very disturbing because of its view of sex. Dell should write in the poetic vein in which he excels and avoid "exaggeratedly detailed realism."

327 F[ARRAR], J[OHN]. Review of The Novel of Tomorrow. The Bookman, 57 (March), 82.
Very brief review. The essays are more illustrative of the author's personalities than they are illuminating to the novels considered. Dell's and Joseph Hergesheimer's essays are liked best.

328* FITZGERALD, F. SCOTT. Letter to Bernard Vaughan. St. Paul Daily News (23 December), sec. 2, p. 5.
Cited in no. 1094, pp. 137-38. Not available from the St. Paul Public Library or the Minnesota Historical Society. Reprinted in no. 1094.

329 FREEMAN, JOSEPH. "A Blind Rebel in a Trap." The Liberator, 6 (April), 29-30 [29].
Review of John H. Lawson's play "Roger Bloomer." On the first page Felix Fay is mentioned briefly as an example of an escapee from the Midwest. Names Dell with U. Sinclair, T. Dreiser, S. Lewis, S. Anderson, and B. Hecht as authors of a literature of revolt containing conflict and a reason for conflict.

330 GIBSON, LYDIA. Sketch of Floyd Dell. The Liberator, 6 (April), 21.
Identifies Dell as author of "The Outline of Marriage," Moon-Calf, and The Briary-Bush.

331 GORMAN, HERBERT S. Review of Wilfrid Scawen Blunt's Collected Poems. The Literary Digest International Book Review, 1 (June), 24.
Dell's selection is "judicious" but Blunt's unevenness as a poet is apparent.

332 HANSEN, HARRY. Midwest Portraits; A Book of Memories and Friendships. New York: Harcourt, Brace, pp. 97, 103, 112-13, 118, 119-20, 122, 123-24, 193, 208-16, 217.
Places Dell in the Chicago milieu. Relates his enthusiasm for Sherwood Anderson and his help in getting Anderson's first novel published. Includes part of a review of Moon-Calf, reminiscences, and a brief biography.

333 KRUTCH, JOSEPH WOOD. "Impasse." New York Evening
Post Literary Review (17 November), p. 255.
Review of Janet March. The novel is verbose and its
characters are neither interesting nor important. It is a
grim effort to deal with Dell's own adolescent development,
something which Moon-Calf failed to do. Krutch focuses on
Dell's lack of development as a novelist. He remains provincial, lacking ironic detachment. Although he has won
freedom from literary and social conventions, he now finds
"that he has nothing to say. With the world before him he
can do nothing except turn back and describe once more
how he prepared himself to write the novels which he has
never written."

334 LEWISOHN, LUDWIG. Review of King Arthur's Socks and
Other Village Plays. The Nation, 116 (27 June), 755.
These plays are part of the dramatic movement born in
Greenwich Village. Brief comments on individual plays.
All raise problems. The form of dramatic writing in each
is worthy of cultivation. Yet Dell looks on these plays as
part of a "cruder period" in his work.

335 MACDONALD, W.A. "Mostly Books." Attleboro [Mass.] Sun
(23 November), p. 3.
Most of this article is a review of Janet March. Tells
plot. The character Roger speaks for Dell. The book has
few ideas. "There is no pulse in it, no absorbing current
of being."

336 MENCKEN, H[ENRY] L. "Fifteen Years." The Smart Set
(December), pp. 138-44 [142].
Mencken's article resigning from position of book reviewer
after fifteen years. He sums up the experience. Briefly mentions Dell as a writer who has not lived up to his
promise. He has only written "one novel and two doses of
Greenwich Village psychology."

337 MONTGOMERY, ROSELLE MERCIER. "The Younger Generation Grows Older." The Literary Digest International Book
Review, 1 (June), 5-7 [7].
Dell is quoted as an authority on the younger generation
being made obsolete by a still younger group.

338* MORGAN-POWELL, S. Review of Janet March. Montreal Star
(1 December).
Cited in no. 913, p. 558. Not available from the University of Montreal or the National Library of Canada.

339 MORTON, DAVID. Review of Wilfrid Scawen Blunt's Collected Poems. The Bookman, 57 (June), 460.
Mainly commentary on the author. Does not mention Dell,

the editor, by name but says this edition contains all that
the author wanted included.

340 NORTH, RICHEL. "The Limitations of American Magazines."
     The Modern Quarterly, 1 (July), 18-30 [22, 23].
     Pseudonym. See Emmart, A.D., no. 324.

341 OVERTON, GRANT. "The Young Wife's Tale." The Book Re-
     view (November), p. 18.
        Review of Janet March. Novel is well written although
     structure is weak. Heroine fails to evoke readers' empathy.
     "As a chronicler of contemporary manners and as a social
     historian Mr. Dell is possibly the best writer who has given
     us a novel."

342 RASCOE, BURTON. "A Bookman's Daybook." New York Trib-
     une Magazine and Books (18 November), pp. 30, 31 [31].
        Reports November 10 conversation with Somerset Maugham.
     Maugham observes that a number of American writers "flare
     up magnificently with one book, and not only cease to de-
     velop but actually go downhill." Names Dell's Moon-Calf
     as "fine, brave, beautiful, unusual" and The Briary-Bush
     as poor.

343 RICE, CALE YOUNG. Letter to John Farrar, Editor. The
     Bookman, 57 (June), 481-82.
        Comments on Dell's essay "Criticism and Bad Manners" in
     The Bookman, 57 (May 1923), 257-62. Rice believes Dell
     has attacked him personally. Claims Dell is motivated by
     jealousy of Rice's success.

344 ROBERTS, CARL ERIC BECHHOFER. The Literary Renais-
     sance in America. London: William Heinemann, pp. 128, 133.
        Names Dell as having influenced Claude Washburn. Short
     paragraph giving brief plot description of Moon-Calf and
     The Briary-Bush. Praises Dell for encouraging Sherwood
     Anderson to publish his work. See Bechhofer, Carl Eric,
     no. 314.

345 S., J.C. Review of Wilfrid Scawen Blunt's Collected Poems.
     The London Mercury, 9 (November), 100-101.
        Dell has succeeded in selecting Blunt's best work for in-
     clusion.

346 SAYLER, OLIVER M. Our American Theatre. New York:
     Brentano's, pp. 91, 300-301, 333, 334, 335.
        Mentions Dell as a playwright indebted to the Province-
     town Players. Lists "King Arthur's Socks" among impor-
     tant stage productions of the period 1908-1923. Listed
     again among productions of 1916-1917 season together with
     "A Long Time Ago." "The Angel Intrudes" included with
     list of 1917-1918 productions of Provincetown Players.

347 SINCLAIR, UPTON. "Parents Do Not Want to Know the Truth About Young People." New York American (11 November), sec. LII, p. 5.
Review of Janet March. Highly critical of novel for its lack of realism and morality. It does not inveigh against promiscuity and abortion, nor does it warn against venereal disease. Yet Dell is "one of the ablest literary minds of our time." The story is "absorbingly interesting" and is written from a "genial, kindly and humane" point of view.

348 THE MIDDLEBROW. Review of Janet March. Town Topics, 40 (29 November), 17.
Short. The plot is difficult. Criticizes large number of characters and excessive historical background information.

349 WILDE, PERCIVAL. The Craftsmanship of the One-Act Play. Boston: Little, Brown, p. 227.
In discussing the supernatural, "The Angel Intrudes" is mentioned in a footnote. While it is "impossible," it is "delightful." See no. 859 for augmented edition.

350 WILSON, EDMUND. "Late Violets from the Nineties." The Dial, 75 (October), 387-390 [387].
A brief comparison of Carl Van Vechten to Floyd Dell.

1924

351 AMET, RUTH F. "Once-a-Week Book Chat." San Jose [Cal.] Mercury-Herald (10 February), p. 20.
Long quotation from Dell on his life prior to becoming literary editor of the Chicago Evening Post. Identifies him as author of Moon-Calf, The Briary-Bush, and the "delightful fantasy 'The Kitten and the Masterpiece' in the February Century."

352 ANON. Review of Janet March. The Dial, 76 (January), 92.
Short. "The book will seem to most adult readers merely a sentimental celebration of immature passion and unripe ideas."

353 ANON. "Among the Magazines." Greensboro [N.C.] Daily News (3 February), sec. 3, p. 10.
Brief comment on Dell's story "The Kitten and the Masterpiece" in the February 1924 Century. Says the story is "unusual."

354 ANON. "The Century for February." Rochester [N.Y.] Democrat and Chronicle (3 February), sec. 4, p. 9.
Comment reprinted from no. 368 where it is attributed to Katie Daffan.

355 ANON. "The Liberator." Chicago Evening Post (8 February),
   Friday Literary Review sec., p. 4.
   Mildly satiric article announcing the relocation of The
   Liberator to Chicago. Notes series "Literature and the Ma-
   chine Age" by Dell, "one of the most distinguished of the
   younger critics." Suggests it should also appear in the
   North American Review so non-radicals might read it with-
   out being shocked by the rest of The Liberator's contents.

356 ANON. "Notes on Books and Bookmen." New York World
   (10 February), p. 6E.
   Brief comment on Dell's story "The Kitten and the Masterpiece" in the Feburary 1924 Century. It is "a shrewd and
   happy presentation of the struggle between the artist and
   environment."

357* ANON. Review of Looking at Life. Springfield (MA) Union
   (20 April).
   Cited in no. 913, p. 563. Unlocatable. A librarian at the
   Springfield City Library was unable to find this reference.

358 ANON. Review of Janet March. London Times Literary Supplement (8 May), p. 284.
   The novel's theme is the rise of a family through three
   generations and the "substitution of feminine influences
   for masculine." Dell is inconclusive in his attitude to the
   rights and liberties of children and changing sexual mores.

359 ANON. Review of Looking at Life. The Booklist, 20 (June),
   330.
   Brief. Describes and lists contents. "Discerning and
   appreciative."

360 ANON. "The Gossip Shop." The Bookman, 59 (August),
   759-68 [759].
   A brief mention of Dell having finished This Mad Ideal
   and leaving Croton-on-Hudson for a summer in Massachusetts.

361 ANON. Review of Looking at Life. The Dial, 77 (August),
   173.
   Praises "elfish, pucklike quality" in essays. Dell is example of serious American who is also popular. He does
   well "as a leader for Rand School intellectuals."

362 ANON. Review of Looking at Life. The Open Shelf (September-
   October), p. 68.
   Brief. Mentions two individual essays. "Mr. Dell is
   more adult and satisfying as an essayist looking at life than
   as a novelist and is perhaps most convincing of all as a
   literary critic discussing books in a fashion which involves
   a good deal of his personal philosophy."

363 ANON. Review of Looking at Life. London Times Literary
Supplement (11 December), p. 844.
    Dell here writes like a journalist, but he cannot detach
his personal emotion. He writes dogmatically. "His sensi-
bility is that of the pre-war intellectual whom the ideal of
social reform affected with the intensity of an aesthetic emotion." He "dogmatizes."

364 BALDWIN, CHARLES C. "Floyd Dell," in The Men Who Make
Our Novels. New York: Dodd, Mead, pp. 129-33.
    Biographical treatment. Quotations from Dell. Short
commentary on Moon-Calf and The Briary-Bush. Praises
early parts of Moon-Calf. The Briary-Bush is less interesting.
Dell is "the mildest of the radicals" and "the most persua-
sive." Reprinted no. 984.

365 BOYD, ERNEST. "Readers and Writers; A Literary Causerie."
The Independent, 112 (26 April), 230.
    One third of this article is a review of Looking at Life.
Dell's ideas are outdated. Even when first printed in 1914,
the feminist ideas were "antiquated theory." "In 1924 it
is almost incredible that a young man could print it." The
reprinting of his ideas on prohibition "in this present year
of grace is the final proof that Mr. Floyd Dell is impervious
to facts. He is living in the fairyland of late-Victorian Socialism."

366 C., J. W. "Dell Looks at Floyd." New York World (6 April),
p. 6E.
    Review of Looking at Life. Highly critical. Shows "striv-
ings of a literal and hesitant man to be ultimate and deci-
sive." Dell lacks humility and is too dogmatic. His own
shortcomings become standards by which he judges Walt
Whitman. He cannot understand Whitman and others.

367 D., M. Review of Looking at Life. St. Louis Library Bulletin (October), p. 350.
    Very brief. Lists subjects of these "frank reflections."

368 DAFFAN, KATIE. "Literary Talk." Houston Chronicle (27
January), sec. 1, p. 26.
    Includes brief comment on Dell's short story "The Kitten
and the Masterpiece" in the February 1924 Century. "The
excellence of Century fiction is well upheld by Floyd Dell
in his delightful phantasy." Comment reprinted no. 354.

369 DAVISON, FRANK C. "Contemporary Literature." New York
Evening Post Literary Review (24 May), p. 771.
    Review of Looking at Life. Dell is discussing not neces-
sarily contemporary life but contemporary literature. In
contrast, Anatole France claimed to look at literature but

really commented on life. Dell, though limited in outlook,
"observes with consistent detachment" and with "candor,
modesty, [and] good sense." "Not Without Dust and Heat"
is given particular attention. Dell is not brilliant or human
enough to have "achieved that final, post-graduate amoral
viewpoint." Reprinted in no. 370.

370 DAVISON, FRANK C. "Contemporary Literature." The Literary Review of the Public Ledger (Philadelphia) (25 May),
p. 3.
Reprinted from no. 369.

371 [FARRAR, JOHN]. "Floyd Dell," in The Literary Spotlight.
New York: George H. Doran, pp. 65-76.
Essay contrasting Dell's contemporary personality with his
personality before being psychoanalyzed. He was socially
naive, insensitive, and bold, yet natural and spontaneous.
"His intention was not so much to shock the bourgeoisie as
to let the bourgeoisie know that its ideas profoundly shocked
him." While his intellectual ideas are the same, his emotional nature has become more conservative. His novels deal
with human emotions in contemporary life. Includes anec-
dotes and, on p. 318, a brief biography and bibliography.

372 F[ARRAR], J[OHN]. "The Real Literary Pulse." The Bookman, 59 (June), pp. 458-59.
Review of Looking at Life woven with reviews of six other
volumes of essays. Dell is in the American tradition, a fol-
lower of Emerson. These essays pit the literary conservative against the political radical.

373 FORMAN, HENRY JAMES. The Outline of Literature; A Plain
Story Simply Told. Edited by John Drinkwater. Vol. 3.
New York: G. P. Putnam's Sons, pp. 983, 988.
Names Dell as a novelist of "this new and stern realistic
creed in America." Lists Dell, S. Lewis, Z. Gale, and
F. S. Fitzgerald as novelists in revolt against the glorifi-
cation of the village. They "burst into a sort of legitimate
Walpurgis Night revel for the long suppressed desires."

374 G. "Poet and Prosateur of Young Love." The Stratford
Monthly, 1 (June), 294-95.
Review of Looking at Life woven with review of A. D.
Ficke's Out of Silence and Other Poems. Dell is a natural
essayist. He is "frankly, engagingly himself." His prose
is clear. Recommended to youth. Dell, "pre-eminently a
speculator upon ideas," lacks emotional involvement in his
novels.

375 G[IBSON], L[YDIA]. "A Magic Mirror." The Liberator,
7 (May), 30.

Review of Looking at Life. Complains that Dell does not
credit The Masses and The Liberator with first publishing
these essays. Praises Dell's unique approach to many
facets of life. Notes his fantasy, mockery, and relevance.

376 HAHN, MANNEL. Review of Looking at Life. St. Louis Post
Dispatch (19 April), p. 8.
Short. Written as dialogue between "Physician" and
"Lawyer." Criticizes book for being a rehash of old ideas
instead of presenting new modern ideas.

377 LOVETT, ROBERT MORSS. Review of Looking at Life. The
New Republic, 39 (28 May), 23.
Dell expounds journalistic criticism emphasizing the critic,
his interest and curiosity, not the artist, the work, or the
audience. Describes contents of volume.

378 MCAFEE, HELEN. "What Are They Reading in Books?" The
Bookman, 58 (January), 513-18 [516].
Notes the "book talk" in Janet March. Dell quotes from
Edna Millay and Walt Whitman and mentions several books.
Allows the author to comment on the characters through
their choice and understanding of literature.

379 MENCKEN, H[ENRY] L. Prejudices: Fourth Series. New
York: Alfred A. Knopf, p. 291.
Mentions Dell as a writer of promise who is not taking
advantage of the freedom from censorship to become a
serious writer.

380 MORSE, CHLOE. Review of Janet March. The Bookman,
59 (March), 124.
Discusses character portrayal in fiction. Dell's method
is ponderous. The book is significant in Dell's career as
the first to break away from autobiography.

381 MOUNT, GRETCHEN. "Open Letter to Floyd Dell." Detroit
Free Press (11 May), Magazine sec., pp. 3-4.
Review of Looking at Life. Although versatile, Dell is
fundamentally a critic, and books such as this one are his
métier. It is a personal spiritual history and a literary
history. Dell's personality has remained intact through
time and changing circumstance. His philosophy is successful because he has been able to live by it.

382 POWYS, LLEWELLYN. "Mr. Dell Gazes Wistfully Out upon
Life." New York Times Book Review (20 April), p. 14.
Review of Looking at Life. Praises Dell's conversation,
but highly critical of his writings. As an essayist, Dell
is totally lacking poetic imagination. His "flippancy of
tone" puts much of his writing outside the bounds of

literature. Praises his expression of sociological concerns as "simple and unaffected." Dell has forgotten that he is a model to youth in matters of writing, aesthetics, morals, and politics.

383 S., H. "An Anthology? No!" New York World (10 February), p. 6E.
Review of The Bookman Anthology of Essays edited by John Farrar. Authors chosen because of their names, not their essay-writing capabilities. Dell's contribution is justified on belief that "the essay form is probably regarded as an illegitimate one that may be treated with levity or indifference."

384 SAPIR, EDWARD. "Twelve Novelists in Search of a Reason; A Sort of Review." The Stratford Monthly, (1 May), 191-96.
Short play. Conversation among twelve contemporary novelists banished by editors of The New Republic. Dell is one.

385 SMALL, FLORENCE S. Letter to the Editor. The Bookman, 59 (July), 615.
Commentary on article by Dell on R. W. Emerson in May 1924 Bookman. Dell patronizes Emerson and is too concerned with himself to understand Emerson.

386 SMERTENKO, JOHAN J. Review of Looking at Life. The Nation, 119 (29 October), 472.
Dell does not give a profound discussion. The essays are shallow and dull. "In Looking at Life his purpose is to educate the Philistines rather than to discourse with civilized people." Short discussion of Dell's ability to "personalize an abstract problem."

387* SUTTON, EVELYN. Review of Looking at Life. San Francisco Journal (11 May), n.p.
Cited in no. 913, p. 563. This date is missing from the San Francisco Public Library.

1925

388 A[DAMS], F[RANKLIN] P[IERCE]. "Song of Travel: Being a Corollary to Floyd Dell's Song of Travel in Yesterday's Conning Tower." New York World (29 October), p. 19.
Doggerel stanzas on glories of European versus American living. In response to Dell's work in Adams' "The Conning Tower" on October 28, 1925.

389 ANON. The Borzoi, 1925: Being a Sort of Record of Ten

Years' Publishing. New York: Alfred A. Knopf, p. 291.
Lists Dell's books that were published by Knopf beginning
with Were You Ever a Child? and ending with This Mad Ideal
in 1925.

390 ANON. "Staled Modernity." New York Times Book Review
(22 February), pp. 8-9.
Review of This Mad Ideal. Highly critical. Dell does not
present new ideas. He is here an iconoclast wrecking the
old ideas of Greenwich Village. Language, style, and narrative are "colorless." Praises Dell's telling of the story
as opposed to his constructing of it. The psychology of
Judith is convincing.

391 ANON. Review of This Mad Ideal. The Outlook, 139 (18
March), 424.
Short. Dell is becoming "quaint" "with his ingenuous
variations on much-worn themes." The heroine is "real,"
but lacks substance and importance.

392 ANON. Review of This Mad Ideal. The Independent, 114
(21 March), 331.
Brief. Praises the characterization of the heroine and
the "delicacy and tenderness" of the first part of the
novel.

393 ANON. "Finds Excitement Injures the Race." New York
Times (29 March), p. 16.
Briefly mentions that a message from Dell was presented
to a conference on birth control. Dell is identified as a
"novelist."

394 ANON. "The Gossip Shop." The Bookman, 61 (April),
249-56 [249].
Brief mention of Dell and Louis Untermeyer talking "vio-
lently" throughout a lunch.

395 ANON. Review of This Mad Ideal. The Bookman, 61 (April),
216.
Very brief. Included on list of recent fiction. Especially recommended. "As good as Moon-Calf if not better."

396 ANON. Review of This Mad Ideal. Edited by Mary Katharine
Reely. Wisconsin Library Bulletin, 21 (April), 112.
Brief statement on plot. "Slight but well told."

397 ANON. Notice of This Mad Ideal. Saturday Review of Literature, 1 (11 April), 677.
Very brief. Title listed under younger generation novels.

398 ANON. Notice of This Mad Ideal. The Nation, 120 (15

April), 448.
    The novel is included in a list of notable fictional works
for spring 1925.

399 ANON. Review of This Mad Ideal. The New Yorker, 1 (18
     April), 26.
        The execution of the novel is not criticized but Dell's
     point of view is "immature." He does not sentimentalize
     his story, but he does simplify it too much. "His sympathy
     with Judith ignores any deeper reason for her conduct."

400 ANON. Review of This Mad Ideal. The Booklist, 21 (May),
     302.
        Brief recounting of plot. "More conservative than his
     earlier novels and contains none of their realistic detail."

401 ANON. Review of The Best Short Stories of 1924. The
     Dial, 78 (June), 520.
        Brief mention of Dell's contribution being part of "the
     best of what there is."

402 ANON. Review of This Mad Ideal. The Dial, 78 (June), 520.
        Brief. Dell uncritically favors the younger generation in
     this mock battle between youth and age. "The author is
     lost in admiration of her [the heroine], but in the end, the
     reader still has his compass. Judith emerges untamed, but
     --untested."

403 ANON. Review of This Mad Ideal. The Open Shelf (June),
     p. 67.
        Short. Describes character of Judith. Hopes Dell's
     censors will not impede the broadening of his fiction's moral
     foundation.

404 ANON. Review of This Mad Ideal. London Times Literary
     Supplement (23 July), 497.
        Short. Tells plot. Heroine's search for freedom is the
     mad ideal "which Mr. Floyd Dell raises to the level of in-
     spired sanity."

405 ANON. "Books That May Have Escaped You." The Book-
     man, 62 (September), 73.
        Were You Ever a Child? included in list of five books.
     Very brief description. "A wise and sturdy little book
     on education."

406 ANON. Review of This Mad Ideal. The Spectator, 135 (5
     September), 382.
        Brief. "The book is interesting, and the heroine should
     serve as a useful warning to all young people not to be
     afraid of life."

407 ANON. "The Gossip Shop." The Bookman, 62 (October),
231-40 [233].
Brief mention of Dell having returned from London and
Paris.

408 ANON. "An Older 'Moon-Calf.'" New York Times Book Review (4 October), p. 8.
Review of Runaway. "Possibly there is a statement of
values somewhere in Runaway, but the only impression is of
hopeless confusion and a complete lack of inner necessity on
the author's part. It would appear that Mr. Dell has come
to distrust his former shibboleth of romantic incompetence
and has failed altogether to bring himself to accept as its
alternative the very standards which he has consistently
resisted. Mr. Dell is himself the 'runaway.'"

409 ANON. "Novelist Ill on Voyage." New York Times (14 October), p. 27.
Short article stating that Dell, who had gone to Europe
for inspiration for another novel, returned home because
of illness. En route he was again ill. Dell identified as
"American novelist."

410 ANON. Review of Runaway. The Independent, 115 (31 October), 508.
Short. Cites the characterization, drama, good writing,
and suggestion of profundity as admirable qualities of the
novel. Yet as a whole it is unrealistic.

411 ANON. "The Gossip Shop." The Bookman, 62 (November),
359-68 [359].
Brief mention of Dell's opinion of London tea time and of
Michael Arlen's Mayfair. Says Dell is doing research. Includes clipping about G. B. Shaw sent by Dell.

412 ANON. Review of Runaway. The Bookman, 62 (November),
328.
Very brief. Notes "romantic and highly colored" plot.

413 ANON. Review of Runaway. The Open Shelf (November),
p. 107.
Short. Brief plot summary. Notes plot complications
and interesting philosophy. "A much more mature book"
than previous Dell works.

414 ANON. "The Gossip Shop." The Bookman, 62 (December),
517-28 [523].
Brief mention of Dell writing to Heywood Broun on the
subject of censorship. Quotes part of letter.

415 ANON. Review of Runaway. The Booklist, 22 (December),
116.

Brief retelling of plot. "The plot is thin, but the characterization is excellent." More mature than earlier novels.

416 ANON. Review of Runaway. Edited by Mary Katharine Reely.
Wisconsin Library Bulletin, 21 (December), 309.
Brief. Tells plot. "Very much the best novel this author
has done. More mature, more impersonal."

417 ANON. "These Wild Young Women." The Bookman, 62 (December), 370-71 [370].
Dell is included among writers who have treated the subject of the revolt of women. Mentions the heroine of Runaway. Although modern, her actions are extremely conservative. Sees Janet March as example of shocking but not
truly modern female.

418 BECKER, MAY LAMBERTON. Review of Runaway. Saturday
Review of Literature, 1 (21 November), 328.
Brief. "It is a study of the rebound from radicalism."

419 BECKER, MAY LAMBERTON. Review of This Mad Ideal.
Saturday Review of Literature, 1 (9 May), 749.
Brief. This is Dell's best novel. The heroine is be-
lievable.

420 BELL, LISLE. "The Ogre of Convention." The Nation, 120
(15 April), 436-37.
Review of This Mad Ideal. Dell's characters are inflexible
idealists who take pleasure in being unconventional. Dell
does not resolve the situation created by his heroine's
idealism.

421 BJORKMAN, EDWIN. "The Dell Ideal." New York Evening
Post Literary Review (21 March), pp. 3-4.
Review of This Mad Ideal. Praises the novel as Dell's
best so far. In this work Dell is finally able to be less
righteous and self-interested. While he seems to write for
pleasure rather than for didactic purpose, he retains a
"spontaneous grace." His style is much improved. "It is
crisper, more dynamic, less literary." The characters are
more human and less representations of Dell. The heroine
is convincing because of small traits, her "unconscious
grace," and her self-knowledge. The reviewer looks for
a sequel.

422* BROUN, HEYWOOD. Comment on Runaway. New York World.
Unlocatable. Cited in no. 913, p. 567. Date uncertain.
Placed under 1925 because that is the year the novel was
published.

423 BULLETT, GERALD. Review of This Mad Ideal. The Saturday Review, 140 (11 July), 45.

Brief recounting of plot. The characters are not sufficiently well-defined or individualized. "The flavour of Mr.
Floyd Dell's work is pleasant but not distinctive."

424 DAVISON, EDWARD. "Middle-Class Life." Saturday Review
of Literature, 2 (17 October), 210.
Review of Runaway. The novel is "subtle, stimulating,
and well-wrought" and a "mature piece of craft." Briefly
tells plot. Discusses the desire for a romantic life as dem-
onstrated in American novels. Defines the nature of the
"romance" in Runaway. Dell's minor characters are well
portrayed.

425 DICKINSON, THOMAS H. Playwrights of the New American
Theatre. New York: Macmillan, p. 277.
Includes "The Angel Intrudes" in list of meritorious one-
act plays.

426 F[ARRAR], J[OHN]. "Strong and Deep." The Bookman,
61 (April), 219.
Compares the fine writing of A. Hamilton Gibbs' Soundings
to that of Maugham's The Painted Veil, Dell's This Mad Ideal,
and Lewis' Arrowsmith.

427 F[ARRAR], J[OHN]. "Two Novels with Touches of Poetry."
The Bookman, 61 (April), 219-20.
Review of This Mad Ideal. Compares it to Robert Nathan's
Jonah. Praises language and the love story. This is Dell's
best novel since Moon-Calf. The marriage-career conflict is
not resolved but presented with "flares of passion and truth."

428 FUESSLE, KENNETH. "Two Generations of Floyd Dell's Idealists." Literary Digest International Book Review, 3 (June),
pp. 475, 487.
Review of This Mad Ideal. The characters are "less a
defense than a vindication" of contemporary young people.
Dell succeeds in a disinterested treatment. The restraint
and direction of the book make it one of the outstanding
novels of the season. Extended retelling of plot.

429 G., R. D. "Floyd Dell's Mad Ideal." Boston Evening Transcript (25 March), part 3, p. 4.
Review of This Mad Ideal. Relates the plot, sarcastically
emphasizing the melodrama. The reader does not know what
the mad ideal is. Includes portrait.

430 HANSEN, HARRY. "The Prodigal Son." Chicago Daily News
(4 February), p. 16.
Reports New York reception given by Ben Huebsch to
honor Sherwood Anderson. Many of the most important
literary figures of the day attended, including Dell. Names
some of the guests.

431 KREYMBORG, ALFRED. Troubadour: An Autobiography.
New York: Boni and Liveright, pp. 306, 307, 313, 314.
Brief mentions of Dell's relationship to the Provincetown
Players.

432 KRONENBERGER, LOUIS. "Paving the Way." Saturday Review of Literature, 1 (30 May), 786-87.
Review of This Mad Ideal. Compares it to Moon-Calf.
The former "is only a reworking of the old material, less
effective and less convincing because it rather seems written from a formula." The main character, Judith Valentine, is not fully realized. Unless Dell moves beyond the
subject matter of youth, he will remain a minor novelist.

433 LANGFELD, WILLIAM R. Review of Runaway. Literary Digest International Book Review, 4 (December), 56.
Runaway is inferior to Dell's previous novels. He seems
to aim for popularity, and the reviewer predicts his success. The plot is recapitulated. "One finds at times in
Runaway the old Floyd Dell of striking phrase, of poetic
description, of humorous irony." "Gone is the atmosphere
of spontaneity, of fervid dissent, of honest, heartfelt protest. Instead of enthusiasm and surrender to his art, one
finds clever craftsmanship, reworking old materials into a
form that may entertain pleasantly while it disappoints artistically."

434 LITTELL, ROBERT. Review of Runaway. The New Republic, 44 (11 November), 313.
Short. "Watery discourse, unconvincing incident, and
flat people" make for a plodding novel. It does not live
up to Dell's intelligence and sensitivity.

435 LOVEMAN, AMY. Review of Runaway. Saturday Review of Literature, 1 (17 October), 224.
Very brief. Lists the book with those which show less
bitterness than those of the recent past.

436 LOVETT, ROBERT MORSS. Review of This Mad Ideal. The New Republic, 42 (22 April), 243.
Short. Dell's heroines are becoming similar in type. The
secondary characters and scene also "seem warmed over."

437 P., E. L. Review of This Mad Ideal. The Outlook, 139 (18 March), 424.
Short. Dell cannot keep up with the advancing standard
of indecency. Instead, he is becoming "quaint" with "his
ingenuous variations on much-worn themes." The heroine
lacks substance.

438 THE RAVEN. "Popularizing Burton's 'Melancholy.'" T.P.'s and Cassell's Weekly (London), 4 (1 August), 472.

Notes Dell's presence in London and his work with "Gordon-Smith" (sic) in translating all the Latin in The Anatomy of Melancholy. Quotes Dell on Burton as a precursor of Freud. Includes photo.

439 S., K. "Runaway; Floyd Dell Now the Author of a Pleasant Story." Boston Evening Transcript (10 October), part 8, p. 5.
Tells plot. Says Dell, in this novel, is trying to get beyond the pessimism and eccentricity of the post-war period. In making this "radical change," Dell has not produced his best work. The hero, Michael Shenstone, "is admirably conceived and described by Mr. Dell and his portrait is one of the best things he has done." Other characters, however, are not so believable.

440 SHERMAN, STUART P. "The Coast of Bohemia." New York Herald Tribune Books (15 March), pp. 1, 2, 3.
Review of This Mad Ideal. Gives overview of Dell's work up to this volume. Sees him as a bohemian dreamer, not truly a socialist. Brief biography. His novels are poetic in that they are " 'impassioned recollection' " of his own childhood and youth. Points out the existence of a child-like secret house in each novel, which serves as a symbol for Dell's view of the happy life and the ideal relationship. This Mad Ideal does not advance the theme, but is "a marked falling off in his artistic resources." He must develop his theme by showing its relationship with reality. His "weakness as a writer of fiction and also as a feminist seems at the moment due to a kind of indolence or apathy or lack of courage in the use of the realistic imagination." See no. 511 for reprint.

441 SMITH, ALISON. "A Feminine Moon-Calf." New York World (8 March), p. 6m.
Review of This Mad Ideal. Relates the plot. This female version of Felix Fay is not as realistically portrayed as the original Moon-Calf. "She is less a human being than a limp bundle of theories." The male characters are more believable.

442 SMITH, HARRISON. "Page Mr. Dell." New York Herald Tribune Books (1 November), p. 4.
Review of Runaway. Relates plot. Finds book decidedly inferior to Dell's first two novels. His usual themes of love and escape are here in "motley." The minor characters are "automatons," and all characters "conventional." Dell has lost his frankness. Instead of an understanding of the erotic, in this book one finds "the conventionalized standards, the hypocritical suggestiveness which is the stock in trade of the editors of women's magazines."

443 TAGGARD, GENEVIEVE. "May Days," in May Days; An Anthology of Verse from Masses-Liberator. Edited by Genevieve Taggard. New York: Boni and Liveright, pp. 1-15 [7-8, 10, 11].
Links Dell, Max Eastman, and John Reed in their work on the Masses. They were "the most significant group that ever managed to dominate, for a time, an entire generation." Dell's role was a teacher to youth. Discusses their devotion to social concerns and the conflict with their sense of themselves as artists. Quotes Dell on "escape" from social responsibility. Discusses Masses trial.

444 VAN DOREN, CARL, and MARK VAN DOREN. American and British Literature Since 1890. New York: Century, pp. 87, 320.
Moon-Calf is representative of the realistic novels examining contemporary American life which began to appear in 1920. Whereas in the past Felix Fay would have been considered unworthy, he is now accepted because of his goals and persistence. Recommends Moon-Calf to the reader.

445 WALDMAN, MILTON. Review of This Mad Ideal. The London Mercury, 12 (August), 435.
Relates plot briefly. The book will not add to Dell's European reputation. It is "a very thin piece of work." Comments on sex relationships as seen in modern lives and novels.

446 WANN, LOUIS. "The 'Revolt From the Village' in American Fiction." Overland Monthly and Out West Magazine, 83 (August) 298-99, 324-25 [299].
This article treats the revolt against provincialism and small town life that occurred among writers in the 1920s. Dell "portrays, in Moon-Calf and The Briary-Bush, the difficulties of the poetic soul amid the restrictions of provincialism." Classifies Dell with F. Scott Fitzgerald and Sherwood Anderson among others.

447 YUST, WALTER. "Introducing Floyd Dell in the Act of Escaping." New York Evening Post Literary Review (21 November), p. 3.
Review of Runaway. Retells plot. Highly praises book for its portrait of "victims of circumstance." Cites the disillusion and beauty in the world's imperfections.

1926

448 A., H. B. "Vagabondage; Floyd Dell Writes an Apologia for the Intelligentsia." Boston Evening Transcript (19 June), part 6, p. 4.

Explains Dell's effort to defend his own generation's literature. Many of the ideas are "'dated.'" "It is not yet time to write just the book that Floyd Dell wanted to write. But we know of no attempt to discover the bases of a mental attitude somewhat foreign but still recognizable, which exhibits so much literary excellence, such fluid grace and constant charm as this volume." Dell "is informative and amiably, urbanely profound."

449 A[DAMS], F[RANKLIN] P. "The Conning Tower." New York World (22 May), p. 15.
Says he read Love in Greenwich Village on May 15, 1926. It is "good" and "sentimental." Praises poem "The Ballad of Christopher Street" and wishes Dell would write more like it.

450 A[DAMS], F[RANKLIN] P. "The Conning Tower." New York World (11 December), p. 11.
Brief mention of Adams meeting Dell at Adams' house on December 9, 1926.

451 ANON. "The Gossip Shop." The Bookman, 62 (January), 629-40 [630].
Brief mention of a party where Dell, Elinor Wylie, and William Rose Benét chanted Shelley's odes in unison.

452 ANON. Review of Runaway. Monthly Bulletin of the Carnegie Library of Pittsburgh, 31 (January), 5.
Brief retelling of plot.

453 ANON. Review of Runaway. London Times Literary Supplement (21 January), p. 42.
Mainly tells plot. Although the characters are stock figures, they are "lively and amusing." "The story is well written and moves briskly, and the reader who looks for entertainment will not be defrauded."

454 ANON. Review of Intellectual Vagabondage. Saturday Review of Literature, 2 (27 March), 674.
Brief. Describes the younger generation and the times with which Dell's book deals. The volume is "witty and truthful." See no. 512 for pseudonym.

455 ANON. "These Literary Rebels." New York Times Book Review (4 April), p. 2.
Review of Intellectual Vagabondage. Dell's assessment of the Victorian period and the past in general is incorrect. Del "magnif[ies] the minor" so that "it usurps the place of the major." The book is not an analysis of the forces effective in this century but is his own autobiography. "Mr. Dell's most obvious talent is facility in writing, not

power of thought. And the facility with which the subject
of the book is handled overshadows all else."

456 ANON. Review of Intellectual Vagabondage. The American
     Review of Reviews, 73 (May), 559.
       Short, descriptive review. Dell's style is "entertaining,
     lucid, and thoughtful."

457 ANON. Review of Intellectual Vagabondage. Saturday Review
     of Literature, 2 (15 May), 791.
       In the first part, Dell draws conclusions not warranted by
     the facts. The second part is the "most important." Dell
     describes sympathetically the route of his generation to
     "spiritual maturity." The intelligentsia of this book includes
     those who "rank ideas by their currency rather than by their
     validity." See no 484.

458 ANON. "Mr. Dell's 'Mood of Playfulness' in 'The Village.'"
     New York Times Book Review (23 May), p. 8.
       Review of Love in Greenwich Village. The book is enter-
     taining but "in every fundamental respect inconsequential."
     Dell is not capable of "sustained flight." His humor and per-
     ception of emotions are praised.

459 ANON. Review of Love in Greenwich Village. Saturday Review
     of Literature, 2 (29 May), 832.
       Brief. Description of contents. Dell is "deft to convey a
     vanished charm and glamour." See no. 513 for pseudonym.

460 ANON. Review of Intellectual Vagabondage. Edited by Ed-
     mund Pearson. The Outlook, 143 (2 June), 187.
       Paragraph summarizing ideas of Dell's book. It is a "stim-
     ulating study."

461 ANON. Review of Love in Greenwich Village. The Independent,
     116 (19 June), 727.
       Dell romanticizes love in the Village. The stories are hard-
     ly immortal but they do have "an unforgettable quality."
     They are derivative.

462 ANON. Review of Intellectual Vagabondage. The Booklist,
     22 (July), 409.
       Brief description of contents. Places Dell in younger
     generation of writers.

463 ANON. Review of Love in Greenwich Village. The Bookman,
     63 (July), 591.
       Very brief. "The sentiments of Bohemia in gay and wist-
     ful array."

464 ANON. "A New Floyd Dell." Saturday Review of Literature,
     2 (10 July), 918-19.

Review of <u>Love in Greenwich Village</u>. Short discussion of the alleged decline of the Village. Describes contents of book. Expresses brief opinions on individual parts. Believes poems should be better. All short stories are good. Essays are appropriate. Here Dell is no longer an "iconoclast and rebel." His ego is "mellowing" and recognizing that he is aging, he is ready for the future.

465 ANON. Review of <u>Intellectual Vagabondage</u>. <u>The Bookman</u>, 63 (August), 719.
Short. "Remarkably penetrating." The intelligentsia does not need an apology for itself. Other readers will find it interesting that the intelligentsia do not wish to see harmony and significance in life. Dell's optimism about the next generation is not shared.

466 ANON. "The Gossip Shop." <u>The Bookman</u>, 64 (September), 127.
Says Dell recovered his health while the guest of Arthur Davison Ficke in Santa Fe, New Mexico. Briefly notes that after much consideration the hero of <u>An Old Man's Folly</u> has been named. Dell calls his novel "a realistic romance."

467 ANON. Review of <u>An Old Man's Folly</u>. <u>The Bookman</u>, 64 (October), 219.
Brief plot summary. Especially recommended.

468 ANON. Review of <u>Love in Greenwich Village</u>. <u>The Booklist</u>, 23 (October), 38.
Brief. Notes general contents and author's attitude to the Village.

469 ANON. "<u>An Old Man's Folly</u> and Other New Works of Fiction." <u>New York Times Book Review</u> (24 October), p. 6.
Review. The first third of the novel is Dell's best work. The rest of the book, in trying to mix realism with romance, becomes "dull and sentimental, even a trifle mawkish." It is "unworthy of a man like Floyd Dell." Before it is too late, Dell should try to regain the promise and achievement of his first novel by dealing with the subject of the mature, not the aged, man.

470 ANON. Review of <u>An Old Man's Folly</u>. <u>The Booklist</u>, 23 (December), 133.
Brief plot summary. "The story is long and discursive."

471 ANON. Review of <u>Intellectual Vagabondage</u>. <u>The Open Shelf</u> (December), p. 128.
Short. Summarizes purpose and subject in quotes from the book.

472 ANON. Review of Love in Greenwich Village. The Open Shelf
(December), p. 137.
Briefly describes contents.

473 ANON. "A Frustrated Life." Saturday Review of Literature,
3 (4 December), 364.
Review of An Old Man's Folly. Dell has turned away from
his former rebelliousness and has embraced the bourgeois
world. The first part of the novel demands attention.
"Here, crisply presented and accurately observed," are the
experiences of a character with whom the reader sympathizes.
The tale is "admirably realized." With Mr. Windle's change
in life style, he loses his central place in the novel, "and
with him go the only authentic and original elements in the
story." The minor characters are "quenched and colorless
people."

474 ANON. "A Shirtsleeves History." Saturday Review of Literature, 3 (18 December), 450-51 [450].
An overview of recent literary history. Dell mentioned as
a member of the Chicago group that welcomed Sherwood
Anderson. Includes portrait with caption calling Dell the
"young Lochinvar of The Chicago Evening Post." See no.
506 for pseudonym.

475 BOYD, ERNEST. "Readers and Writers." The Independent,
116 (3 April), 397.
Review of Intellectual Vagabondage. Discusses format.
Questions whether Dell at age thirty-nine can speak for the
younger generation. Finds evidence that he can. But believes Dell's ideas are dated. "I am greatly pleased by Mr.
Dell's coherent, frank, and not too solemn diagnosis of the
faiths and illusions of his youth, even though he does see
himself as a still romantic herald of a dawn which was ob-
scured with remarkable efficiency on August 4, 1914."
Summarizes contents.

476 BRADLEY, WILLARD KING. Review of Love in Greenwich
Village. The Literary Digest International Book Review,
4 (July), 486.
The title and subject matter are dramatic in the vein,
respectively, of musical comedy and grand opera. Praises
"The Kitten and the Masterpiece." Recommends volume to
those interested in history of Greenwich Village.

477 BRAITHWAITE, WILLIAM STANLEY, ed. Anthology of Magazine Verse for 1926 and Yearbook of American Poetry.
Boston: B. J. Brimmer, p. 12 in biography section.
Brief biography of Dell and list of publications included
among biographies of American poets.

478 BURGESS, ERNEST W. "The Romantic Impulse and Family
     Disorganization." The Survey, 57 (1 December), 290-94
     [293, 294].
         This article is a survey of the growth of the notion of
     romantic love as the basis for marriage. Mentions Love in
     Greenwich Village as a discussion of the attempt in the
     Village to rationalize love. Long quotation. The book
     shows that free love was successful to the extent that it
     remained a theory rather than a practice. The experience
     described by Dell will not be convincing to contemporary
     youth who will wish to draw their own conclusions.

479 CALVERTON, V. F. "The New Society." The Nation, 122
     (26 May), 585.
         Review of Intellectual Vagabondage. The book deals with
     the past rather than with the present or future. The first
     section is "scintillating" and clever but vague. The sub-
     stance is correct but the lyricism detracts from its criti-
     cism. Indeed, Dell is essentially an essayist, not a critic.
     The second section is briefly described.

480 CALVERTON, V. F. Review of Love in Greenwich Village.
     New Masses, 1 (October), 28.
         "Floyd Dell is a vivid example of the inadequacy and fail-
     ure of our literary radicals." "Instead of battling for a
     revolutionary art, he has devoted himself to the trifling pas-
     time of writing sexy novels for adolescent Menckenians and
     jaded bourgeoisie." Love in Greenwich Village has some
     appeal because Dell has captured some spirit of abandon,
     some sense of beauty as a way of life. "Yet he is now
     sacrificing his economics to sex-playboying. He seems to
     be on the path by which, in America, our literary radicals
     reach ineffectuality, sterility, and a place in Who's Who."

481 COBLENTZ, STANTON A. "Mr. Dell Tells Why He and Other
     Writers Are Intellectual Vagabonds." New York Evening
     Post Literary Review (22 May), p. 5.
         Review of Intellectual Vagabondage. Dell attempts to
     describe the forces and influences that have formed modern
     writers. Dell cannot treat the whole subject in the small
     space allotted and he speaks only for a limited group.
     Praises his sincerity, open-mindedness, and understanding
     of the milieu of modern literature. The book is valuable
     for elucidating many aspects of modern writing.

482 COURNOS, JOHN. "Floyd Dell's Nice Old Hero Mr. Windle,
     Has a 'Complex.'" New York Evening Post Literary Re-
     view (6 November), p. 7.
         Review of An Old Man's Folly. The first part of the
     novel is superior to the last part. In the second half,

Dell speaks in his own voice on a variety of topics instead
of incorporating them into his characters' personalities.
Relates the plot. Dell has a gift for "noble grotesque."
"With some compression the author might have achieved
astonishing results."

483 CUNNINGHAM, NORA B. "Floyd Dell Writes the Autobiography of a Generation." The Literary Digest International
Book Review, 4 (September), 636.
Review of Intellectual Vagabondage. Extended summary
of Dell's argument. Little commentary. The book is an
autobiography of the author as well as of his generation.

484 CUNNINGHAM, NORA B. "The Intelligentsia." Saturday Review of Literature, 2 (19 June), 878.
Letter to the editor in regard to review of Intellectual
Vagabondage appearing in Saturday Review of Literature.
Takes reviewer to task for his definition of intelligentsia.
Writer sees their role as testing accepted ideas. Dell's
hope that the younger generation may produce a great
literature may be extravagant. But the intelligentsia's
freedom to explore may bring forth achievement. See no.
457.

485 DEUTSCH, BABETTE. "The Deserted Village." New York
Herald Tribune Books (27 June), p. 3.
Review of Love in Greenwich Village. Long description
of contents illustrative of Dell's attitude to the Village.
Yet the reader feels that it is Dell, not the Village, who
has changed. He has adopted middle-class values of home,
children, and stability.

486 DEUTSCH, BABETTE. "The Spirited Autobiography of an
Intellectual." New York Herald Tribune Books (11 April),
p. 4.
Review of Intellectual Vagabondage. The book is "full
of pith and provocation." It accounts for Dell's generation's failure and challenges the next generation to do
better. The first half of the book succeeds in pointing
out the relationship between life and literature but fails
due to lack of space to treat adequately individual intellectuals. The second half of the book is not convincing in
its application to a group. Instead, Dell seems to speak
for himself. He becomes prophetic at the end in his search
for an art that will explain and interpret life.

487 DONDORE, DOROTHY ANNE. The Prairie and the Making of
Middle America; Four Centuries of Description. Cedar
Rapids, Iowa: Torch Press, p. 406.
Dell classified with Sherwood Anderson and Sinclair Lewis
as young rebellious realist. To Dell the Midwest is a "minor

issue," important not in itself but as background in the biographical treatments in Moon-Calf and The Briary-Bush.
In his search for "culture," Felix Fay is the latest type
through which literature has reflected the development of
the Midwest.

488 DREW, ELIZABETH A. The Modern Novel; Some Aspects of
Contemporary Fiction. New York: Harcourt, Brace, p. 96.
Brief mention of the character "Mooncalf" as representative of self-centered youth. Such characters in novels lack
proportion because there is little detachment of the author
from the character.

489 EDWARDS, ROBERT. Review of Love in Greenwich Village.
The Greenwich Village Quill, 18, no. 7 (July), 39-40.
Humorous refutation of sentiment Dell attached to free
love in the Village. Though Dell believes the Village is
gone, only the radical Village is dead. "It is a delightful
book. Dell is an artist, a suave and tricky writer, and it
does give a real picture of a certain set in the old glamorous Village which is not dead, not by a damn sight--but
around some other corner."

490 F[ARRAR], J[OHN]. Review of An Old Man's Folly. The
Bookman, 64 (October), 223-24.
Short. Notes radicalism and attitudes to war and international situation. Highly laudatory. Mr. Windle is "one of
the most delightful of fiction characters." This is Dell's
"richest" tale. "It shows him a novelist of proportions
which have never before been fulfilled." The story is
"poignant, compelling," and nonpartial in treatment of politics.

491 GOLD, MICHAEL. "May Days and Revolutionary Art." The
Modern Quarterly, 3 (February-April), 160-64 [160, 161,
163].
Review of May Days edited by Genevieve Taggard. Cites
the presence of Dell's work in the anthology and recalls his
outstanding prose work in the Masses. Important for Gold's
view of Dell. Although Dell's thinking on individualism and
communism was confused, he and Max Eastman were "the
best teachers youth could have found during those years."
Gold gratefully acknowledges his debt.

492 GRATTAN, C. HARTLEY. Review of Intellectual Vagabondage.
The New Republic, 47 (23 June), 145.
Highly critical. This book deals with the sentimental intelligentsia. The book is not valuable as a defense. Dell's
historical review of intellectuals in the two preceding centuries as well as those of the twentieth-century causes the
reader to believe they have all been fools, ignorant, di-
vorced from reality, and prejudiced.

493 HANSEN, HARRY. "Pathos of Bohemia." New York World
     (16 May), p. 4m.
         Mainly a review of Love in Greenwich Village. Believes
     Dell is happy in his present life despite his nostalgia. Dell's
     book helps build an image of the Village which will live on
     because it appeals to people's fancy. Describes individual
     pieces. Brief review of Intellectual Vagabondage. Recom-
     mended for its overview of the intelligentsia. Brief descrip-
     tion of material covered. It is "informal and engaging,"
     and "gently discursive."

494 LAWRENCE, ISABELLE WENTWORTH. "Love Today in Green-
     wich Village." Boston Evening Transcript (3 July), part 6,
     p. 4.
         Review of Love in Greenwich Village. Tells history of
     the Village, the story of the Liberal Club, and several
     tales from Dell's book. "It is his astonishing and exhila-
     rating ability to reproduce this lightsome atmosphere which
     makes this novel Floyd Dell's most outstanding achievement
     so far."

495* LAWRENCE, I[SABELLE] W[ENTWORTH]. Review of Love in
     Greenwich Village. New York Herald Tribune Books (27
     July), p. 3.
         Unlocatable. Cited in Book Review Digest for 1926. May
     be the same as no. 494.

496 LOVEMAN, AMY. Notice of An Old Man's Folly. Saturday
     Review of Literature, 3 (16 October), 222.
         Brief mention of novel as one by a novelist who is al-
     ready known.

497 LOVEMAN, AMY. Review of Love in Greenwich Village. Sat-
     urday Review of Literature, 2 (10 April), 712.
         Very brief. The volume represents "the no longer young-
     er generation."

498 M., T. Review of An Old Man's Folly. The New Republic,
     48 (3 November), 307.
         Short. Summary of plot. The story might "easily have
     degenerated into rank sentimentality had not the author
     done it with such fine restraint. It is the best of Mr.
     Dell's recent novels."

499 N., R. W. "In Greenwich Village." Springfield Sunday Union
     and Republican (4 July), p. 7f.
         Review of Love in Greenwich Village. The book is evi-
     dence that Dell is "outgrowing his prolonged immaturity."
     Captures the spirit of the Village.

500 N., R. W. "Pleasing Fantasy Surrounded with Irrelevance

in Mr. Dell's Novel." Springfield Sunday Union and Republican (31 October), p. 7f.
Review of An Old Man's Folly. The novel's plot and structure are weak. The youthful, radical ideas are not sufficiently grounded in character development. Rather they seem employed for their own sake. Yet the book has a purpose and a dual theme. The "poetic element" of the novel is most impressive. "In the poetry and fancy of this conception is the appeal of Mr. Dell's book. Forget the rest."

501 PARSONS, ALICE BEAL. "Mr. Windle's Wild Oats." New York Herald Tribune Books (7 November), p. 4.
Review of An Old Man's Folly. Facetious account of plot. "A pleasant amiable story, a very literary story, with charm and whimsicality and spice. A very up-to-date story that ripples engagingly along and never once ... makes any of those disturbing revelations that exalt or terrify, stripping reality bare for the startled eye."

502 PEARSON, EDMUND. Review of Intellectual Vagabondage. The Outlook, 143 (2 June), 187.
Short. Summarizes the contents of "this stimulating study in literature."

503 PRESTON, KEITH. "The Confessions of a Literary Lotus Eater." Chicago Daily News (7 April), p. 18.
Review of Intellectual Vagabondage. Dell has tried and praised "all the panaceas of our time," but now finds none sufficient to modern times. He finds the intelligentsia bankrupt. Dell is confused from reading too much. Reviewer believes "wish-fulfillments" of intelligentsia superior to those "pseudo adult" ones put forth by Dell.

504 P[RESTON], K[EITH]. "The Periscope." Chicago Daily News (26 May), p. 14.
Short review of Love in Greenwich Village written in form of doggerel. Criticizes Dell for taking part in bohemianism of Village, then settling down to stable marriage.

505 QUERCUS, P. E. G. "Trade Winds." Saturday Review of Literature, 2 (16 January), 498.
A list of trivia includes the information that the Chaucer Head book store has for sale Dell's copy of The Green Hat for $7.50.

506 QWERTYWOP. "A Shirtsleeves History." Saturday Review of Literature, 3 (18 December), 450-51 [450].
Pseudonym. See no. 474.

507 RAINE, WILLIAM MACLEOD. "Two Widely Different Books Carry Theme of Youth's Revolt." Denver Rocky Mountain News (13 June), magazine section, n.p.

Reviews of Love in Greenwich Village and Intellectual Vagabondage. The review of the first names Dell the "logical
historian" of the Village. Review deviates to describing
spirit of the Village. Praises "The Ballad of Christopher
Street" which Raine claims to have heard Dell read at Antibes.
Review of Intellectual Vagabondage relates Dell's history of
intellectual despair which became vagabondage.

508 RASCOE, BURTON. "Contemporary Reminiscences." Arts
and Decoration, 25 (July), 48, 68, 74 [48, 68].
Short discussion of Love in Greenwich Village. The book
preserves "the pathos of distance" that separates Dell from
his Greenwich Village days. "Dell's prose is always caress-
ing, but to me the chief interest in the book lies in the fallacy of its assumptions. Dell imagines that the glamorous
and romantic ... Greenwich Village is gone, whereas it is
only gone for him."

509 ROBINSON, LANDON. "Love in 'The Village' About the Same
as When Floyd Dell Lived There." New York Evening Post
Literary Review (5 June), p. 7.
Review of Love in Greenwich Village. Describes contents.
Dell has nothing new to relate. His mourning for the old
Village is unjustified. The title is inappropriate since the
book does not deal with a variety of love unique to the
Village.

510 S., R. E. Review of Intellectual Vagabondage. St. Louis
Library Bulletin, June, p. 170.
Very brief. Describes it as a "defense of the younger
generation in art and literature."

511 SHERMAN, STUART. "Floyd Dell on the Coast of Bohemia,"
in Critical Woodcuts. New York: Charles Scribner's Sons,
pp. 49-62.
Reprinted with title change from no. 440.

512 THE PHOENICIAN. Review of Intellectual Vagabondage.
Saturday Review of Literature, 2 (27 March), 674.
Pseudonym. See no. 454.

513 THE PHOENICIAN. Review of Love in Greenwich Village.
Saturday Review of Literature, 2 (29 May), 832.
Pseudonym. See no. 459.

514 [WILSON, EDMUND]. "The All-Star Literary Vaudeville."
The New Republic, 47 (30 June), 158-63 [158].
Dell mentioned with Mencken, Hackett, and Untermeyer
as a reviewer from "the early days of the present era"
whose writing "set an example of honesty and boldness."
Reprinted in nos. 515, 875, 901, and 998.

515 WILSON, EDMUND. "The All-Star Literary Vaudeville," in
American Criticism 1926. Edited by William A. Drake. New
York: Harcourt, Brace, pp. 337-58 [338].
Reprinted from no. 514. Reprinted in 998.

1927

516 A[DAMS], F[RANKLIN] P. "The Conning Tower." New York
World (29 January), p. 11.
On January 26, 1927, Adams had Dell and others to dinner at his house. Records conversation with Dell on topic
of young people and talkativeness of young girls.

517 ANON. Review of An Old Man's Folly. London Times Literary Supplement (27 January), p. 61.
Recites plot. Finds the "moral" to be the triumph of ordinary life over avant-garde aspirations. The novel shows
"that it is just as easy to apply the sentimental touch to
new conditions as to the old."

518 ANON. "The Gossip Shop." The Bookman, 64 (February),
763.
Dell on California. Now lectures to women's clubs.
Writes poetry but does not publish it. Tells how he avoided
keeping regular business hours when employed in Chicago.

519 ANON. "Lecture Audiences." The Bookman, 64 (February),
658-59 [658].
Notes that audiences respond favorably to conservative
authors of the past, but are most interested in the modern
radical novel. Tells Dell's experience when giving his current lecture. Although he and the audience laugh at E. E.
Cummings, the audience is eager to read Cummings.

520 ANON. "The March Number." New Masses, 2 (February), 3.
Dell's question on the proper proletarian revolutionary attitude to sex has provoked comment from radicals.

521 ANON. Review of An Old Man's Folly. Monthly Bulletin of
the Carnegie Library of Pittsburgh, 32 (February), 54.
Briefly quotes no. 473. Tells plot, praises execution.

522 ANON. Review of Intellectual Vagabondage. Edited by Mary
Katharine Reely. Wisconsin Library Bulletin, 23 (March),
77.
Brief description. "The author interprets the ideals of
his own generation."

523 ANON. "Critics of America Stir Controversy." New York
Times (27 March), sec. 2, p. 4.

Summarizes Dell's views expressed in the April issue of
Current History. Dell defends America's intellectuals.

524 ANON. Review of The Outline of Marriage. The Saturday
Review, 143 (11 June), 915.
Dell outlines the modern attitude to marriage. "He presents his case well, with vigour, pungency and wit, and a
brevity in no way indicating a lack of matter."

525 ANON. "Errata." New Masses, 3 (July), 3.
Corrects misprinted phrase in Dell's June 1927 review in
New Masses of Robert Wolf's Springboard.

526 ANON. Review of The Outline of Marriage. London Times
Literary Supplement (14 July), p. 411.
Short. Reports Dell's thesis. Dell's skill as a novelist
contributes to his expression of his concern with marriage
problems.

527 ANON. Review of Upton Sinclair. The Independent, 119
(30 July), 117.
Short. Sinclair's importance to his times justifies Dell's
book. But his social pamphlets are treated uncritically and
with too much enthusiasm. The volume is an "extraordinarily interesting story."

528 ANON. Review of Upton Sinclair. Edited by Edmund Pearson. The Outlook, 146 (24 August), 547-48.
Comments on Sinclair as an author. Dell is "intellectual-
ly and temperamentally fitted to deal sympathetically" with
his subject.

529 ANON. Review of Upton Sinclair. New York Times Book
Review (4 September), pp. 14-15.
Centers on Dell's interpretation, not Sinclair's life. The
biography is "very capable." Dell uses psychological interpretation well. He fails to see that Sinclair's admitted flaws
as a novelist probably account for his lack of commercial
success.

530* ANON. "Our First Speaker--Floyd Dell." Chicago Woman's
Aid Bulletin, 11 (28 September), 2.
Unlocatable. Cited in no. 913, p. 602, as a news story
or editorial comment.

531 ANON. Review of An Unmarried Father. New York Times
Book Review (30 October), p. 7.
Dell should not be criticized for not creating a diversity
of characters. He deals with variations of his own psyche.
Dell is weak in presenting interior conflict, but he writes
well on the subject of young love. Short plot summary.

532 ANON. Review of Upton Sinclair. The Booklist, 24 (November), 65.
   Brief description of how Dell treats Sinclair in this biography.

533 ANON. Review of Upton Sinclair. Boston Evening Transcript (5 November), part 8, p. 3.
   Describes contents of book. "It is a fair question if the 'Socialistic preconceptions' of Upton Sinclair really prevent his being hailed as 'the greatest American novelist.' There is a partisan touch on these pages, together with a good deal of what is and is intended to be cold and dispassionate judgment by a literary critic." One paragraph devoted to comment on Sinclair's lack of humor.

534 ANON. Review of An Unmarried Father. The New Republic, 52 (9 November), 321.
   Short, highly critical. The book is criticized for not giving the reader "the gist of the matter" or "the gist of the people." Dell is a disappointment who has not lived up to his earlier promise. Compares him to Compton Mackenzie.

535 ANON. Review of An Unmarried Father. The Independent, 119 (12 November), 485.
   Summarizes plot. Dell's work does not encourage immorality but encourages morality. Dell is a "sincere" artist who sees literature as an art, not a profession, and who deserves a better audience.

536 ANON. "An Unmarried Father; Floyd Dell Reverses an Age-Old Conventional Plot." Boston Evening Transcript (12 November), part 8, p. 3.
   Places the novel within the contemporary interest in "masculine freedom from parental responsibility" desired by women. Tells plot. The first half of the novel is the most successful. "The author has a sound thesis and he builds upon it well. What he lacks in style he attains in vigor and movement." However, in the final chapters, the author seems anxious to disengage himself from the ethical questions, and the result is an "inartistic slashing." The end "borders perilously close upon farce."

537 BATES, ERNEST SUTHERLAND. "Blithe Fantasy." Saturday Review of Literature, 4 (17 December), 452.
   Review of An Unmarried Father. The first half is superior to the second. The novel "is the most spontaneous, the most readable, and, perhaps, the best of Mr. Dell's works."

538 BECKER, MAY LAMBERTON. "The Reader's Guide." Saturday Review of Literature, 4 (6 August), 29.

Moon-Calf included in list of books containing a librarian
as a character.

539 BECKER, MAY LAMBERTON. Review of Upton Sinclair.
     Saturday Review of Literature, 3 (23 July), 999.
         Very brief. Mentions "bold" beginning for the publisher.

540 BECKER, MAY LAMBERTON. Review of Upton Sinclair.
     Saturday Review of Literature, 4 (3 September), 93.
         Brief. "A sympathetic exposition of his work as he lives
     it and his life as he writes it." Represents one point of
     view about Sinclair.

541 BOYD, ERNEST. "Readers and Writers." The Independent,
     119 (20 August), 187.
         Review of Upton Sinclair. Dell was a good choice to
     write Sinclair's biography because the two men differ in
     personality but agree in radicalism. Dell does not suffi-
     ciently explain Sinclair's fame abroad. He does not make
     Sinclair interesting or convince the reader of his merits
     as a writer.

542 BRODY, ALTER. "The Case of Floyd Dell and Others."
     The Nation, 125 (7 December), Holiday Book Section, pp.
     652, 654.
         Review of An Unmarried Father. The novel is "original
     and absorbing." Yet Dell does not handle his characters
     like an artist. Lacking a sense of the mystery of life, Dell
     knows too much about his characters. "His vision is of a
     sane, sanitary, well-lighted world, swept by reason and
     knowledge, in which there are no dark corners."

543 CALVERTON, V. F. "Sex and Economics." New Masses,
     2 (March), 11-12 [11].
         Names Dell briefly as one who initiated question which
     this essay attempts to answer. It is "what is the prole-
     tarian, revolutionary attitude toward sex?" However,
     oblique comments in the essay surely refer to Dell's per-
     sonal acceptance of bourgeois marriage. One paragraph
     appears to summarize Dell's career. His "economic radical-
     ism becomes nothing more than an empty, spiritless ges-
     ture." Attacks the radical who cannot accept the moral
     implications of his philosophy.

544 DEUTSCH, BABETTE. "A Moot Point." New York Herald
     Tribune Books (28 August), p. 3.
         Review of Upton Sinclair; A Study in Social Protest.
     Dell has produced "an attractive history" of Sinclair, but
     he over-estimates his worth as a novelist. Dell "will not
     concede that a novelist wields a strong weapon in the cause
     of human liberty and justice by paying attention to his
     craft rather than by engaging in emphatic propaganda."

545 DIAMANT, GERTRUDE. Review of The Outline of Marriage.
     New Masses, 3 (July), 30-31.
         Relates Dell's ideas. "Excellent exposition." "Dell legiti-
     mizes sex ... as the basis of the marriage contract."

546 FAGIN, N. BRYLLION. The Phenomenon of Sherwood Ander-
     son; A Study in American Life and Letters. Baltimore:
     Rossi-Bryn, p. 45.
         Mentions Dell's name and gives a lengthy quote from
     Looking at Life about the effect of Windy McPherson's Son
     on Dell.

547 FARRAR, JOHN. "Anonymously." The Bookman, 66 (Decem-
     ber), 424-28 [426, 428].
         Two brief mentions of Dell in this long article. Briefly
     recalls a faux pas on the part of Dell. Notes that Dell's
     youngest son is named Christopher after the character
     Christopher Robin.

548 FEIPEL, LOUIS N. Notice of Upton Sinclair. The Library
     Journal, 52 (August), 771.
         Brief mention of book's publication as part of Murray
     Hill Biographies series.

549 FREEMAN, JOSEPH. "The Wilsonian Era in American Litera-
     ture." Modern Quarterly, 4 (June-September), 130-36
     [132-33, 134, 136].
         Discussion of fiction in the Wilsonian Era, its subjectiv-
     ity, pride in America, struggle with Puritanism, and inter-
     est in the singular individual. Cites Dell as a critic who
     wrote "what was probably the first socialist literary criti-
     cism in America." His creative work diverges to deal with
     the attempts of individuals to adjust idealistic concepts of
     love and marriage to bourgeois standards. The divergence
     represents "an unsolved bipolarity."

550 GARD, WAYNE. Book Reviewing. Edited by Nelson Antrim
     Crawford. Borzoi Handbooks of Journalism. New York:
     Alfred A. Knopf, p. 86.
         This is a book on how to write book reviews. Dell's re-
     view of Spoon River Anthology is offered as an example.
     Notes that Dell was one of a few who saw the importance
     of Masters' work. The actual review by Dell follows.

551 GLASPELL, SUSAN. The Road to the Temple. New York:
     Frederick A. Stokes, pp. 180-82, 188, 191, 195, 204, 212,
     218, 221-22, 247.
         Short references to Dell in this biography of George
     Cram Cook by his last wife. Subjects treated include re-
     lationship of Cook and Dell on Cook's Iowa farm, Dell's
     conversion of Cook to socialism, Dell's challenge to Cook's

intellect, nature of their Monist Society, Cook as Dell's associate on the Friday Literary Review, Cook as part of Dell's group in Chicago, and Dell at the Masses office.

552 GOLD, MICHAEL. "A New Masses Theatre." New Masses, 3 (November), 23.
Calls for establishment and support of New Playwrights' Theatre to propagate theories of revolt of workers. Names Dell, an editor of the old Masses, as a founder of the Provincetown Players.

553 HERMAN, ARTHUR. "Floyd Dell's New Novel." New York Evening Post (8 October), sec. 3, p. 11.
Review of An Unmarried Father. Tells plot. Dell is at his best when expressing revolutionary thoughts on marriage and sex. The book "suffers from colorlessness of style and aridity of characterization. One longs for the glow and fire that lift an effort of the imagination out of the muck of the mediocre. Perhaps this is asking too much of a novel in which character and situation are creakily superimposed upon a thesis; yet somehow one feels that is not asking too much of Floyd Dell."

554 KELLOGG, FLORENCE LOEB. "Floyd Dell Studies a Pink." The Survey, 58 (1 May), 171-72.
Review of An Old Man's Folly. Tells plot. The character of Windle is influenced by the early H. G. Wells. The novel is the first to deal with America during the war years of 1917-1918. It focuses on persons for whom the radical movement is an extertainment, not a way of life. Dell is an excellent writer. "His prose is smooth and lively." "There are a dozen fine episodes that could stand alone." But his important ideas are expressed in a trivial manner. This novel takes "an important background and concentrate[s] trivially on unimportant persons and their actions. It would be a pity to conclude that this is the only novel of those recent days that our radical movement can produce."

555 LEE, B. VIRGINIA. Review of An Unmarried Father. Overland Monthly, 85 (December), 376.
The title and the author suggest a book about sex, but the story deals instead with psychology. Dell treats the problem of unwed pregnancy from the unconventional point of view of the father. Until the end, the book is "one of the most fascinating of documents to come from the Dell typewriter, and a study in character as original as it is interesting." Praises the writing, the thinking, and the humor.

556 LOHRKE, EUGENE. "Turn to the Almanac." New York Herald Tribune Books (9 October), p. 2.

Review of An Unmarried Father. Dell places excessive reliance on statistics at the expense of a real grappling with the subject. "In his earlier works, a certain enthusiasm for the unreal gave wings to Mr. Dell's introspective fantasies. Now, having lost those wings, he is floundering. He needs a re-orientation with respect to the vital and important." Yet the book manages to keep the reader's interest to the end.

557 MACY, JOHN. Review of Upton Sinclair. The Bookman, 66 (October), 216-17.
Highly praises the biography. Dell is not guilty of excessive adulation. Sinclair is "portrayed with objective fidelity and the imaginative skill of the true artist in biography." Discusses Sinclair as writer and reformer.

558 S., A. A. Review of An Old Man's Folly. The World Tomorrow, 10 (January), 36.
Short. Tells plot. The first half is best because "Windle is there shrewdly observed and well presented." The novel reflects what is happening in Dell's life. Speculates that his radicalism is a young man's folly.

559 SINCLAIR, UPTON B. Money Writes! New York: Albert and Charles Boni, pp. 103, 147, 176, 185-88.
Several brief mentions and a short chapter devoted to Dell in this book on American literature from an economic point of view. Mentions his friendship with Dell and their conflict over whether such books as Cabell's Jurgen inspire people to action. Notes Dell's excellent literary taste. Dell's opinion of The Hairy Ape is reactionary. Dell is the best literary critic in America. As a novelist his main concern is adolescent sexual adjustment. Discusses Janet March. Sinclair wishes Dell would deal with adult matters. Sees An Old Man's Folly as a roman à clef.

560 SINCLAIR, UPTON B. Review of Janet March. Money Writes! New York: Albert and Charles Boni, p. 186.
Janet is a young woman who does not earn her own way. Dell, in failing to mention that her "sex-code would expose her to venereal disease," "was failing in his duty to youth." This is a summary of the original review which Sinclair says he "contributed" to the Hearst Sunday supplements. Perhaps it was not published. It does not appear in the supplement to the San Francisco Examiner and is not mentioned in Joseph Caer's Upton Sinclair: Bibliography and Biographical Data.

561 VAN DOREN, CARL. "Floyd Dell," in Contemporary American Novelists 1900-1920. New York: Macmillan, pp. 166-71.
Dell is one of several writers who have detached them-

selves from small town standards. Describes Moon-Calf
and The Briary-Bush. The first embodies beauty, "lucid-
ity," and "grace." The Briary-Bush is more profound
than Moon-Calf. "It hovers over the dark waters of the
unconscious on perhaps the surest wings an American novel
has ever used." Significantly, Van Doren devotes five pages
to Dell and one and two-thirds to F. Scott Fitzgerald.

562 WHIPPLE, LEON. "Portrait of a Seeker." The World Tomorrow, 10 (September), 376.
Review of Upton Sinclair. Much of the review deals with
Sinclair. Includes pointed statements on Dell's handling of
his subject. Too much attention to "thin-spun analysis."
He does not devote enough space to Sinclair's pamphlets.
He fails to examine Sinclair's ability with words, and he
does not elucidate Sinclair's unique qualities. There is excessive eulogy. Dell's style is "undistinguished."

563 WHIPPLE, LEON. Review of An Unmarried Father. The
Survey, 59 (1 December), 325-26.
Tells plot. Dell treats human situation in a "taut spare
plot." Praises character delineation. Motivation is frequently implausible or unclear but "it has an authenticity,
biological and social, that excuses inconsistency."

564 WHIPPLE, LEON. Review of Upton Sinclair. The Survey,
59 (1 October), 52.
Short. "Dell is inadequate on Sinclair's biography, and
he underestimates him as a rambunctious pamphleteer." He
succeeds in showing the duality of Sinclair's poet and soci-
ologist natures.

565 WOOD, CHARLES W. "Don't Fight with Sex." New Masses,
2 (February), 7-9, 31 [7].
This article is written to answer Dell's question "What
is the correct revolutionary proletarian attitude toward
sex?" Names Dell. He asked the question of Wood, V. F.
Calverton, Upton Sinclair, Scott Nearing, and Michael Gold.

566 WOODWARD, W. E. "Upton Sinclair." The Nation, 125 (12
October), 392, 394.
Review of Upton Sinclair. Concentrates mainly on Sinclair but short comments on Dell and his work. Since
Sinclair is still alive, Dell could not be as penetrating as
he might be. Instead of focusing on the man, he attends
to his works. Though the biography is "formal and literary," it is also excellent "in style and manner" and in
"perception."

1928

567 A[DAMS], F[RANKLIN] P. "The Conning Tower." New York
World (13 October), p. 11.
Reports Adams' activities on October 9, 1928. He saw
"Little Accident" and greatly enjoyed the performance.
Dell not mentioned by name.

568 ANON. "Floyd Dell Developing in Direction of Comedy."
Springfield Sunday Union and Republican (8 January),
p. 7f.
Review of An Unmarried Father. Relates plot. Notes
humor in the story and looks to Dell to continue developing
his sense of humor. Had the author not been so concerned
with studying maternal and paternal instinct, the story
might have been even more humorous.

569 ANON. Review of The Anatomy of Melancholy. New York
Times Book Review (26 February), p. 8.
Burton's book is edited by Dell and Paul Jordan-Smith.
Mainly comments on Burton. On subject of editing, says
the two "have performed a labor (we fear a labor largely
of love)."

570 ANON. "In the Bookman Office." The Bookman, 67 (March),
iv, vi, viii [iv].
There is a brief introduction of Dell, a contributor to
this issue. His play from An Unmarried Father is soon
to be produced. He has published a new edition of Burton's Anatomy of Melancholy. He is presently on a lecture
tour on the Pacific coast.

571 ANON. "'Little Accident,' Adaptation of Dell Novel, Booked
at Broad." Newark Evening News (8 September), Magazine Section, p. 6x.
Announces opening of play at Broad Street Theater.
Briefly tells plot and lists actors. Identifies Dell as novelist and lists some of his works.

572 ANON. "'Little Accident,' New Play, Is Footlighted at Broad."
Newark Evening News (11 September), p. 8.
Review of performance. Discusses actors and production
and relates some of plot. The title should be changed. The
third act is the weakest. The authors handle the subject
matter with good taste and sincerity. The work is not a
great one, but it is interesting and will prove to be a success on Broadway.

573 ANON. "New Plays in the Provinces." New York Times (16
September), sec. 9, p. 2.

Brief mention of "Little Accident," a dramatic version of Dell's An Unmarried Father, having been produced.

574 ANON. Review of Upton Sinclair. London Times Literary Supplement (4 October), p. 712.
The book is "a sound and honest, though not particularly distinguished, piece of work." Dell is correct to concentrate on Sinclair's social protest activities. Dell presents a case for "'social revolutionary criticism' as a function of imaginative literature."

575 ANON. "Cast and Forecast." New York World (10 October), p. 17.
Includes picture of Katherine Alexander with caption indicating she is cast as heroine in "Little Accident." No mention of Dell by name.

576 ANON. "Comedy and Farce in 'Little Accident.'" New York Times (10 October), p. 32.
Review of performance of "Little Accident." Comments on actors and tells plot. The first two acts are superior to the "rather rickety" third act. Dell and Mitchell "have contrived a thinnish but prepossessing piece that is a mixture of comedy, farce and what might be material for a deeper play of human relationships, but fortunately isn't."

577 ANON. "'Light of Asia' at Hampden's; 'Little Accident' Is a Boy." New York Daily News (10 October), p. 39.
Review of performance. Recites plot. Notes audience's response to jokes. Briefly names Dell as co-author.

578 ANON. "'Little Accident' Has Parenthood as Theme of Plot." New York American (10 October), p. 17.
Mainly relates plot. Names Dell as co-author of play.

579 ANON. "Cast and Forecast." New York World (13 October), p. 12.
Briefly mentions that Crosby Gaige has successfully managed "Little Accident."

580 ANON. Review of "Little Accident." Theatre, 48 (December), 46-47.
Lists cast. Finds the comedy "spirited and clever." Tells plot briefly. "Had Floyd Dell's novel been followed closely we should have had another 'problem' drama, but ... it is saved from the pathological doldrums and becomes one of the most amusing minor comedies on Broadway."

581 BELLAMY, FRANCIS R. "The Theatre." The Outlook and Independent, 150 (24 October), 1031.

Includes a review of performance of "Little Accident."
Tells plot. Praises deftness of writing and genuineness of
emotion. The story is convincing. "'Little Accident' is so
far the season's most entertaining comedy."

582 BENCHLEY, ROBERT. Review of "Little Accident." Life, 92
(2 November), 21.
Review of performance. Notes that the subject matter
could not have been treated on the stage a decade ago.
Finds the ending unsuitable. In all, "a gay little comedy."

583 BRACKETT, CHARLES. Review of "Little Accident." New
Yorker, 4 (27 October), 34, 36.
Review of performance. The novel was serious, but the
play is entirely comedy. The last act is not as good as
the first two but the play is "charming."

584 C., E. Y. "Rebirth of a Classic." Chattanooga News (25
February), sec. 2., p. 11.
Review of The Anatomy of Melancholy. Discusses con-
tents and Burton's method. Describes present edition.
Praises translation, index, and beauty of volume. The book
is appropriate to the scholar as well as to the casual reader.

585 C., M. Review of An Unmarried Father. The Modern Quarterly, 4 (May-August), 416.
Dell's sexual freedom is not revolutionary but reactionary.
Janet March was "a female monstrosity" ruled by conventional societal dictates. The plot of An Unmarried Father
allows for revolutionary behavior on the part of the mother,
but Dell "subjects her to psycho-analysis" and finds her
behavior springs from conventionality.

586 CARB, DAVID. Review of "Little Accident." Vogue, 72 (24
November), 76-77, 122.
Review of performance. Does not mention Dell by name.
Comments on actors. "The farce is badly over done. The
authors have followed the Rialto recipe scrupulously: re-
peat every laugh several times, let comedy and sentiment
alternate mathematically." Yet the play is amusing. Praises
the humor, the theme, and the "fresh and ingenious" situ-
ations.

587 COHEN, JULIUS. "'Little Accident,' Good Comedy at Morosco." The Journal of Commerce (10 October), p. 24.
Review of opening night. Tells plot. Discusses actors'
performances. Praises comedy format with "thoroughly
human people."

588 COLEMAN, ROBERT. "'Little Accident' Big Hit." New York
Daily Mirror (11 October), p. 23.

Review of performance. Tells plot, comments on actors.
Names Dell. The play is "one of the outstanding hits of the
new season. It is a diverting, human, continuously amusing
show, packed with laugh wallops."

589 D., N. H. "Burton on Melancholy." Boston Evening Transcript (28 January), Book Section, p. 2.
Review of The Anatomy of Melancholy. Mainly describes
Burton's work. "We must congratulate the editors on the
admirable success of their heroic experiment."

590 DICKINSON, ASA DON. The Best Books of Our Time, 1901-
1925. Garden City, New York: Doubleday, Doran, pp. 81-
82, 346, 351, 382.
Descriptions of Moon-Calf and The Briary-Bush. Lists
authorities endorsing the books. Lists number of endorse-
ments, nationality, and literary form.

591 DUDLEY, BIDE. "'Little Accident.'" New York Evening
World (10 October), p. 18.
Review of first performance. Tells plot. Names Dell as
co-author. It is a genuine hit, neither "pretentious" nor
difficult. It was received with "spontaneous laughter" and
applause.

592 FARRAR, JOHN. "Anonymously." The Bookman, 66 (February), 656-60 [656].
Briefly mentions that Dell finished the dramatic version
of An Unmarried Father and claims to write as well in the
country as the city. Farrar doubts being able to write
well on "companionate marriage" while playing with the new
baby Christopher.

593 FREEMAN, JOSEPH. "Notes on American Literature." The
Communist, 7 (September), 570-78 [575, 576].
This article deals with three generations of contemporary
American writers. Briefly mentions Dell as member of the
left-wing group. He continues to write novels, but shows
no new trends in his work. He is one of three authors
(the others are U. Sinclair and V. F. Calverton) to write
a book with a social interpretation of literature. Intellectual Vagabondage is narrow and too subjective to be critical.

594 LIPPMANN, WALTER. "Upton Sinclair." Saturday Review of
Literature, 4 (3 March), 641-43.
Highly negative review of Upton Sinclair. Dell's socialist orientation clouds his view of Sinclair. Sinclair is neither an accurate interpreter of American life nor a great
realist as Dell claims. Criticizes Dell's use of psychoanalysis in interpreting Sinclair's life. "Mr. Dell's uncritical

certainty that Upton Sinclair is a 'great realistic novelist'
leads, I think, to the ruin of what started out to be a
searching study of an extraordinarily interesting human
being."

595 MICHAUD, REGIS. The American Novel To-day; A Social and
Psychological Study. Boston: Little, Brown, pp. 22, 254.
Brief mention of Dell as one of a number of writers "ob-
sessed by the problems of Puritan inhibitions and their influence on human conduct." Dell is cited as "one of the
most original writers of to-day." Criticizes The Runaway
for ending "like a popular 'movie.'" Reprinted in nos.
990 and 1079.

596 MOREHOUSE, WARD. "Broadway After Dark." New York
Sun (11 October), p. 40.
Lists persons who attended the opening night performance
of "Little Accident." No mention of Dell.

597* NATHAN, GEORGE JEAN. Review of a Broadway Play.
Judge, pp. 19, 27.
Unlocatable. Cited in no. 913, p. 603.

598 P., N. S. "'Little Accident,' at Morosco, Is Sophisticated
Comedy." New York Journal (10 October), p. 19.
Review of performance. Tells plot at length. Names
Dell as co-author. Describes play as "spirited, uproarious
and sophisticated comedy." Predicts a long run for the
play.

599 RATHBUN, STEPHEN. "'Little Accident.'" New York Sun
(10 October), p. 26.
Review of performance. Comments on differences between
book and play. The novel is "sociological." The play is a
farce. The device of kidnapping in the play is a mistake.

600 SMITH, ALISON. "Another New Play." New York World (11
October), p. 13.
Review of performance of "Little Accident." The play is
"uncommonly deft and ingratiating." Contrasts humor in
play with seriousness of An Unmarried Father, "an unquali-
fiedly serious study." Recounts plot and comments on actors.

601 STAGG, HUNTER. "Galley Sheets in the Wind." Richmond
News Leader (5 March), p. 18.
Review of The Anatomy of Melancholy. Mainly describes
Burton and his book. Praises the readability of this edi-
tion.

602 STOCKBRIDGE, FRANK PARKER. "Main Street Wants to

Know." The Bookman, 66 (January), 546-51 [551].
Article on the changing taste of readers from 1919 to 1928.
Briefly mentions Moon-Calf as being popular during that
period of time.

603 VAN DOREN, MARK. "First Glance." The Nation, 126 (29
February), 241.
Review of The Anatomy of Melancholy. Concentrates on
Burton. One paragraph on Dell/Jordan-Smith edition.
Praises the Latin translations. Finds no edition of Burton
to surpass in beauty or desirability this one.

604 WALDORF, WILELLA. "'Little Accident.'" New York Evening Post (10 October), p. 14.
Review of opening night performance. Cites Dell as co-
author. Notes the humor throughout, especially in the
second act. Retells plot, comments on acting.

605 WATTS, RICHARD, JR. "'Little Accident' Stage Version of
Floyd Dell's Novel." New York Herald Tribune (10 Octo-
ber), p. 20.
Review of performance. Tells plot. It is a "mild" farce.
The conclusion "falters." Due to lack of sufficient plot there
are digressions but they are entertaining.

606 YOUNG, ARTHUR. On My Way: Being the Book of Art
Young in Text and Picture. New York: Horace Liveright,
pp. 276, 279, 280, 281, 293.
Memoirs of Art Young, contributor to the Masses and
"co-conspirator" in the trial with Dell. Describes Dell's
physical appearance, his contribution as editor of the
Masses, his position in the artists' revolt, and his reading
of manuscripts.

607 YOUNG, GORDON RAY. "A Torrent of Education." Los
Angeles Times (22 January), sec. 3, pp. 16, 17.
Review of The Anatomy of Melancholy. Praises this "admirably distinctive" edition for its translation of Latin,
printing, index, bibliography, and biographical notes.
"With care and deftness," the editors have woven their
translations with the text. Discusses Burton and his work
apart from this edition.

608* ZIMMERMANN, KATHARINE. New York Telegram (10 October), p. 14.
Cited in no. 913, p. 603. No circulating copies are
available.

1929

609 ANON. "A Middle-Aged Mooncalf." New York Times Book
Review (17 February), p. 7.
Review of Souvenir. Rather than exploiting dramatic possibilities, Dell has frequently chosen to write as an essayist
in this novel. "Mr. Dell has not sought, with the implacable
application of the top-rung novelist, to make the mind's
motives clear in their complexity, either by the method of
analysis or by the drama that renders analysis unneces-
sary." He reached his height as a novelist with Moon-Calf
and Janet March, novels of confession.

610 ANON. "Floyd Dell's Thin Souvenir." New York World (17
March), p. 11m.
Review of Souvenir. Brief plot summary. The wit, the
feminine characters, and the author's social opinions are
foremost to the book. The plot is secondary. The book
is not unified. "It is Mr. Dell in his usual manner spread
unusually thin." The book is often more like a series of
essays than a "serious narrative."

611 ANON. Review of Souvenir. The Booklist, 25 (April), 285.
Brief recounting of plot.

612 ANON. Review of Souvenir. The Bookman, 69 (April), xxiv.
Short. Briefly tells plot and delineates point of view.
"Mr. Dell only half succeeds in making Felix Fay's reac-
tions plausible." "The most satisfactory sections of the
book deal with the Village, on which Mr. Dell is an authority."

613 ANON. Review of Souvenir. Among Our Books, 34 (May), 40.
Brief plot summary.

614 ANON. "Floyd Dell; Author of Souvenir." Wilson Library
Bulletin, 3 (June), 662.
Biography. Says Dell made the Friday Literary Review
"into one of the livest and most stimulating [book sections]
that any newspaper has ever published."

615 ANON. "Six Playwrights Who Have Thumb-Printed Contempo-
rary Drama." Theatre, 49 (June), 39.
This page has six drawings of playwrights with captions.
Indicates all belong in a Broadway Hall of Fame. Dell is
identified as a "modernist novelist" responsible, with Thomas
Mitchell, for the "highly successful American comedy "Little
Accident."

616 ANON. "'Little Accident' Wins the Megrue Prize." New York
Times (18 June), p. 29.

Short article naming Dell and Thomas Mitchell as recipients of cash award as co-authors of play which cheers up audiences.

617 B., W. S. Review of Souvenir. Boston Evening Transcript (16 February), book section, p. 4.
　　Tells plot. Main interest of the story is in the father's reaction to his son's return. Praises book for its "unpretentious, but vibrant and precise prose."

619 BECKER, MAY LAMBERTON. "The Reader's Guide." Saturday Review of Literature, 5 (23 March), 815.
　　Brief mention of Souvenir. It shows the new morality against the old.

619 BRAY, ELIZABETH MCCULLOUGH. "Poet, Critic and Novelist Round Out Local Group of Which Mrs. Bray Writes." Davenport Democrat and Leader (21 April), pp. 4, 9.
　　Sketches and appraisals of Arthur Davison Ficke, Harry Hansen, and Floyd Dell, all one-time residents of Davenport, Iowa. Briefly reviews Dell's career and his associations with the town. Quotes from Moon-Calf. Says he is "known as the socialist novelist." Dell complains of not being taken seriously. He claims "Little Accident" is a problem play, not a farce as it has been seen by critics and audiences.

620 BYRON, MILTON. Review of Souvenir. Edited by Frances Lamont Robbins. Outlook and Independent, 151 (13 February), 269.
　　Briefly summarizes plot. Character development is better than in Moon-Calf and The Briary-Bush. "Tragic and pathetic without being sentimental."

621 CARTER, JOHN. "The Aging Radical." Saturday Review of Literature, 5 (23 March), 799.
　　Review of Souvenir. The book is one of Dell's best. If not profound, it is true. The writing is competent and the theme is treated effectively. "A calmly ironic study."

622 FARJEON, HERBERT. Review of "Little Accident." The Graphic, 124 (13 April), 64.
　　Review of London Apollo Theater performance. Tells plot and praises star actor. The authors lack the "touch of confidence" because they fall back on social convention for the ending. They have not defined the play as farce or comedy. The audience does not care about the fate of the hero or the child's mother. "But even when the entertainment fails, you are left with entertaining glimpses of its possibilities." Dell not mentioned by name.

623 GOLD, MICHAEL. "Floyd Dell Resigns." New Masses, 5
(July), 10-11.
Cruel and vitriolic attack on Dell on the occasion of his
resigning from his position on the New Masses. Dell has
never been a true revolutionary or a good writer. The
money he has made from writing has made him a greedy
capitalist who wears dress suits. The characters in his
novels are "silly and worthless people." Dell is "a skimmer
of surfaces, a dilettante." Dell's character is indecent.

624 LEISY, ERNEST ERWIN. American Literature; An Interpreta-
tive Survey. New York: Thomas Y. Crowell, p. 259.
Dell's name included in a list of contemporary writers.

625 MANGEL, MAX. "Don't Become a Success." New Masses,
5 (July), 22.
Letter to the editor praising Mike Gold's articles. "Here's
hoping he never becomes a financial success like Floyd
Dell."

626 MANLY, JOHN MATTHEWS, and EDITH RICKERT. Contemporary American Literature; Bibliographies and Study Outlines.
Revised by Fred B. Millett. New York: Harcourt, Brace,
pp. 157-58, 349, 352, 356, 358, 361, 363, 366.
Brief biography, bibliography of Dell's works, and list of
studies and reviews. Includes Dell's name in lists of authors. Revised from no. 291. This is an expanded version of the 1922 publication. Reprinted in no. 1059.

627 MILLETT, FRED B. "Introduction to Contemporary American
Literature," in John Matthews Manly and Edith Rickert's
Contemporary American Literature; Bibliographies and Study
Outlines. Revised by Fred B. Millett. New York: Har-
court, Brace, pp. 3-99 [30].
Brief mention of Dell's first two novels as representative
of the revolt against convention.

628 MORGAN, CHARLES. "Broadway Plays Abroad." New York
Times (28 April), sec. 9, p. 1.
Review of London performance of "Little Accident." Concentrates on production and acting style. Little comment on
play itself. Speculates that it may originally have been
serious but became a farce by "ingenuous alterations." Described as "a curious admixture of seriousness, farce and
blatant sentimentalism." Dell not named.

629 ORTON, VREST. Dreiserana; A Book About His Books. New
York: Chocorua Bibliographies, p. 35.
Says Dell, a novelist and poet, was selected at Dreiser's
suggestion to edit The "Genius" after it had been accepted
by John Lane Co. He eliminated 100 pages in proof.

630 PARSONS, ALICE BEAL. "Second Generation." New York
Herald Tribune Books (10 February), p. 4.
    Review of Souvenir. Compares Felix Fay to an omniscient
God. The book shows Dell's "shrewd insight into human motives." Though his characters are realistic, "there is no
depth of emotion, no particularity of description." Not one
of the scenes is actually realized. Dell "gives us the appearance of things, all the outer planes and surfaces of
life as we know it, a deceptive oversimplification which it
is the business of the artist to pierce with truth."

631 RASCOE, BURTON. A Bookman's Daybook. Edited by C.
Hartley Gratton. New York: Horace Liveright, pp. 68,
136, 152.
    Brief mentions of Dell in this selection of Rascoe's "Day-
book" columns from the New York Herald Tribune. Mentions Dell's association with the Chicago Evening Post's
Friday Review of Literature and notes its accomplishments.
Believes the Chicago renaissance was stimulated by this
publication. Says Dell could dance like a Russian cossack.
Quotes Somerset Maugham's opinion of Dell's first two novels.

632 SKINNER, SERENA. Review of "Little Accident." The Com-
monweal, 9 (13 February), 431.
    The comedy is well written for the stage, but it lacks
plausibility. Serious matters of life should not be lightly
treated in a farce. "It is rather startling cowardice when
we fight off reality with farce."

633 SPECTOR, HERMAN. "Weiss Is Wrong." New Masses, 5
(August), 22.
    Letter to the editor. Mentions pleasure given by Mike
Gold's article on Dell. See no. 623.

634 TRASK, C. HOOPER. "Broadway to Berlin." New York
Times (22 September), sec. 9, p. 4.
    This article discusses the spring-summer production of
American plays in Berlin. "Little Accident," translated
ineptly by Hans Rothe, was produced at the Komodie. The
reviewer finds the second act to have "real originality" and
the third to contain good farce. But this production was
poorly staged and aimed for slapstick rather than the real
farce involved.

635 WRIGHT, CHARLES. "Yours for the Revolution." New
Masses, 5 (August), 22.
    Letter to the editor from a communist sympathizer prais-
ing Dell's resignation from the New Masses. Dell is no
longer a revolutionary and his resignation was a "relief."

636 ZEITLIN, JACOB, and HOMER WOODBRIDGE. Life and Let-
     ters of Stuart P. Sherman. Vol. 2. New York: Farrar
     and Rinehart, pp. 706, 711.
         Quotes Dell on Sherman's alleged change of literary stand-
     ards and change of position. Notes Dell's humor. Sher-
     man's praise of Dell and others does not indicate he entire-
     ly approves of their work. Instead the praise comes from
     appreciation of their outlook on life.

1930

637 ANDERSON, MARGARET. My Thirty Years' War. New York:
     Covici, Friede, pp. 36-38, 39, 41, 42, 47, 49, 83.
         Memories of Dell and his literary circle in Chicago. De-
     scribes Dell's conversation. He boosted the Little Review
     in the Chicago Evening Post and he begged contributions.

638 ANON. "Chronicle and Comment." The Bookman, 70 (Janu-
     ary), 529-44 [542].
         A survey of the 1920s. Dell is named as a midwestern
     author whose career encompassed more aspects of the
     1920s than any other person's. Lists the aspects. Moon-
     Calf was only surpassed by Main Street in literary sensa-
     tion over a realistic novel.

639 ANON. Review of Love in the Machine Age. Science
     News-Letter, 17 (26 April), 271.
         Short. Describes the treatment of the thesis. This is a
     "thorough and scholarly survey" of the science of human
     behavior. Dell, "a leading novelist" brings "human sym-
     pathy" to his study.

640 ANON. "Urge Mental Tests in Criminal Suits." New York
     Times (11 May), sec. 2, pp. 1-2 [2].
         Reports on events of International Congress on Mental
     Hygiene meeting. Indicates Dell's participation in discus-
     sions of sex and civilization led by Dr. Otto Kauders of
     Vienna. Quotes Dell on defense of modern civilization in
     its effect on marriage. Identifies Dell as a "novelist."

641 ANON. Review of Love in the Machine Age. Boston Evening
     Transcript (4 June), part 3, p. 2.
         Restates Dell's thesis.

642 ANON. Review of "Little Accident." The Saturday Review,
     150 (30 August), 258.
         Review of movie version. Does not name Dell, but men-
     tions the play of the same name. The movie is "weary
     drizzle."

643 ANON. Review of <u>Souvenir</u>. <u>The Saturday Review</u>, 150
(4 October), 409.
Short. Tells plot. Novel places contemporary issues
against a Greenwich Village style background.

644 ANON. "Floyd Dell Answers Bertrand Russell on Do Men
Want Children?" <u>Parents' Magazine</u>, 5 (November), 14-15
67 [14, 15].
Actual article is by Dell, but an introductory commentary
refers to Dell and Russell as "two famous men" who are
"thinkers." Includes photos of Dell and his children.

645 ANON. Review of <u>Love in the Machine Age</u>. <u>The Booklist</u>,
27 (November), 92-93.
Brief statement of book's thesis. The author's ideas
are "almost Utopian."

646 ANON. Review of <u>Love in the Machine Age</u>. London <u>Times
Literary Supplement</u> (6 November), p. 903.
Restates Dell's thesis.

647 ANON. Review of <u>Love in the Machine Age</u>. <u>The Saturday
Review</u>, 150 (8 November), 608-609.
The book claims to have wider scope than it does. It
is "a rehash of the elements of contemporary psychology."
It does not bring psychology to bear on history and sociology as it claims. The bibliography is "uncommonly pretentious" yet does not refer to Jung.

648 ANON. Review of <u>Souvenir</u>. London <u>Times Literary Supple-
ment</u> (20 November), p. 992.
Short. Tells plot. The story is occasionally slow, but
the reader retains an interest in the characters. Dell's
method is to keep his characters in the context of a social
problem. All of his writing is "sensible and well-balanced."

649* ANON. Review of <u>Love in the Machine Age</u>. <u>Times of India</u>
(Bombay) (25 November).
Cited in no. 913, p. 579.

650* BARNES, HARRY ELMER. Review of <u>Love in the Machine
Age</u>. New York <u>Telegram</u> [?]
Unlocatable. Cited in no. 913, p. 579.

651 BRINKLEY, FRANCES WILLIAMS. "Sex and Its Cure." <u>Sat-
urday Review of Literature</u>, 6 (31 May), 1090.
Review of <u>Love in the Machine Age</u>. Recounts Dell's
main points. Short discussion of the changes in sexual
mores and their appearance in different generations.
Notes Dell's reliance on psychology in his history and finds

his book to be an example of the "trend toward the merging of disciplines."

652 CAIRNS, WILLIAM B. A History of American Literature. Revised edition. New York: Oxford University Press, p. 527.
Short paragraph on Dell gives brief biography and lists some of his novels. Says Dell writes " 'daring' " books of "sensational frankness." The first edition of this book was published in 1912, before Dell became known as a writer.

653 COLTON, ARTHUR. "An All-English Burton." Saturday Review of Literature, 6 (26 April), 986-87.
Review of The Anatomy of Melancholy, edited by Dell. Criticizes the edition for rendering Burton's Latin in English. Because of the Renaissance attitude to Latin the original should not be translated. Compares Burton to Sir James Fraser as compiler and Burton to Montaigne as quoter of Latin. For reply, see no. 667.

654 COWLEY, MALCOLM. "Happiness Made Easy." The New Republic, 62 (30 April), 304-305.
Review of Love in the Machine Age. Compares Dell's presentation of his material to an old-time medicine show. Ridicules Dell's idea that most of society's problems could be solved by giving youth liberty. If this were so, society would be populated by mediocre people and ruled by the law of survival of the fittest.

655 EDMAN, IRWIN. "Moon-Calf Grown Up." The Forum, 83 (June), xii, xiv.
Review of Love in the Machine Age. Dell has assumed the moral responsibilities conferred by his popularity as a novelist. "The book is a model of lucid organization, of sober statement, of documented common sense." Summarizes Dell's thesis. Praises his conclusions and prophecy of the future. His synthesis of psychiatry, social science, history, and morals is "plausible, entertaining, and convincing."

656 FORMAN, HENRY JAMES. "Achieving Emotional Adulthood in the Modern Age." New York Times Book Review (28 September), p. 11.
Review of Love in the Machine Age. Cites Dell's interest in social problems and his wide knowledge of psychology. Restates and discusses his thesis. Finds the book "over-written" because the young already have freedoms advocated by Dell. But the book will stimulate the reader to read and think on his own. Dell is "always an interesting writer."

657 H., G. Review of Love in the Machine Age. New Yorker, 6
     (19 April), 102.
       Short. Like others writing on sex in modern life, Dell
     looks to primitive tribes for examples. Notes his "enthu-
     siasm" and "gusto."

658 HANSEN, HARRY. Review of Love in the Machine Age. New
     York World (4 April), p. 14.
       The book intends to be popular, not scholarly. Describes
     Dell's method which is to examine research in hopes of
     freeing the reader from repressions. Reviewer does not
     judge the validity of conclusions because of own ignorance
     of psychology.

659 LOVEMAN, AMY. Notice of Love in the Machine Age. Sat-
     urday Review of Literature, 6 (19 April), 968.
       Very brief. Title only.

660 MEAD, MARGARET. "Floyd Dell Urges Education for Love in
     a Machine Age." New York Evening Post (5 April), p. 10m.
       Review of Love in the Machine Age. Describes the book
     and restates Dell's thesis. Dell makes "a sane, balanced,
     delightful plea" for his ideas on childrearing. His analyses
     are marred by his lack of familiarity with anthropological
     findings and theory. Dell is successful in using other
     theory to substantiate his propagandistic point of view.
     The best part of the book is that which deals with actual
     problems in raising children. The book is "exceedingly
     readable, often revealing, intelligent pleading" for Dell's
     ideas.

661 PARRINGTON, VERNON LOUIS. Main Currents in American
     Thought: The Beginnings of Critical Realism in America,
     1860-1920. Vol. 3. New York: Harcourt, Brace, p. 386.
       Brief section on youthful, rebellious writers. Highly
     critical description of these "poseurs"--Fitzgerald, S. V.
     Benet, Dell, and B. Hecht. Dell is "the most serious and
     ablest" in the group of intellectual rebels.

662 PATTEE, FRED LEWIS. The New American Literature 1890-
     1930. New York: Century, pp. 23, 153, 154.
       Dell's name included in quote from Harry Hansen's Mid-
     west Portraits (see no. 332) concerning the Chicago liter-
     ary community. Names Dell as Upton Sinclair's biographer
     and quotes from the biography.

663 PHELPS, WILLIAM LYON. Commentary on The Anatomy of
     Melancholy. Scribner's, 87 (February), 219-20.
       Phelps reviews the popularity of Burton's book. Praises
     the Dell/Jordan-Smith edition which translates the Latin
     as a "noble undertaking."

664 PRUETTE, LORINE. "Happy and Successful Lives." New York Herald Tribune Books (6 April), p. 3.
Review of Love in the Machine Age. Long restating of Dell's major points. Short commentary notes Dell's idealization of family life and proposes that it may be a major sociological trend. The book is scholarly and interesting.

665 ROSS, MARY. "Mental Hygiene Looks at the World." The Survey, 64 (15 June), 262-64, 287 [287].
Brief mention of Dell speaking at the formation of the International Committee for Mental Hygiene. He "brilliantly" showed how the development of the system of land owning delayed the development of children. Dell identified as a novelist and author of Love in the Machine Age.

666 SEABURY, FLORENCE GUY. Review of Love in the Machine Age. Outlook and Independent, 155 (28 May), 149.
Short restatement of Dell's thesis.

667 SMITH, PAUL JORDAN. "'Doctoring' Burton." Saturday Review of Literature, 7 (16 August), 58.
Reply to no. 653. Says presenting the Latin translated into English makes the volume readable to the majority of readers. The book is intended for the layperson, not the collector or the researcher.

668 SNOW, FRANCIS. Review of Love in the Machine Age. Current History, 32 (May), 214.
Short. "The book as a whole is as sickening as it is futile."

669 WHITE, WILLIAM A. Review of Love in the Machine Age. The Annals of the American Academy of Political and Social Science, 149, part 3, "Some Social Aspects of Mental Hygiene," edited by Frankwood E. Williams (May), 201-203.
Reprinted from no. 670.

670 WHITE, WILLIAM A. Review of Love in the Machine Age. Mental Hygiene, 14 (April), 469-72.
Relates the book to the psychoanalysis and mental hygiene movements and finds it "the most altogether satisfying, constructive, and profoundly significant" "in recent years." Restates the thesis of the work. "I cannot think of another work on mental hygiene which is its equal." Reprinted in no. 669.

671 YUST, WALTER. "'Of Making Many Books.'" Philadelphia Public Ledger (9 April), p. 11.
Review of Love in the Machine Age. Places it in current flurry of opinions on marriage and life-styles. Dell is unique in his acceptance of the machine age. The book

is "a highly serviceable experience in this day and time; one of the most uncompromisingly honest, clarifying and truly eloquent investigations of a vexed problem of daily living." Long quotation.

1931

672 ANON. "Finds Young Love Has Rough Path." Cleveland Plain Dealer (1 April), p. 13.
    Report of a speech based on Love in the Machine Age made by Dell to the Hospital Social Workers Association. Summarizes and quotes from speech which deals with the economic inability of young people to marry. Dell identified as novelist and playwright.

673* ANON. Photograph of Dell. Parents' Magazine, 6 (May), 28.
    Cited in no. 913, p. 604.

674 ANON. Review of The Anatomy of Melancholy. Journal of Nervous and Mental Disease, 74 (August), 243-44.
    Highly praises the "real, complete and authentic translation" of the entire work. "Floyd Dell and Paul Jordan-Smith have done a splendid bit of scholarly work." Describes Burton and the nature of his book.

675 ANON. "'Cloudy with Showers,' New Comedy, at the Broad." Newark Evening News (15 August), Magazine section, p. 7.
    Announces opening of the play at the Broad Street Theater. Tells plot and lists actors. Names Dell as co-author and identifies him as a "fictionist."

676 ANON. "'Cloudy with Showers,' a Merry Comedy, Presented at the Broad." Newark Evening News (18 August), p. 14.
    Review of first performance of play in Newark. Tells plot in detail. Lists actors and comments on their performances. The authors concentrate on sex and produce a comedy with "exhilarating moments."

677 ANON. "Thomas Mitchell, Comedian and Playwright, Born in Elizabeth." Newark Evening News (20 August), p. 7.
    Brief mention of Dell as co-author with Mitchell of "Cloudy with Showers."

678 ANON. "Two Plays En Route to Broadway." New York Times (23 August), sec. 8, p. 2.
    One-half of this article deals with "Cloudy with Showers." Most of the section is a quotation from the Newark Evening News account of a production of the play. See no. 676. Notes Dell's part as co-author.

679 ANON. Announcement of Article. Parents' Magazine, 6 (September), 28.
     Briefly announces Dell's coming article in this magazine. Says Moon-Calf and Love in the Machine Age prove Dell understands youth. Includes picture of Dell.

680 ANON. "McNutt in Cast of Own Play." New York Times (17 September), p. 14.
     Brief. States that play producer has minor role. Says Dell and Mitchell have introduced new final act to "Cloudy with Showers."

681 ANON. Review of "Cloudy with Showers." Life, 98 (18 September), 18.
     Brief. "This play isn't lousy, it's terrible." Review of performance.

682 ANON. "The Play of the Month." The Sketch Book Magazine, 8 (October), 21.
     Review of performance of "Cloudy with Showers." Tells plot. Names Dell as author. It is a "good farce." Praises humor. The dialogue is "copious and intimate, and frequently sparkling."

683 ANON. "Mr. Dell's Mooncalves." New York Times Book Review (18 October), p. 7.
     Review of Love Without Money. Tells plot. Dell is at his best in treating the adolescent Peter. The novel is old-fashioned in spite of its modernism because it deals with a generation that has already grown up. The revolt of Peter and Gretchen is without meaning and their flight to Chicago is pathetic because they believe in its significance.

684 ANON. Review of Love Without Money. Saturday Review of Literature, 8 (26 December), 415.
     Dell writes skillfully about adolescence. His characters are realistic. He has not progressed beyond that ability. Reviewer sees central problem of book to be Peter and Gretchen's desire for a room of their own. "The problem resolves itself into no problem at all, and this conscious limitation of the author's scope restricts the book, draws it down to extremely small dimensions, and militates against any real importance it might otherwise have achieved as an exposition of a human problem. It makes delightful reading."

685 ATKINSON, J. BROOKS. "Professor's Coming of Age." New York Times (2 September), p. 17.
     Review of performance of "Cloudy with Showers." Tells plot, comments on acting. The play might be improved by considering the unities and by being reduced to two acts.

"In many respects it is a clever skit with amusing ideas and comic dialogue." "But the task of keeping the prank in motion fairly exhausts the fun before the play is over."

686 BENCHLEY, ROBERT. Review of "Cloudy with Showers."
      New Yorker, 7 (12 September), 30, 32, 34.
          Praises the humor in the first act. Acts two and three lack cohesion. The play is a farce.

687 BIRRELL, AUGUSTINE. "The Analyst of Moods." The New Statesman and Nation, 1 (28 February), literary supplement sec., pp. xii, xiv.
          Review of Burton's The Anatomy of Melancholy. Long account of the history of the book's publication. Praises the translation of Latin passages: "This edition has one striking feature of its own which it owes to the courage of its two American editors, who though themselves scholastic personages, have the courage of their opinions."

688 BUTCHER, FANNY. "Another Novel by Floyd Dell Depicts Youth." Chicago Daily Tribune (13 October), p. 21.
          Review of Love Without Money. Dell deals with the same subject matter here as in his early novels, but here the treatment is humorous rather than serious. Love Without Money could be staged as a farce comedy like "Unmarried Father." "Mr. Dell has achieved a new popularity in his writing which ought to bring him fortune without doing anything drastic to the fame which is already his as a novelist." Includes photo.

689 C., R. M. Review of Love Without Money. New Yorker, 7 (31 October), 79-80.
          Harsh. Tells plot. Dell has "remarkably little of any substance to say." In his first novels his style was "beguiling," but he has lost that skill. He is "aggressively callow," "determinedly adolescent." Ridicules Dell's use of Chicago as the scene of his novels. Complains about a few pages that are excessively frank about sex. Is not a book for young people.

690 CHATFIELD-TAYLOR, OTIS. Review of "Cloudy with Showers." Outlook and Independent, 159 (16 September), 86.
          Review of New York performance. Tells plot and comments on acting. It is a "somewhat labored farce" and is structurally weak. Yet it provides good entertainment.

691 CLARAGE, ELEANOR. Review of Love Without Money. Cleveland Plain Dealer (22 October), p. 13.
          Brief. "The champion of the younger generation does another of those intense things about the sex life of the adolescent, which can interest no one but adolescents."

692 DAWSON, MARGARET CHENEY. "Rebellion of Youth." New
York Herald Tribune Books (18 October), p. 7.
Review of Love Without Money. The main characters,
Gretchen and Peter, are not fully realized. They remain
"paper dolls." Their actions are not as momentous as the
author seems to think. The best characterization is that of
Mrs. Cedarbloom. Dell is no longer identified with seriousness but with a "warm sympathy" toward his characters and
a willingness to accept their flatness.

693 DE CASSERES, BENJAMIN. Review of "Cloudy with Showers."
Arts and Decoration, 36 (November), 51, 72.
Review of performance. Describes action in each act.
The third act is not up to the first two. Cites "shrewd and
brilliant dialogue." The play is the season's first hit.

694 FERGUSSON, FRANCIS. Review of "Cloudy with Showers."
The Bookman, 74 (October), 186-87.
Praises humor and acting. Complains that Dell argues
"too grimly" about seduction. The writers are shrewd and
quiet. Praises the character sketches.

695* FREEMAN, MARILLA. "Books and Articles by and about Mr.
Dell." Cleveland Public Library, 4 mimeographed pages.
March 1931.
Cited in no. 913, p. 600. The Cleveland Public Library
has no record of this article.

696 KUNITZ, STANLEY J. "Floyd Dell," in Living Authors; A
Book of Biographies. New York: H. W. Wilson, pp. 101-
102.
Biography. Gives the facts of Dell's life. Lists his publications. Physical and character description. As editor
of the Friday Literary Review, he built it "into one of the
livest [sic] and most stimulating that any newspaper has
ever published." See Dilly Tante, no. 700, for pseudonym.

697 LOVEMAN, AMY. "Books of the Fall, II." Saturday Review
of Literature, 8 (24 October), 236.
Very brief mention of Love Without Money as fiction.

698 PARRY, ALBERT. "Soul Flights of the Village." The American Mercury, 24 (October), 189-97 [190, 194, 195].
Third article in Perry's series on the Village for the
Mercury. Brief mentions of Dell. Says Dell gave a pseudonym to the founder of the Liberal Club when writing about
the Village in his memoirs. Names Dell as pupil of George
Cram Cook, who, though once a revolutionary, now makes
money writing about sex. Compares paths of Dell and
Howard Brubaker.

699 SLOSSON, PRESTON WILLIAM. The Great Crusade and After, 1914-1928. Edited by Arthur M. Schlesinger and Dixon Ryan Fox. A History of American Life, Vol. 12. New York: Macmillan, p. 420.
Briefly mentions Moon-Calf in list of books reflecting America's post-World War I discontent with herself.

700 TANTE, DILLY. "Floyd Dell," in Living Authors; A Book of Biographies. New York: H. W. Wilson, pp. 101-102.
Pseudonym for Stanley J. Kunitz. See no. 696.

1932

701 ANON. Notice of Diana Stair. The Nation, 135 (19 October), 379.
Lists Diana Stair among notable books of the season.

702 ANON. Review of Diana Stair. The Nation, 135 (23 November), 509-10.
The heroine is not convincing and becomes a "meaningless cipher," nor is the historical setting convincing. The novel is an apology for present liberal tendencies. It "can hardly stand on its intrinsic value."

703 ANON. Review of Diana Stair. The Atlantic Monthly, 150 (December), Christmas Book section, 30.
Very briefly tells plot.

704 BRITT, GEORGE. "Montmartre in Manhattan." New York World-Telegram (16 May), sec. 2, p. 13.
First of series of articles on Greenwich Village. Brief mention of Dell and Edna St. Vincent Millay together in Washington Square. Notes that Dell named the "Pagan Routs" costume parties staged by the Liberal Club. Includes photo of Dell.

705 BRITT, GEORGE. "Montmartre in Manhattan." New York World-Telegram (19 May), sec. 2, p. 19.
Fourth of series of five articles on Greenwich Village. Discusses periodical publications. Brief mention of Dell's part on the Masses. Includes Art Young's description of him.

706 BRITT, GEORGE. "Montmartre in Manhattan." New York World-Telegram (20 May), sec. 2, p. 17.
Last article in series. This one centers on theater development in Greenwich Village. Cites Dell as member of Provincetown Theatre group. His play, "King Arthur's Socks," was on the group's first New York bill. The next year "The Angel Intrudes" was presented.

707 BUTCHER, FANNY. "Free Woman Is Floyd Dell Theme Again."
     Chicago Tribune (12 December), p. 19.
         Review of Diana Stair. Tells plot. Short description of
     Diana as typical Dell heroine, liberated and independent.
     The novel could have been shorter, "but it is written with
     such complete seriousness, such ardor, that its importance
     is inherent. One does miss, however, the delicate humor
     and humanity and charm of Moon-Calf." The heroine as
     well as the novel are "a little too tractlike at times to be
     always deeply, humanly appealing."

708 CALVERTON, V. F. The Liberation of American Literature.
     New York: Charles Scribner's Sons, pp. 450, 455-56.
         Cites Dell's contribution in guiding the Masses in expres-
     sion of proletarian ideology. Finds Dell's essays on "Liter-
     ature and the Machine Age" to be the most significant work
     published by The Liberator. "Those essays marked the
     first appearance in the United States of social criticism,
     projected from a radical point of view." Short discussion
     of Dell's disfavor among radicals because of his novels.

709 DUDLEY, DOROTHY. Forgotten Frontiers; Dreiser and the
     Land of the Free. New York: Harrison Smith and Robert
     Haas, pp. 257-58.
         Paragraph on Dell and his recognition and praise of
     Jennie Gerhardt.

710 GRATTAN, G. HARTLEY. "Upton Sinclair on Current Liter-
     ature." The Bookman, 75 (April), 61-64 [64].
         Summary of a conversation between Sinclair and Grattan
     about current American literature and writers. Sinclair
     wishes his friend Dell could devote himself to serious fic-
     tion. Sinclair likes the early Dell books.

711 HATCHER, HARLAN. "The Inner Compulsion." Saturday
     Review of Literature, 9 (12 November), 237.
         Review of Diana Stair. Since The Briary-Bush Dell's
     works have been criticized for sentimentality and triviality,
     but Diana Stair supports the former acclaim given Dell.
     The historical setting allows the author to project and treat
     modern problems. The narrative is "well conducted and
     often dramatic." The minor characters are "more vividly
     realized than the complex Diana." Gives brief overview of
     plot and theme.

712 LEWISOHN, LUDWIG. Expression in America. New York:
     Harper and Brothers, pp. 370, 412-14, 472.
         Brief mention of Dell as rebel and as apologist for Upton
     Sinclair. Small section on his artistic and historical sig-
     nificance. For the first time in the United States experi-
     ence and expression were integrated. Dell is the symbol

of the renaissance in American letters. Comments on his writing in the Masses, his autobiographical novels, and Janet March, a book which sums up the hopes of the feminist movement. Reprinted in no. 802.

713 LOVEMAN, AMY. Listing of Diana Stair. Saturday Review of Literature, 9 (17 December), 333.
Very brief mention of the novel as suitable for a Christmas gift.

714 M., D. L. "A Widowed Heroine in the Boston of a Century Ago." Boston Evening Transcript (26 November), Book Section, p. 1.
Review of Diana Stair. Mainly devoted to telling the plot. Finds Diana the only well developed character. Praises the depiction of nineteenth-century American life.

715 MANTLE, BURNS. The Best Plays of 1931-1932 and the Year Book of the Drama in America. New York: Dodd, Mead, pp. 6, 384-85, 531.
Briefly mentions "Cloudy with Showers" as less successful than "Little Accident." Lists characters and actors of "Cloudy with Showers" and gives plot summary. The play is listed as one of the best for 1928-1929.

716 PANGBORN, H. L. "Mr. Dell and the Utopian Spirit." New York Times Book Review (23 October), p. 6.
Review of Diana Stair. Finds some chapters well done but believes the novel would profit from condensation. Though the historical setting is probably accurate, it appears more as scenery than as the product of imagination. Some of the minor characters are more convincing than the major ones. Tells much of the plot.

717 PRUETTE, LORINE. "A Lady Not So Genteel." New York Herald Tribune Books (23 October), p. 6.
Review of Diana Stair. Diana is realized as a person, not an illustration. There are many "vivid characterizations, the best ones chiefly of women." The last section of the book represents "brilliant story telling." Tells the plot.

718 SINCLAIR, UPTON. American Outpost; A Book of Reminiscences. Station A, Pasadena, Cal.: Published by the Author, pp. 48, 125-28, 140.
Sinclair's autobiography. Brief mentions of Dell in his capacity as Sinclair's biographer. Long quotation of Dell's opinion of another work.

719 THURNAU, H. C. "Old Wine in a New Bottle." The Modern Language Journal, 17 (December), 188-94.
This article compares the plot of Dell's short story "The

Blanket" to that of the Grimm story "Der alte Grossvater und der Enkel." Traces the occurrences of this plot back to an ancient Greek story. Lists the national literatures which have a form of the story.

1933

720 ANON. Review of Diana Stair. The Booklist, 29 (January), 143-44.
Brief. Describes heroine and her adventures. Diana is a "convincing character" and her milieu is appropriate to "a one person novel."

721 ANON. "His Latest Book Is Autobiography." Davenport Times (7 October), p. 3.
Photo of Dell. Briefly identifies him as "former Davenporter and author of Moon-Calf."

722 ANON. Notice of Homecoming. The Nation, 137 (18 October), 460.
Homecoming included in list of notable books of the season.

723 ANON. Review of Homecoming. The Booklist, 30 (November), 76.
Brief description. "It is mainly a literary autobiography, peopled with writers, and marked by restraint and dignity."

724 ANON. Review of Homecoming. The Open Shelf (December), p. 14.
Very brief. Identifies book as by the author of Moon-Calf and Diana Stair.

725 ANON. Review of Homecoming. Edited by Mary Katharine Reely. Wisconsin Library Bulletin, 29 (December), 262.
Short. Includes brief biography. Stresses Dell's search for himself and for the "enduring values of life."

726 ANON. Review of Homecoming. The Nation, 137 (6 December), 659-60.
Because Dell has written about his life since his first novel, this volume "had best be regarded as the definitive edition up to this date." Dell has learned little from his experiences. He feels older than he is, but does not give up considering himself part of the young generation. His book is honest but trivial.

727 BRICKELL, HERSCHEL. Review of Homecoming. The North American Review, 236 (December), 573.
Short. Describes contents. "It is a good book."

728 BUTCHER, FANNY. "Critical Times Cause Readers to Seek
Facts." Chicago Tribune (29 September), p. 15.
Review of Homecoming. Half the article deals with the
public's interest in autobiographies. Relates Dell's early
history. "Homecoming is impressive, vivid, frank ..., but
in emphasizing those very virtues it lacks the delicious vice
of occasional wholly inconsequential charm."

729 CHAMBERLAIN, JOHN. "Books of the Times." New York
Times (29 September), p. 17.
Review of Homecoming. The book is a recapitulation of
previous works. The individual portraits are "remarkable."
Dell as a socialist cannot be taken seriously. "The book is
important, in the last analysis, for what Dell saw, not for
what he was and is."

730 DUFFUS, R. L. "Floyd Dell, Symbol of a Period." New York
Times Book Review (8 October), p. 5.
Review of Homecoming. This autobiography is "excellent."
It is the story of Dell's personal movement from instability
to stability. Besides being Dell's story, the book is also
the story of an era, the period from 1893 to 1933.

731 ESTORICK, ERIC ELY. "Dell Autobiography Interesting Volume." Akron Beacon Journal (7 October), p. 5.
Short review of Homecoming. "This autobiography is a
careful, meticulous, and logically sound re-living of a personal evolution of growth in a complex social organism; it
is a psychological interpretation over a social-historical
analysis of a literary ferment in American letters, which the
author encountered in the course of his many artistic en-
deavors."

732 FREEMAN, JOSEPH. "Greenwich Village Types." New Masses,
8 (May), pp. 18-20 [18].
This article deals with the evolution of the bohemian intellectual from Greenwich Village days until contemporary
times. The outlook is Marxist. Brief mention of Freeman
going to the Village in 1921 to meet Dell and others. Includes long quote from Dell in 1920 about the nature of his
generation.

733 FULLER, HAROLD DE WOLF. Review of Homecoming. Literary Digest, 116 (28 October), 38.
Short. Finds Dell's early life most interesting because of
its sharp contrast with what he was to become. Credits
Dell with "intellectual curiosity and some poetic talent."
His personal achievement in drama, the novel, and verse
are not out of the ordinary. His relations with American
writers of the teens and twenties prove an interesting aspect of literary history.

734 H., H. H. Review of Homecoming. Durham [N.C.] Herald-
     Sun (8 October), sec. 1, p. 5.
        Briefly retells Dell's life story. Notes autobiographical
     nature of Moon-Calf. Dell is "eternally young."

735 HAPGOOD, HUTCHINS. "The Instinct to Conform." The
     New Republic, 77 (29 November), 80.
        Review of Homecoming. Dell's motivation is the desire
     to conform. Thus he criticizes George Cram Cook as a
     failure because Cook did not conform. The book is read-
     able, sensitive, intelligent, but it does not reveal a con-
     crete personal life. "There seems no personality behind
     his writing." This is also characteristic of his book re-
     views in the Masses.

736 HICKS, GRANVILLE. The Great Tradition; An Interpretation
     of American Literature Since the Civil War. New York:
     Macmillan, p. 212.
        Moon-Calf, This Side of Paradise, and Stephen Benet's
     The Beginning of Wisdom "expressed the bewilderment and
     hopelessness of youth." Groups Dell with the middle gen-
     eration of writers active in the American renaissance, 1912-
     1925. These writers were no longer political muckrackers.
     They attacked much of American life. Revised in no. 776.

737 LONG, FORREST C. Letter to the Editor. Progressive
     Education, 10 (February), 109-10.
        Comments on Dell's essays in Progressive Education of
     November 1932 and January 1933. Attacks his assumptions
     that education is for adult living and that school curricula
     are rigid. Praises suggestion on use of schools. Dell is a
     "competent critic."

738 LOVEMAN, AMY. Notice of Homecoming. Saturday Review
     of Literature, 10 (14 October), 189.
        Brief mention among books of note to those interested in
     contemporary fiction.

739 M., D. L. "What Life Means to Reminiscent Mr. Dell."
     Boston Evening Transcript (4 November), book section,
     p. 1.
        Review of Homecoming. Sharply criticizes Dell for con-
     stantly writing about himself. Accuses him of desiring
     publicity and of suffering from a "deep-laid egotism." "The
     wisdom he has to impart is small." "It is his close-ups of
     the well-known figures of our period rather than his own
     growth which provide the true substance of this autobiog-
     raphy."

740 N., E. A. Review of Homecoming. Mason City [Iowa] Globe-
     Gazette (25 November), p. 7.

The book is important because Dell represents the changing literary taste of America and the rebellion against middleclass mores. Focuses on his life in Davenport.

741 NORTH, STERLING. "He Not So Much Kissed As Told."
Chicago Daily News (27 September), p. 15.
Review of Homecoming. Unlike Diana Stair, Homecoming deals with something familiar to Dell and is thus praised. Compared favorably to Moon-Calf, "the sensation of the year." Dell "is easily the Rousseau of his generation, as well as the Mr. Isadora Duncan." Dell's success as a novelist was based on the same appeal as "confession magazines." Notes discrepancy between Dell's radical image and his monogamous life. Praises chapters on Chicago.

742 PARRY, ALBERT. Garrets and Pretenders. New York:
Covici-Friede, pp. xiv, 16, 187, 189, 190, 200, 270, 277, 278, 287-89, 293, 297, 302, 355, 361.
Dell's socialism is "more academic than barracadic." He is a "talented but not gigantic writer." "The early brilliance that was his is now largely gone, dissipated in a skillful effort to ennoble the petty passions of the American intelligentsia." Revised edition, no. 925.

743 PRUETTE, LORINE. "How the Mooncalf Found His Way Home."
New York Herald Tribune Books (1 October), p. 5.
REview of Homecoming. Relates Dell's life story. Finds book interesting for insight it gives into biography's relation to artistic invention. Dell's major concern is continuity and stability of vocation and love. He gives an "honest psychological appraisal of his own life."

744 REDMAN, BEN RAY. "Moon-Calf Grows Up." Saturday Review of Literature, 10 (30 September), 141, 145.
Review of Homecoming. Dell has written a frank portrait of himself. Summary of his activities. Compares Homecoming to Moon-Calf in terms of self-revelation. They are Dell's best works.

745 RIEBACK, WILLIAM H. Review of Albert Parry's Garrets and Pretenders. American Literature, 5 (May), 196-98 [196].
See no. 742. Includes Dell in list of names which "in themselves constitute a literary history of America."

746 ROBINSON, TED. "'Homecoming' Reveals Floyd Dell as Shy Writer Naively Surprised at His Own Fame." Cleveland Plain Dealer (15 October), Women's Magazine and Amusement Section, p. 15.
Review of Homecoming comprises one-third of this article.

The reviewer, personally acquainted with Dell, finds his autobiography interesting in itself and in its portraits of Dell's contemporaries. Praises his simplicity of style, "the power he has to create interest, and the artistic expertness of his construction." Believes the work is "a big book."

1934

747 ANON. Notice of The Golden Spike. Saturday Review of Literature, 11 (6 October), 194.
   Very brief mention.

748 ANON. Review of The Golden Spike. Christian Century, 51 (17 October), 1314-15.
   The theme is well presented, although the campus life lacks plausibility. The novel does not reflect Dell's radical opinions.

749 ANON. Notice of Diana Stair. The Booklist, 31 (November), 93.
   Novel listed among Grosset and Dunlap's dollar reprints.

750 ANON. Review of The Golden Spike. Boston Evening Transcript (17 November), book section, p. 2.
   Mainly devoted to recounting plot. Dell's ability to deal with typically American characters accounts for his popularity. Diana Stair is his best work.

751 BENET, WILLIAM ROSE. "The Earlier Lewis." Saturday Review of Literature, 10 (20 January), 421-22.
   Briefly mentions Dell's editorship of the Masses as though this were representative of an era. Article deals with Benét's youthful recollections of Sinclair Lewis. Reprinted in no. 903.

752 BRICKELL, HERSCHEL. Review of Homecoming. North American Review, 237 (January), 95.
   Brief. The reviewer expressed "great admiration" for the book.

753 BRICKELL, HERSCHEL. Review of The Golden Spike. North American Review, 238 (December), 573.
   Very brief. "Contains a repetition of a Dellian pattern familiar from Moon-Calf on, and not a great deal more."

754 CHAMBERLAIN, JOHN. "Books of the Times." New York Times (12 October), p. 23.
   Review of The Golden Spike. Briefly tells plot. The campus phase is unrealistic. There are no "vivid climaxes." The author is too wordy with conversations and too unselec-

tive with incidents. The hero Harvey is not always believable. Characterization in general lacks authenticity because
Dell projects 1934 ideas on pre-war rebels.

755 COWLEY, MALCOLM. Exile's Return; A Narrative of Ideas.
New York: W. W. Norton, pp. 171, 188, 190.
Quotes a 1923 letter by Cowley expressing the desire for
a dramatic action out of keeping with "petty literary wars"
with Dell, Ezra Pound, and Robert McAlmon. Quotes Burton Rascoe on Dell's ability to perform a Russian cossack
dance. Recalls plan to burlesque Dell. Revised in nos.
847 and 897.

756 DAVENPORT, BASIL. "The Opening Wedge." Saturday
Review of Literature, 11 (13 October), 202-203.
Review of The Golden Spike. Commends Dell's presentation
of Harvey Claymore and of his times. Questions the role of
money in marriage. The story is "convincing and moving."
"It is a full, rich book, which handles a young love story
with tenderness, a college campus with penetrating irony,
and a whole host of characters with sympathy." Dell reiterates throughout the theme of the rich taking away from
the poor.

757 DAWSON, MARGARET CHENEY. "The Domination of Gold."
New York Herald Tribune Books (14 October), p. 4.
Review of The Golden Spike. Relates the plot. The book
is concerned with the exploitation of the poor by the rich.
Dell piles detail on detail and follows the story to its source.
"He makes a shameless use of platitudes and finally allows
the terms of his conflict to become so conventional that they
cease to be very effective." Yet the book is based on a
knowledge of human nature and is worth reading.

758 EASTMAN, MAX. "Bunk About Bohemia." Modern Quarterly,
8 (May), 200-208 [207].
Eastman defends his bohemianism against the "myth-makers"
on the New Masses. Brief mention of Dell as associate editor
of the old Masses and of the role of the editors in chosing
material to be included in that publication. Continued in
no. 760.

759 EASTMAN, MAX. "Floyd Dell's Double Life," in Art and the
Life of Action with Other Essays. New York: Alfred A.
Knopf, pp. 134-57.
Extended commentary on Love in the Machine Age. Restates Dell's thesis. Cites the dichotomy between ideas expressed in this book and beliefs held by Dell in his youth.
The book is lifeless and detached from the facts of real
life. It is neither "objectively scientific" nor "morally
wise." His "program of adult matehood ... derives not

from biology at all, but from a Puritan theological tradition and some need in his own nature for an escape from the emotional complexities of the actual problem."

760 EASTMAN, MAX. "New Masses for Old." Modern Quarterly, 8 (June), 292-300 [297, 298].
Continuation of no. 758. Briefly mentions Dell and Eastman resisting anarchism and bohemianism for its own sake in the Masses. Notes Dell's role in the artists' revolt of March-April 1916.

761 HARTWICK, HARRY. The Foreground of American Fiction. New York: American Book, pp. 130, 219, 220.
Moon-Calf mentioned as an example of a Freudian novel. Janet March represents the feminist struggle. The Briary-Bush examines contemporary marriage and divorce. The later two are protest novels.

762 HILLQUIT, MORRIS. Loose Leaves from a Busy Life. New York: Macmillan, pp. 222, 224, 225, 226, 228, 232.
Autobiography of lawyer who acted for the defense in the Masses trial. Brief mentions of Dell in the account of the trial. Says evidence against defendants included Dell's defense of conscientious objectors. Claims Dell, at the time of the trial, was no longer opposed to the war, but had registered for the draft. Dell was "an excellent witness."

763 KRONENBERGER, LOUIS. "Floyd Dell's 'The Golden Spike' and Other Recent Works of Fiction." New York Times Book Review (28 October), p. 6.
Half of this article is devoted to a review of The Golden Spike. Here Dell treats his familiar subject of young people learning of life and love. It is a good picture of Harvey's "personal attitude toward the world." Dell's excessive use of detail makes the novel seem old-fashionedly realistic. "'The Golden Spike' is lifelike and consistent and faithful, the work of a man who has caught sight of life on certain levels and at certain moments. It is also, to do it justice, easy and pleasant to read. But it misses, by a wide margin, being literature."

764 LOVEMAN, MAY. "The Clearing House." Saturday Review of Literature, 10 (2 June), 735.
Diana Stair included in list of recent novels using Boston as a background.

765 LOVEMAN, AMY. "The Clearing House." Saturday Review of Literature, 11 (29 September), 149.
Brief mention of Moon-Calf together with This Side of Paradise, Three Soldiers, Hemingway's fiction, and Wines-

burg, Ohio as examples of youthful postwar revolt and dis-
illusionment.

766 LUCCOCK, HALFORD E. Contemporary American Literature
and Religion. Chicago: Willett, Clark, pp. 5, 145-46,
192.
Brief mentions of Janet March as a dated flapper heroine.
Quotes Dell on Edna St. Vincent Millay's attitude to World
War I. Cites Dell as the historian of the Greenwich Village
period in American history. In spite of his other work and
his contributions to education, he is best known for his
first three novels. Notes themes of Moon-Calf and The
Briary-Bush. These novels are "a realistic treatment of
youth's effort to find itself and to find meaning in life."
They manifest "a sense of tragic bafflement."

767 M., D. R. "The Wives and Mistressses of Floyd Dell." Des
Moines Register (7 January), Sunday magazine sec., p. 4.
Review of Homecoming. Concentrates on Dell's life in
Davenport. Dell is "a romantic."

768 P., R. Review of The Golden Spike. The New Republic,
81 (28 November), 83.
Short. The book is "disappointing." The material is
worthy but it lacks focus.

769 ROBINSON, TED. Review of The Golden Spike. Cleveland
Plain Dealer (25 November), Women's Magazine and Amusement Section, p. 13.
Short. Mainly plot summary. The book is "of absorbing
interest." It is not clear if the reviewer has read the
novel.

770 SMITH, PAUL JORDAN. For the Love of Books; The Adventures of an Impecunious Collector. New York: Oxford University Press, pp. 153-54, 168-69.
Relates Dell's "brilliant discovery of the source of Keats'
'Ode on Melancholy.'" Dell's article on "Keats' Debt to
Robert Burton" (The Bookman, March 1928) showed "the
organic kinship existing between the central thought of the
ode" and ideas from Burton's Melancholy. Dell has "an
amazing familiarity" with English poetry. Tells how and
why he and Dell, after translating and editing Burton's
Melancholy, produced an index to the book. Reprinted in
no. 1016. Revised editions in which Dell receives exactly
the same treatment, nos. 804 and 828.

771 SYMES, LILLIAN, and TRAVERS CLEMENT. Rebel America;
The Story of Social Revolt in the United States. New York:
Harper and Brothers, pp. 265, 282, 283, 303, 306.
This book studies those revolutionaries who wished dras-

tically to change the social order. Dell is quoted on the
extraordinary nature of the year 1912. Lists his concerns
while editor of the Masses, stressing his feminist outlook.
Recalls his endorsement of President Wilson's peace proposal
and the Masses trial.

1935

772 ADAMS, FRANKLIN P. The Diary of Our Own Samuel Pepys.
Vol. 1. New York: Simon and Schuster, 267, 295.
    Collection of Adams' articles. Brief mention of having
read Moon-Calf, a "fine," "earnest," and well-written book.
Says he began The Briary-Bush, a promising book.

773 ADAMS, FRANKLIN P. The Diary of Our Own Samuel Pepys.
Vol. 2. New York: Simon and Schuster, 619, 684, 698,
832.
    Collection of Adams' articles. Brief commentary on Love
in Greenwich Village. Wishes Dell would write more poetry.
Mentions conversation with Anthony, Dell's son. Relates
conversation at dinner party at his home attended by Dell.
Dell and Adams discuss why girls are more talkative than
boys. Brief commentary on "Little Accident."

774 FREEMAN, JOSEPH. "The Tradition of American Revolutionary Literature," in American Writers' Congress. Edited by
Henry Hart. New York: International Publishers, pp. 52-
58 [54-55].
    Historical synopsis of revolutionary literature and develop-
ment in America of this form. Dell is example of romantic
revolutionary. Notes his view of proletarian literature as
part of development of American revolutionary literature.

775 HATCHER, HARLAN. Creating the Modern American Novel.
New York: Farrar and Rinehart, pp. 9, 60, 75-79, 81, 82.
    Appraisal of Dell. Cites his fight against censorship and
his midwestern origins. Compares Dell to F. Scott Fitzgerald. Discusses Dell's personal rebellion and his contribution to post-war writing reflecting the younger generation. Comment on each novel. His work has not grown
since the first novel. His novels do not include "the
permanent searching of the soul" that assures continued
reading.

776 HICKS, GRANVILLE. The Great Tradition; An Interpretation
of American Literature. Revised edition. New York: Macmillan, p. 212.
    Revised from no. 736. Revised in no. 1011. Information
on Dell is identical.

777 LOVEMAN, AMY. "The Clearing House." Saturday Review of
Literature, 11 (19 January), 438.
Brief mentions of Moon-Calf and The Briary-Bush among
books which use Chicago as a setting.

778 STEARNS, HAROLD E. The Street I Know. New York: Lee
Furman, p. 138.
Stearns' autobiography. Says that in late 1916 Floyd Dell
was in New York working on his first novel.

779 SULLIVAN, MARK. Our Times; The United States 1900-1925.
Vol. 6. New York: Charles Scribner's Sons, 548, 565.
This volume deals with the twenties. Lists Moon-Calf and
The Briary-Bush as popular books of 1920 and 1921.

780 VORSE, MARY HEATON. A Footnote to Folly: Reminiscences.
New York: Farrar and Rinehart, p. 42.
Describes artists' and writers' meetings to select material
for the Masses. Some were held in Vorse's home. Tells
how Dell read contributions to the group.

1936

781 ATKINS, ELIZABETH. Edna St. Vincent Millay and Her Times.
Chicago: The University of Chicago Press, pp. 15, 64.
Biography of Millay. In discussing the narrowness of
Millay's reading as a child, the author compares her to Dell.
"At the same age Floyd Dell was nervously gulping every-
thing that had been said and thought in the world, and
was thrown into a literary colic that killed the poet in him."
Brief mention of Dell as a youthful social reformer in Green-
wich Village. Reprinted in no. 960.

782 FREEMAN, JOSEPH. An American Testament; A Narrative of
Rebels and Romantics. New York: Farrar and Rinehart,
678 pp., passim.
Personal narrative of how one man embraced communism.
As Dell's friend and sometime houseguest, Freeman places
him in the revolutionary, literary, and socialist milieu of
the first third of the century. Sympathetic observations
on Dell's personality, socialist views, and contribution to
revolutionary causes. Dell discussed in connection with the
Masses, the Liberator, and the New Masses. Sees Dell as
a modern universal man and as a leading writer of the nineteen-twenties.

783 GREGORY, HORACE. "The Education of an American Radical." New York Herald Tribune Books (18 October), p. 7.
Review of Joseph Freeman's An American Testament. See

no. 782. Notes Freeman's acquaintance with Dell who, with Max Eastman, became his mentor. Through Dell and East-man he saw American social democracy develop through muckraking and socialism to post-World War I characteris-tics. The three men shared a "schizophrenia in esthetic thinking" whereby writing and criticizing poetry became unreal acts. Gregory states his appreciation to Freeman for pointing out "Dell's clean-cut vigor as a political pam-phleteer; his editorials in the old 'Masses' and in the 'Lib-erator' should be reread as models of radical journalism."

784 HICKS, GRANVILLE. John Reed: The Making of a Revolu-tionary. New York: Macmillan, pp. 110, 208, 214, 219, 231, 240, 304, 308.
Biography of John Reed. Brief mentions of Dell. Cites his role in the artists' revolt on the Masses, his review of Reed's The War in Eastern Europe, a dinner meeting with Reed, the Masses trial, his position in Frank Harris' scheme to found a new magazine. Reprinted in no. 1002.

785 MANTLE, BURNS. The Best Plays of 1928-1929 and the Year Book of the Drama in America. New York: Dodd, Mead, pp. vi, 8, 252, 282, 350, 394-95.
Briefly notes that "Little Accident" was the only success-ful light comedy in the year and is the first American play to deal partially seriously with the paternal instinct. De-scribes the play and its performance, includes text of script. Brief biography of Dell. Lists characters and actors and gives plot summary.

1937

786* ANON. Comment on a Dell Essay. Education Research Serv-ice Circular, No. 2, p. 3.
Unlocatable. Cited in no. 913, p. 585.

787 BRAGMAN, LOUIS J. "The Case of Floyd Dell; A Study in the Psychology of Adolescence." American Journal of Psy-chiatry, 93 (May), 1401-11.
The author, a medical doctor, gives an overview of Dell's work, concentrating on how it reflects Dell's growth from childhood through adolescence to adulthood and on how this process is reflective of a universal human development. Comments on many of Dell's works. "He points the way, through mental hygiene, for the avoidance of conflicts, and the achievement of stability. Having experienced all the major problems of youth, he proceeds to clarify them for others. His works are the literary representations of his own psychological experiences."

788 CANTWELL, ROBERT. "Upton Sinclair," in After the Genteel

Tradition; American Writers Since 1910. Edited by Malcolm Cowley. New York: W. W. Norton, pp. 37-51 [43].

Essay assessing Sinclair. Brief mention of Dell. Says his "biographical essay, while interesting for its facts, was written in a period when estheticism was dominant in American literature, and is primarily devoted to establishing the social value of Sinclair's books."

789 CLEATON, IRENE, and ALLEN CLEATON. Books and Battles; American Literature, 1920-1930. Boston: Houghton Mifflin, pp. xvii, 65, 74, 95, 100, 110, 159, 160, 180, 202, 213.

Dell is frequently mentioned as an example of trends in the twenties in this "lively" history of the period. Several mentions of the censorship of his novels. Dell as a public speaker, Dell as a literary critic, and Dell's Greenwich Village days are treated. Reprinted in no. 1021.

790 COWLEY, MALCOLM, ed. After the Genteel Tradition; American Writers Since 1910. New York: W. W. Norton, pp. 214, 222, 242, 251.

Brief mention of Dell's socialism. Dell identified as a critic. Names Dell as example of a writer who can shift from one focus to another. Lists Moon-Calf as a 1920 novel attacking the genteel tradition. Brief note of Dell's friendship with Sherwood Anderson.

791* JOHNS, ORRICK. Time of Our Lives: The Story of My Father and Myself. New York: Stackpole Sons.

This autobiography is reprinted in no. 1047.

792 LOGGINS, VERNON. I Hear America ...; Literature in the United States Since 1900. New York: Thomas Y. Crowell, pp. 153, 252, 355.

Names Dell as member of Chicago group of writers and friend of Sherwood Anderson. Cites Dell as a "propagandist" in art. Moon-Calf, Janet March, Love in Greenwich Village, and Intellectual Vagabondage are included in a recommended reading list.

793 LOVEMAN, AMY. "The Clearing House." Saturday Review of Literature, 16 (24 July), 17.

Moon-Calf and The Briary-Bush listed among works of fiction dealing with American newspaper or newspaperman.

794 LOVETT, ROBERT MORSS. "Sherwood Anderson," in After the Genteel Tradition; American Writers Since 1910. Edited by Malcolm Cowley. New York: W. W. Norton, pp. 74-82 [74, 75].

A reexamination of Anderson. Notes Dell's presence at Ernestine Evans' Chicago studio when Anderson gave a reading. Says Dell "saw with his usual discernment the promise in this attempt." Credits Dell with helping get Windy McPherson's Son published. Reprinted in no. 966.

795 RASCOE, BURTON. Before I Forget. Garden City, N.Y.:
Doubleday, Doran, pp. 318-19, 351.
Brief mention of Dell as editor of Chicago Evening Post's
literary section. Rascoe did not meet Dell until after both
moved to New York. Mentions Dell's review of Cabell's
Beyond Life in the Liberator as important in promoting
Cabell.

796 SMITH, BERNARD. "Van Wyck Brooks," in After the Genteel
Tradition; American Writers Since 1910. Edited by Malcolm
Cowley. New York: W. W. Norton, pp. 64-78 [65, 69].
In this assessment of Van Wyck Brooks, there are two
uses of Dell's name as an example. First, "the Masses
group led by Floyd Dell" is given credit for being a prime
objector to the genteel tradition. Next, Dell is cited as a
persistent, vigorous advocate of the need for socialism before a great twentieth-century art can arise.

1938

797 MANTLE, BURNS. "Floyd Dell, Thomas Mitchell," in Contemporary American Playwrights. New York: Dodd, Mead,
pp. 254-55.
Short biography. Compares Dell to Mitchell.   '

798 MONROE, HARRIET. A Poet's Life; Seventy Years in a Changing World. New York: Macmillan, pp. 252, 254, 310.
Monroe's autobiography. Names Dell as among those poets
first invited to contribute to Poetry. Quotes Dell on Poetry
and quotes his editorial of April 3, 1913 on Ezra Pound's
"Contemporania."

799 TIETJENS, EUNICE. The World at My Shoulder. New York:
Macmillan, pp. 17, 18, 23, 39, 131.
Tietjens' memoirs relate her experience in Margery Currey's
and Dell's apartment when poetry was read. Describes the
rooms. Recalls that Dell first showed her Carl Sandburg's
early poems.

1939

800 HAPGOOD, HUTCHINS. A Victorian in the Modern World.
New York: Harcourt, Brace, pp. 312, 314-16, 374.
In his autobiography, Hapgood cites Dell's important place
in journalism. Suggests Dell may have initiated the little
theater idea. Short discussion of theme of his plays written
for the Liberal Club. Long quote from his own review of
Homecoming. See no. 735. Contrasts Max Eastman and
Dell. "Floyd lacked the ego and was humanly sympathetic

and genuinely appreciative of things that he was not." But he was unable to achieve "an indistinguishable temperamental activity" to reveal in his writing. Claims Dell was assistant to George Cram Cook on the Chicago Evening Post.

801 HERRON, IMA HONAKER. The Small Town in American Literature. Durham, N.C.: Duke University Press, pp. xvi, 353, 369, 370, 391-94.

Dell is a "disillusioned and pessimistic" writer who deals with rebellious youth in a small town atmosphere. Discusses Moon-Calf, The Briary-Bush, This Mad Ideal, and Runaway in terms of rebellion against restrictions of provincial life. Dell is an "original writer" who has contributed to modern fiction the figure of the youthful dreamer. He "takes high rank as one of the most significant interpreters of American small town characters during the twenties."

802 LEWISOHN, LUDWIG. The Story of American Literature. The Modern Library. New York: Random House, pp. 370, 412-14, 472.

Reprinted from no. 712.

803 SMITH, BERNARD. Forces in American Criticism; A Study in the History of American Literary Thought. New York: Harcourt, Brace, pp. 159, 184, 296, 297-301, 302, 308, 314, 369.

Mentions Dell as having outlook opposite to that of William Dean Howells. Notes the "energy and hopefulness" of Dell the critic. Sees Dell, Huneker, and Spingarn as the founders of modern schools of criticism from which all twentieth-century American criticism stems. Cites Dell's appreciation of Dreiser and Anderson. Dell's work was among the little of critical interest in the Liberator after it became a Communist organ in 1922. Extended discussion of Dell as a socialist critic and his movement toward Marxism. "It was Floyd Dell who raised socialist criticism to a plane that would entitle him to be called the true precursor of Marxist critical writing in America."

804 SMITH, PAUL JORDAN. For the Love of Books; The Adventures of an Impecunious Collector. New York: Oxford University Press, pp. 153-54, 168-69.

Revised from no. 770. Dell receives exactly the same treatment here as in the 1934 version. See also nos. 828 and 1016.

805 UNTERMEYER, LOUIS. From Another World. New York: Harcourt, Brace, pp. 48-56, 63, 68, 71, 75, 78, 133, 138, 147, 155-56.

Untermeyer's recollections of Dell in this autobiography. Mentions Dell's association with the Masses, the Masses trial, and his friendship with and opinion of Vachel Lindsay. Quotes Dell's letters to Untermeyer on poverty.

806 YOUNG, ART. Art Young, His Life and Times. Edited by John Nicholas Beffel. New York: Sheridan House, pp. 297, 324, 328, 332, 336, 391, 392.
Autobiography of Dell's associate, an artist who contributed to the Masses. Cites Dell's contribution to a statement about the Associated Press's coverage of a West Virginia labor strike. Mentions Dell in relation to the Masses trial. Notes his part in merging the Liberator with the Workers' Monthly.

1940

807 ANON. Commentary and Introduction. Parents' Magazine, 15 (January), 16.
Preface to article by Dell in this issue. Identifies him as author of Love in the Machine Age and Moon-Calf. His own "stormy and insurgent youth" is given as his qualification to interpret in his article the "conflicts and the social and political activities of youth." Includes photo.

808 ANON. "A Mail Man with an Influence on Literature." Davenport Democrat and Leader (13 Febuary), p. 14.
Short article on Fred Feuchter who recently died. He was Dell's friend when Dell was a boy in Davenport. Mentions other friends and quotes from Homecoming to show Feuchter's influence on Dell.

809 MILLETT, FRED B. "Floyd Dell," in his Contemporary American Authors; A Critical Survey and 219 Bio-Bibliographies. New York: Harcourt, Brace, pp. 314-16.
Short biography and bibliography of works by and about Dell.

810 WOOD, WILLIAM R., and JOHN D. HUSBAND. Short Stories as You Like Them. Edited by William R. Wood and John D. Husband. New York: Harcourt, Brace, pp. 282, 287-88.
Brief biography. Includes Dell's version of the history of his story "The Blanket."

1941

811 CARGILL, OSCAR. Intellectual America; Ideas on the March. New York: Macmillan, pp. 166, 323, 324, 330, 507, 592, 637-38, 651-60, 662, 665, 763.
Brief mentions of Dell's opinions, his place in the Chicago literary scene, his influence on Windy McPherson's Son, and the similarity of some of his and Edna Millay's poetry.

The longest section gives a short biography and treats the range of his work. Claims he made "the Review the best critical journal in Chicago." Discusses critical misunderstanding of Dell's first two novels as works advocating the new sexual freedom. Moon-Calf is in reality a study of adolescence. Although not great, "it is a very good novel." Moon-Calf and The Briary-Bush are Dell's "most solid achievement." The later fiction is disappointing. Intellectual Vagabondage is historically important as the intellectual chronicle of Dell's generation. Discusses Dell's radicalism and sees his contribution to socialism to be as great as John Reed's up to 1929. Places Love in the Machine Age with Dell's best work. Reprinted in no. 1000.

1942

812 ANDERSON, SHERWOOD. Sherwood Anderson's Memoirs. New York: Harcourt, Brace, pp. 198, 234-35, 236, 237, 239, 240, 241, 243, 248, 249, 251, 293, 460.
Anderson's recollections of Dell. Claims Dreiser got Anderson's first novel published, but calls Dell his "literary father." Mentions Dell's interest in Freud, his opinion of the Winesburg stories, and his influence in Chicago.

813 ANON. "Dell, Floyd," in Twentieth Century Authors; A Biographical Dictionary of Modern Literature. Edited by Stanley J. Kunitz and Howard Haycroft. The Authors Series. New York: H. W. Wilson, pp. 369-70.
Short biography concentrating on Dell's literary accomplishments. Bibliography of works by and about Dell.

814 KAZIN, ALFRED. On Native Grounds; An Interpretation of Modern American Prose Literature. New York: Reynal and Hitchcock, pp. 167, 168, 169, 170, 175, 176, 205, 207, 214.
Brief mentions of Dell in this work on development of modern American prose. Places him in the Chicago literary revival as newspaperman fighting for acceptance of modern European works. Sees him as realist, as socialist, who lacked depth of understanding and conviction.

815 KEMLER, EDGAR. The Irreverent Mr. Mencken. Atlantic Monthly Press Book. Boston: Little, Brown, pp. 58, 81, 82, 121.
Says Willard Huntington Wright encouraged Dell to write candidly about sex. Dell's name mentioned in regard to quarrel between Dreiser and Mencken. Names Dell as part of Chicago literary society.

<u>1943</u>

816 ANON. "Dell and the Monument." <u>Davenport Democrat and</u>
    <u>Leader</u> (25 March), p. 4.
    Reprints Dell poem "On the Washington Monument" from
    the <u>Washington Post</u> of unspecified date. Reprints short,
    early poem by Dell about Davenport. Recalls his life in
    Davenport and briefly states the circumstances of the writ-
    ing of the newest poem.

817 ANON. "Poet Dell Addresses Burleith Citizens in Big, Bor-
    rowed Suit." Washington <u>Evening Star</u> (9 November), p. B6.
    Tells how Dell, caught in a rainstorm, addressed the group
    in an oversized suit. He spoke on "Political Poetry," citing
    examples of British and American poets whose work was in-
    fluenced by politics. He also read some of his own poems.
    Only half the article is devoted to Dell.

818 BUTCHER, FANNY. "The Literary Spotlight." <u>Chicago Sun-</u>
    <u>day Tribune</u> (15 August), book section, p. 13.
    Long article on the Chicago renaissance in literature.
    Centers on Dell and an episode demonstrating his "naughty"
    behavior and his ability to shock people out of complacency.
    Indicates Dell's popularity as editor of the <u>Post</u>'s <u>Friday</u>
    <u>Literary Review</u>.

819 CURTI, MERLE. <u>The Growth of American Thought</u>. New
    York: Harper and Brothers, pp. 710, 711.
    Cites <u>Intellectual Vagabondage</u> for telling of the pre-war
    revolt against the genteel tradition. Names Dell as an author
    whose work evidenced the reaction to conventional Victorian
    sexual morality. Reprinted in nos. 847 and 962.

<u>1944</u>

820 AGEE, JAMES. Review of "Casanova Brown." <u>The Nation</u>,
    159 (16 September), 334.
    Review of movie based on "Little Accident." Briefly men-
    tions Dell as co-author of the farce.

821 ANON. Review of "Casanova Brown." <u>Newsweek</u>, 24 (28
    August), 97-98.
    Review of movie based on Dell and Mitchell's "Little Acci-
    dent." No mention of Dell by name. Relates plot and com-
    ments on acting.

822 ANON. Review of "Casanova Brown." <u>Time</u>, 44 (18 Septem-
    ber), 92, 94.
    Review of movie based on "Little Accident." Mainly con-
    centrates on Gary Cooper's performance. Briefly mentions
    Dell as co-author of "this rattlebang old stage hit."

823 DE VOTO, BERNARD. The Literary Fallacy. Boston: Little, Brown, pp. 51-52.
Brief comment on Intellectual Vagabondage in terms of its attempt to explain the meaning of personality. Dell fails. The book summarized the literary cliché's accepted in the early part of the century.

824 EVANS, BERGEN. The Psychiatry of Robert Burton. New York: Columbia University Press, pp. 45, 108-109.
Mentions Dell's opinion that Burton was a precursor of Freud and argues that Dell's view is incorrect. Also argues that Burton is a better psychiatrist than Dell credits him with being.

825 LEWIS, SINCLAIR. "Fools, Liars, and Mr. DeVoto." Saturday Review of Literature, 27 (15 April), 9-12 [10].
Lewis attacks Bernard DeVoto's The Literary Fallacy. Dell mentioned as an example to show that DeVoto does not deal sufficiently with modern writers. Reprinted with new title, no. 906.

1945

826 FITZGERALD, F. SCOTT. Letter to John Peale Bishop. The Crack-Up. Edited by Edmund Wilson. New York: New Directions, p. 272.
Letter of 1925 notes that Floyd Dell was in Antibes that summer.

827 HOFFMAN, FREDERICK J. Freudianism and the Literary Mind. Baton Rouge: Louisiana State University Press, pp. 56, 70, 235-36, 325.
Credits Dell with introducing psychoanalysis to Greenwich Village. His editorship of the Masses accounts for the publication's association of psychoanalysis with an approaching better life. Quotes from unpublished Dell letter on psychoanalysis in the Village in the teens. Relates Dell's personal experience with psychoanalysis under a Freudian. Notes Dell's association with Sherwood Anderson. Recognizes two divisions of modern attitudes to psychoanalytic sex. One is "the sponsorship by Floyd Dell of an intelligent cultural analysis of sex habits and attitudes in modern times." The other is D. H. Lawrence's "vitalistic sex gospel."

828 SMITH, PAUL JORDAN. For the Love of Books; The Adventures of an Impecunious Collector. Abridged. New York: Oxford University Press, pp. 79-80, 86-87.
Reprinted from no. 804. Abridged from no. 770. The part on Dell is the same as in the 1934 original. See no. 1016.

1946

829 HOFFMAN, FREDERICK; CHARLES ALLEN; and CAROLYN F.
ULRICH. The Little Magazine; A History and a Bibliography.
Princeton, N.J.: Princeton University Press, pp. 7, 8, 29,
30, 37, 53, 69, 71, 150, 151, 240, 252, 253, 254, 260, 271,
375.
Brief mentions of Dell serve to chronicle his association
with and contributions to the little magazine. Cites his
part in making the Masses an inspiration to the proletarian
movement of the 1930's, his intelligent reception of Freudianism, and his acknowledgment of the importance of the unconscious to the writer of fiction. Describes the Masses
under his editorship. Notes his contributions to the Masses,
the Little Review, the Liberator, New Numbers, the Quill,
Slate, The Modern Quarterly, and The Play-Book.

1947

830 CLARK, BARRETT H. "The United States," in A History of
Modern Drama. Edited by Barrett H. Clark and George
Freedley. New York: Appleton-Century-Crofts, pp. 639-
740 [720].
"Little Accident" is indicative of the public's changing
attitude to sex. It is "solid entertainment."

831 MADISON, CHARLES A. Critics and Crusaders; A Century
of American Protest. New York: Henry Holt, p. 237.
Quote from Dell showing his support of Emma Goldman.

832 SNELL, GEORGE. The Shapers of American Fiction 1798-1947.
New York: E. P. Dutton, p. 243.
Names Dell as a realist in the "school of Midwestern writ-
ers." Reprinted in no. 934.

1948

833 ANDERSON, KARL JAMES. "My Brother, Sherwood Anderson." Saturday Review of Literature, 31 (4 September),
6-7, 26-27 [7, 26].
The story of Anderson's life by his brother. Relates how
he met Dell through his brother Karl. Identifies Dell as a
"brilliant and dogmatic young critic." Dell introduced Anderson to other Chicago writers including Dreiser. Tells how
Dell came to read and praise the unpublished Windy McPherson's Son and how the book was finally published. Reprinted in no. 902.

834 CANBY, HENRY SEIDEL. "Fiction Sums Up a Century," in

Literary History of the United States. Edited by Robert E.
Spiller, Willard Thorp, Thomas H. Johnson, Henry Seidel
Canby. Vol. 2. New York: Macmillan, pp. 1208-36 [1235].
  Notes that Dell explored changing sexual mores in Moon-
Calf, was a writer for the Provincetown Players, and achieved
prominence as a novelist. Reprinted in nos. 882, 948, and
1052.

835* DUNCAN, HUGH DALZIEL. "The Rise of Chicago as a Liter-
    ary Center from 1885-1920." Ph.D. dissertation, University
    of Chicago, 1948.
      Cited in no. 963.

836 EASTMAN, MAX. Enjoyment of Living. New York: Harper
    and Brothers, pp. 443-44, 545, 549, 551, 553, 554, 556,
    559, 564, unnumbered page in center section.
      Eastman's memoirs. Cites Dell's excellent work as associ-
    ate editor of the Masses. Recalls how he was recruited for
    the job. Notes influence of World War I on his political
    thought. Discusses artists' revolt on the Masses and Dell's
    part in the proceedings. Recalls playing the part of Lance-
    lot in Dell's "King Arthur's Socks." Includes picture of
    Dell.

837 GAIGE, CROSBY. Footlights and Highlights. New York:
    E. P. Dutton, pp. 230-31.
      Autobiography of producer of "Little Accident." Briefly
    tells how Dell and Mitchell collaborated. Short description
    of opening night. Gaige's opinion of Dell's edition of The
    Anatomy of Melancholy.

838 KRUTCH, JOSEPH WOOD. "Eugene O'Neill," in Literary
    History of the United States: History. Edited by Robert E.
    Spiller, Willard Thorp, Thomas H. Johnson, Henry Seidel
    Canby. Vol. 2. New York: Macmillan, pp. 1237-50 [1239].
      Discussion of O'Neill's place and achievement in American
    literature. Briefly mentions Dell's connection with the
    Provincetown Players as a producer. Stresses that he was
    not professionally connected with the theater but was to be-
    come a novelist. Included in list of "prime movers" in the
    little theater movement. Reprinted in nos. 886, 952, and
    1057.

839 ZABEL, MORTON D. "Summary in Criticism," in Literary
    History of the United States: History. Edited by Robert E.
    Spiller, Willard Thorp, Thomas H. Johnson, Henry Seidel
    Canby. Vol. 2. New York: Macmillan, pp. 1358-73 [1361].
      Brief mention of Dell who, with others, prepared the way
    for Marxist criticism of the 1930's. Reprinted in nos. 888,
    959, and 1063.

1949

840 ELIAS, ROBERT. Theodore Dreiser; Apostle of Nature. New
York: Alfred A. Knopf, pp. 171, 179, 182, 184.
Says Dreiser met Dell in December 1912, was introduced
to Dell's girlfriend Kirah Markham, and was attracted to
her. Cites Dell's important editing of The "Genius" and his
and Dreiser's efforts in getting Sherwood Anderson published. Notes Dell's presence at a party given by Dreiser
for Edgar Lee Masters. Reprinted in no. 1023 as emended
edition. The parts on Dell are the same.

841 STONE, IRVING. The Passionate Journey. Garden City,
N.Y.: Doubleday, pp. 279-80, 297.
Brief mentions of Dell as a novel writer. Describes him
as an "intellectual out of Chicago's newspaper world."

1950

842 ANON. Announcement of acquisition of Dell Papers. The
Newberry Library Bulletin, 2 (July), 139-40.
Brief description of contents of Dell Papers. There are
five hundred letters addressed to him as well as some articles and manuscripts. Notable for "account of Dell's relation to Sherwood Anderson."

843* JACOBSON, JOHN. A Man Who Walked Humbly with God.
Pamphlet NP, pp. 9-11.
Unlocatable. Cited in no. 913, p. 598.

844 POUND, EZRA. The Letters of Ezra Pound. Edited by D. D.
Paige. New York: Harcourt, Brace, pp. 19, 60.
In 1913 letter to Harriet Monroe, Pound says Dell is
"clever" to perceive the Latin tone in "Contemporania" which
was reviewed by Dell in the Chicago Evening Post on April
11, 1913. Another letter to Monroe in 1915 announces a
"Manifesto." Does not ask Dell and others to sign it because editors should not take positions against each other.

845 SUTCLIFFE, DENHAM. "New Light on the Chicago Writers."
The Newberry Library Bulletin, 2 (December), 146-57 [146,
147-50, 151, 155, 156, 157].
Dell mentioned frequently throughout. Describes the Dell
papers in the Newberry Library, concentrating on the letters. Discusses Dell's place in the Chicago Renaissance and
the importance of his letters. Cites Ezra Pound's letter to
Dell and his, as well as others', admiration for Dell's criticism. Notes Dell's friendship with Arthur Davison Ficke
and Ficke's regard for Dell's judgment.

<u>1951</u>

846* ANON. "Floyd Dell Pays a Visit." Greenwich <u>Villager</u> (21
June), pp. 1, 11.
Cited in no. 913, p. 602.

847 COWLEY, MALCOLM. <u>Exile's Return; A Literary Odyssey of</u>
<u>the 1920s</u>. New York: Viking Press, pp. 162, 178, 180.
Revised fron no. 755. See no. 897. The information on
Dell is identical to the 1934 version.

848 CURTI, MERLE. <u>The Growth of American Thought</u>. Second
Edition. New York: Harper and Brothers, pp. 710, 711.
Identical to no. 819. See no. 962.

849 DREISER, HELEN. <u>My Life with Dreiser</u>. Cleveland: World
Publishing, p. 169.
Biography of Theodore Dreiser by his wife. Reports a
1927 farewell dinner in Greenwich Village before Dreiser
left for Russia. Dell gave a speech.

850 GOLD, MICHAEL. "<u>The Masses</u> Tradition." <u>Masses and Main-</u>
<u>stream</u>, 4 (August), 45-55 [50].
This article gives Gold's view of the <u>Masses</u> and of the
people associated with it. Briefly mentions Dell's proletarian
origins and his belief that proletarians would create their
own means of expression.

851 HOFFMAN, FREDERICK J. <u>The Modern Novel in America</u>
<u>1900-1950</u>. Twentieth-Century Literature in America series.
Edited by William Van O'Connor and Frederick J. Hoffman.
Chicago: Henry Regnery, pp. 106, 107.
Cites Dell as part of the "Revolt from the Village." "No
one has left a more sentimental reminiscence of Greenwich
Village than Mr. Dell, nor did any other American novelist
explore with quite his indefatigable interest the possibilities
for fiction of illicit love sentimentally described and defended." Revised in no. 951.

852 HOWE, IRVING. <u>Sherwood Anderson</u>. American Men of Letters Series. New York: William Sloane Associates, pp.
55-56, 57, 58-59, 60, 62, 64, 65, 66, 69, 70, 72, 75, 76,
121.
Biography of Anderson. Relates Anderson's association
with the Chicago literary circle centering on Dell and Dell's
help in publishing <u>Windy McPherson's Son</u>. Dell's rejection
of bohemian freedom in later works. Brief discussion of
Dell's writing in the <u>Friday Literary Review</u>. "His writing
clarified and entertained, but it seldom undercut to that
ultimate insight which alone is the justification of criticism."

853 HUGHES, GLENN. A History of the American Theatre 1700-
      1950. New York: Samuel French, pp. 372, 405.
         Brief mention of Dell being one of the talented persons
      attracted by the Provincetown Players. Lists "Little Accident"
      as popular hit of the 1928-1929 Broadway season.

854 KRUTCH, JOSEPH WOOD. "The New Seacoast of Bohemia."
      Saturday Review of Literature, 34 (30 June), 11, 12.
         Review of Malcolm Cowley's Exile's Return. Dell linked
      with Gorham Munson, Hendrik Van Loon, and Burton Ras-
      coe as group of Americans associated with Bohemia who re-
      ceive incidental reference in Cowley's book. This group
      shows that the 1920's produced Bohemians unrelated to ex-
      traordinary excesses.

855 LANGNER, LAWRENCE. The Magic Curtain: The Story of a
      Life in Two Fields, Theatre and Invention. New York:
      E. P. Dutton, pp. 70, 80, 90-91.
         Author's memoirs. Mentions Dell as member of the Lib-
      eral Club. Says Dell introduced him to Dell's former wife,
      Margery Currey. Recalls his participation in a play rehears-
      al at Theodore Dreiser's apartment directed by Dell.

856 MATTHIESSEN, F. O. Theodore Dreiser. The American Men
      of Letters Series. Edited by Joseph Wood Krutch, Margaret
      Marshall, Lionel Trilling, Mark Van Doren. New York:
      William Sloane Associates, pp. 26, 69, 73, 123-24, 127,
      145, 164, 170.
         Biography of Theodore Dreiser. Brief quotes from Dell
      expressing his opinion of Dreiser's writing. Mentions Dreis-
      er's interest in Dell's unnamed girl friend. Gives Dell's
      review of Jennie Gerhardt partial credit for its success.

857 MIZENER, ARTHUR. The Far Side of Paradise; A Biography
      of F. Scott Fitzgerald. Boston: Houghton Mifflin, pp. 111,
      185.
         Briefly mentions Dell's "Compton Mackenzie quest novel
      about the education of a middle-western socialist" as an act
      typical of the split between literature and Marxism. Quotes
      letter from Fitzgerald to John Peale Bishop saying that Dell
      was in Antibes in the summer of 1925. See no. 972 for new
      edition.

858 SCHEVILL, JAMES. Sherwood Anderson; His Life and Work.
      Denver, Colo.: The University of Denver Press, 1951, pp.
      71-73, 101, 341.
         Tells of Anderson's attendance at Dell's literary parties
      in Chicago. Says Anderson himself showed Dell the manu-
      script of Windy McPherson's Son and Dell was instrumental
      in getting it published. Dell's comment on original title
      of Winesburg, Ohio noted. Quotes from Dell's review of
      Anderson's memoirs and finds it a personal attack.

859 WILDE, PERCIVAL. The Craftsmanship of the One-Act Play.
     Augmented edition. New York: Crown Publishers, p. 227.
     Augmented from no. 349. Information on Dell is the same.

                              1952

860 ANON. "The Second Newberry Library Conference on Ameri-
     can Studies." The Newberry Library Bulletin, 3 (October),
     25-29 [25, 27].
          An account of the conference. Lists Dell in attendance.
     Calls for Dell's opinion of the literary movement in which he
     participated. Quotes his remarks.

861 BELL, DANIEL. "The Background and Development of Marxian
     Socialism in the United States," in Socialism and American
     Life. Edited by Donald Drew Egbert and Stow Persons.
     Princeton Studies in American Civilization #4. Vol. 1.
     Princeton, N.J.: Princeton University Press, 213-405 [316].
          Brief mention of Dell, a socialist, on trial for antiwar prop-
     aganda during World War I.

862 BROOKS, VAN WYCK. The Confident Years: 1885-1915. New
     York: E. P. Dutton, pp. 73, 373-74, 383, 408, 409-11,
     413, 478, 486-87, 488, 489, 490, 494, 496, 526, 540.
          Places Dell in milieu of the time. Dell represents the pre-
     war Greenwich Village spirit and is its spokesman. Mentions
     his opinion of Robert Ingersoll and his admiration of Tolstoy,
     Shaw, and Wells.

863 DAY, DOROTHY. The Long Loneliness; The Autobiography of
     Dorothy Day. New York: Harper and Brothers, pp. 68, 69.
          Recounts Day's association with the Masses and its editors.

864 DUFFEY, BERNARD. "Two Literary Movements: Chicago,
     1890-1925." The Newberry Library Bulletin, 3 (October),
     1-24 [11, 14, 15-17, 20, 22].
          This article treats the rise and decline of the Chicago lit-
     erary renaissance and the genteel literary movement immedi-
     ately preceding it. Dell is named a number of times. Dis-
     cusses the importance of Dell's and Margery Currey's studios
     as a vital cohesive force among Chicago's artists.

865 EGBERT, DONALD DREW. "The Aesthetic Theory and Practice
     of the Liberal Communitarians," in Socialism and American
     Life. Edited by Donald Drew Egbert and Stow Persons.
     Princeton Studies in American Civilization #4. Vol. 2.
     Princeton, N.J.: Princeton University Press, 459-62 [462].
          Descriptive, critical bibliography. "Floyd Dell's imagina-
     tive description of Apple Farm Commonwealth in Diana Stair
     ... shows unusual insight into the crosscurrents of com-
     munitarianism and reform."

866 EGBERT, DONALD DREW. "Socialist Fiction and the Proletarian
    Novel," in Socialism and American Life. Edited by Donald
    Drew Egbert and Stow Persons. Princeton Studies in Ameri-
    can Civilization #4. Vol. 2. Princeton, N.J.: Princeton
    University Press, pp. 473-83 [481].
      This descriptive, critical bibliography mentions Dell as a
    writer who treated the theme of sex. In Moon-Calf Dell "is
    equally concerned with the sex and radical experience of his
    hero, but becomes preoccupied with the marriage question in
    the sequel, The Briary-Bush.

867 HORTON, ROD W., and HERBERT W. EDWARDS. Backgrounds
    of American Literary Thought. New York: Appleton-
    Century-Crofts, pp. 239, 356.
      Brief mention of Dell as Marxist writer between 1914 and
    1924. Includes Dell as writer who incorporated psychoanaly-
    tic thought and Freudianism into his work. Revised in no.
    988.

868 JONES, HOWARD MUMFORD. The Bright Medusa. Urbana:
    University of Illinois Press, pp. 6, 89.
      Dell mentioned as part of Chicago renaissance. Quotes
    Dell on Randolph Bourne.

869 LEWIS, SINCLAIR. From Main Street to Stockholm; Letters
    of Sinclair Lewis 1919-1930. Edited by Harrison Smith.
    New York: Harcourt, Brace, pp. 35, 39, 44, 45.
      A letter to Alfred Harcourt urges him to write to Dell,
    among other "really important critics," concerning the im-
    portance of Main Street. Anderson's thoughts on Dell's
    comments in Heywood Broun's New York Tribune column con-
    cerning Main Street. Quotes Anderson's comparison of Felix
    Fay and Carol Kennicott.

870 MCGRORY, MARY. "Reading and Writing--Why All the Shout-
    ing About the '20s, Wonders Floyd Dell, Noted Survivor."
    Washington Sunday Star (9 November), sec. E, p. 7.
      No. 913 incorrectly attributes this article to the Washing-
    ton Post. The article is the result of an interview with
    Dell, who continued to reside in the Washington, D.C., area
    after his work with the WPA writers' project of the Depres-
    sion. Much of the article quotes Dell or states his opinions
    on the revolt and writing of the 1920's and on contemporary
    novels. McGrory says Dell is "Washington's most distinguished
    survivor of the '20s." Finds Dell disillusioned about the ac-
    complishments of the era.

871 MILLAY, EDNA ST. VINCENT. Letters of Edna St. Vincent
    Millay. Edited by Allan Ross Macdougall. New York: Har-
    per and Brothers, pp. 84, 121, 166, 253-56.
      Brief editorial mention of Dell writing about Millay in Love

in Greenwich Village. Probable humorous reference to Dell as "the Rev. Mr. Dell." Millay tells sister Norma that Dell sent her in England a copy of "Sweet and Twenty." Millay's comments on Homecoming followed by a humorous chastising of Dell for his attitude to the Volstead Act.

872 O'CONNOR, WILLIAM VAN. An Age of Criticism 1900-1950. Twentieth-Century Literature in America series. Chicago: Henry Regnery, p. 117.
Brief mention of Dell in chapter on "Social and Activist Criticism." Names him as editor of the Masses and says his interest was psychoanalysis, not politics.

873 THORP, WILLARD. "American Writers on the Left," in Socialism and American Life. Edited by Donald Drew Egbert and Stow Persons. Princeton Studies in American Civilization #4. Vol. 1. Princeton, N.J.: Princeton University Press, pp. 599-620 [604, 605].
Dell mentioned briefly as an associate of Max Eastman and Piet Vlag on the Masses, a socialist journal. Named as a bohemian who moved to the political left.

874 WAGENKNECHT, EDWARD. Cavalcade of the American Novel; From the Birth of the Nation to the Middle of the Twentieth Century. New York: Henry Holt, p. 314.
Very brief mention of Dell encouraging Sherwood Anderson.

875 WILSON, EDMUND. "The All-Star Literary Vaudeville," in A Literary Chronicle: 1920-1950. Doubleday Anchor Books. Garden City, N.Y.: Doubleday, pp. 76-96 [77].
Reprinted from no. 514.

876 WILSON, EDMUND. "The All-Star Literary Vaudeville," in The Shores of Light; A Literary Chronicle of the Twenties and Thirties. New York: Farrar, Straus and Young, pp. 229-47 [230].
Reprinted from no. 514.

877 WILSON, EDMUND. "Edna St. Vincent Millay: A Memoir." The Nation, 174 (19 April), 370-83 [371].
A memoir of Wilson's acquaintance with Millay. Brief mention of Millay acting with the Provincetown Players in a play by Dell. Repeats Phyllis Duganne's story of Dell chasing Millay in Greenwich Village. Reprinted with slight variations that do not pertain to Dell in no. 878.

878 WILSON, EDMUND. "Epilogue, 1952; Edna St. Vincent Millay," in The Shores of Light: A Literary Chronicle of the Twenties and Thirties. New York: Farrar, Straus and Young, pp. 744-93 [748].

Reprinted with slight variations that do not pertain to Dell from no. 877.

879 WILSON, EDMUND. "Late Violets from the Nineties," in The Shores of Light; A Literary Chronicle of the Twenties and Thirties. New York: Farrar, Straus and Young, pp. 68-72 [69].
Brief comparison of Carl Van Vechten to Floyd Dell.

1953

880 ANDERSON, SHERWOOD. Letters of Sherwood Anderson. Edited by Howard Mumford Jones and Walter B. Rideout. Boston: Little, Brown, pp. 3, 4, 5, 15, 30, 38, 72, 112, 182, 275, 404, 405.
Mentions Dell's recognition of Dreiser's talent. Claims Dell introduced him to Dreiser's and Dostoevski's work. Dell is shallow. Believes Dell wanted to mold him. Claims Dell as his "literary father," but cannot forget Dell's criticism of "Winesburg" stores as too vague and lacking a definite end.

881 BALL, ROLAND CONKLE, JR. "Literary Criticism and Theory in the American Little Magazines." Ph.D. dissertation, University of California at Berkeley, pp. 178-79.
Studies the growth of literary criticism in selected little magazines of the twentieth century. Describes their attack on the prevalent attitudes, the conflict of ideas on what to do about philistinism, the search for a literary tradition, esthetic theory, and the influence of sociological theories. Paraphrases Dell on a Marxist interpretation of literature.

882 CANBY, HENRY SEIDEL. "Fiction Sums Up a Century," in The Literary History of the United States. Edited by Robert Spiller, Willard Thorp, Thomas H. Johnson, Henry Seidel Canby. Revised edition in one volume. New York: Macmillan, pp. 1208-36 [1235].
Identical to 1948 edition. See no. 834.

883 DEDMON, EMMETT. Fabulous Chicago. New York: Random House, pp. 206, 281.
Brief mention of Dell as a member of the Little Room, a literary group which admired the East's genteel tradition. Notes that Dell left Chicago for New York along with other writers. Sees him as a central personage in the bohemian community and as the one who inspired Margaret Anderson to begin The Little Review.

884 DEDMON, EMMETT. "The Flowering of Chicago." Saturday Review, 36 (10 October), 9-10, 48-52 [51].

Article derived from no. 883. Mentions Dell as the head of Chicago's bohemia.

885 DICKINSON, ASA DON. The World's Best Books; Homer to Hemingway. New York: H. W. Wilson, p. 89.
Dell included in list of best authors from 1050 B.C. to A.D. 1950. Identified as journalist and novelist who holds avant-garde opinions. Brief descriptions of Moon-Calf and The Briary-Bush.

886 KRUTCH, JOSEPH WOOD. "Eugene O'Neill," in Literary History of the United States. Edited by Robert E. Spiller, Willard Thorp, Thomas H. Johnson, Henry Seidel Canby. Revised edition in one volume. New York: Macmillan, pp. 1237-50 [1239].
Identical to 1948 edition. See no. 838.

887 SMITH, ALSON J. Chicago's Left Bank. Chicago: Henry Regnery, pp. 13, 18, 25, 33, 34, 156, 243.
Brief mentions of Dell in this study of Chicago's bohemia. Cites his contribution to the Friday Literary Review, his friendship with Ezra Pound, and his membership in the "Little Roomers," a group that met in Ralph Clarkson's studio.

888 ZABEL, MORTON D. "Summary in Criticism," in The Literary History of the United States. Edited by Robert E. Spiller, Willard Thorp, Thomas H. Johnson, Henry Seidel Canby. Revised edition in one volume. New York: Macmillan, pp. 1358-1373 [1361].
Identical to 1948 edition. See no. 839.

1954

889 BODENHEIM, MAXWELL. My Life and Loves in Greenwich Village. New York: Bridgehead Books, p. 62.
Brief mention of Dell's subject in Love in Greenwich Village in Bodenheim's memoirs.

890 HECHT, BEN. A Child of the Century. New York: Simon and Schuster, p. 221.
Brief mention in this memoir of Dell as the former husband of "Marjy Currey." Identified as "a Chicago literary critic in a Windsor tie who had treacherously gone to New York City to become a novelist."

1955

891 BROOKS, VAN WYCK. John Sloan; A Painter's Life. New York: E. P. Dutton, pp. 94, 98.

Biography of Sloan, a painter whose work appeared in the Masses. Mentions Dell as a leader on the Masses and the conflict between the artists and the politically minded contributors to the Masses. Names Dell as one in opposition to Sloan.

892 BROWNE, MAURICE. Too Late to Lament; An Autobiography. London: Victor Gollancz, pp. 128, 129, 150, 201, 240.
The founder of Chicago's Little Theater recalls Dell's contribution to the city's literary climate and his efforts to publicize the Little Theater. Recalls his relationship with Hilda Golightly, his opinion that creative theater must present contemporary unacted plays, and his rejection of Browne's sonnet sequence when he was editor of the Masses.

893 HOFFMAN, FREDERICK J. The Twenties; American Writing in the Postwar Decade. New York: The Viking Press, pp. 9, 16-17, 18, 90, 96-98, 197, 204, 328, 347, 350, 351, 381, 403, 466.
Dell's contribution to the character of the 1920's is mentioned in terms of his writing. Sympathy with youth, movement from small towns to the city, and the retreat from the Midwest are reflected in his novels. Brief discussion of the temporary popularity of some novels. Includes brief biography.

894 HOLMAN, C. HUGH. "The Defense of Art: Criticism Since 1930," in The Development of American Literary Criticism. Edited by Floyd Stovall. Chapel Hill: University of North Carolina Press, pp. 199-245 [205, 219].
Brief references to Dell. Notes that the Masses under Dell and Eastman was not "socially doctrinaire" and did not qualify as Marxist criticism. Quotes Dell as example of demands for sexual freedom in the 1930's.

895 RALEIGH, JOHN H. "Revolt and Revaluation in Criticism 1900-1930," in The Development of American Literary Criticism. Edited by Floyd Stovall. Chapel Hill: University of North Carolina Press, pp. 159-198 [170].
Brief mention of Dell. Quotes Van Wyck Brooks' The Confident Years on Dell's opinion of the nature of contemporary literature. Notes that Dell was the hero of Joseph Freeman and other young radicals before World War I.

896 SHANNON, DAVID A. The Socialist Party of America; A History. New York: Macmillan, pp. 9, 208.
Names Dell as a member of the socialist party in New York. Notes his name on list for proposed Social Problems Lecture Bureau speakers. Reprinted in no. 994.

1956

897 COWLEY, MALCOLM. Exile's Return: A Literary Odyssey of
the 1920s. New York: Viking Press, pp. 162, 178, 180.
Revised from no. 755. See no. 847. The information
on Dell is the same.

898 DUFFEY, BERNARD. The Chicago Renaissance in American
Letters; A Critical History. East Lansing: Michigan State
University Press, 285 pp., passim.
Important examination of Dell's place in the literary ren-
aissance which took place in Chicago in the first decades
of this century. He and his wife "provided the essential
vitality" of the artist colony which included his friends
Sherwood Anderson and Margaret Anderson. Discusses his
outlook and achievement in the Friday Literary Review.
Named as one of Chicago's more important novelists.

899 HANSEN, HARRY. "The World of Reading." The Palimpsest,
37 (April), 208-17 [215].
Article deals with Hansen's boyhood in Davenport, Iowa,
including his memory of Dell. Names him in connection with
George Cram Cook. Identifies him as newspaper reporter,
literary editor, and successful poet.

900 TAYLOR, WALTER FULLER. The Story of American Letters.
Chicago: Henry Regnery, p. 343.
Brief mention of Sherwood Anderson's connection with
Dell's Chicago literary friends. Notes their interest in
Freud.

901 WILSON, EDMUND. "The All-Star Literary Vaudeville," in
A Literary Chronicle: 1920-1950. Garden City, N.Y.:
Doubleday, pp. 76-92 [77].
Reprinted from no. 514.

1957

902 ANDERSON, KARL. "My Brother, Sherwood Anderson," in
The Saturday Review Treasury. New York: Simon and
Schuster, pp. 325-32 [329].
Reprinted from no. 833.

903 BENET, WILLIAM ROSE. "The Earlier Lewis," in The Saturday Review Treasury. New York: Simon and Schuster,
pp. 30-35 [33].
Reprinted from no. 751.

904 DRAPER, THEODORE. The Roots of American Communism.

Communism in American Life series. Edited by Clinton Ros-
siter. New York: The Viking Press, pp. 49, 124, 127-29,
404, 406, 419.
Brief mentions of Dell. Names him as a member of the
editorial board of The New Review in 1913 and 1914. Identifies him as one of a group of nonscientific men who tried to
equate Communism with science. Sees Dell and Max Eastman
as from an older era of communists who did not give up art
for politics. Cites Dell's social interpretation of literature.
Quotes his opinion of Bertrand Russell's fall from communism.

905 KIRSCH, ROBERT R. "The Book Report." Los Angeles Times
(7 October), sec. 3, p. 5.
Brief review of Moon-Calf, one of Sagamore Press's American Century Series in paperback. The novel "still retains
its power." Finds similarities between post-World War I world
and post-World War II world.

906 LEWIS, SINCLAIR. "Mr. Lewis' Reply." Saturday Review
Treasury. New York: Simon and Schuster, pp. 272-81
[276].
Reprinted from no. 825. Title altered in reprint.

907 RIDEOUT, WALTER B[ATES]. The Radical Novel in the United
States, 1900-1954; Some Interrelations of Literature and Soci-
ety. Cambridge, Mass.: Harvard University Press, pp. 54,
95, 102, 104, 111, 124, 125-26, 127, 132, 151, 225.
Brief mentions throughout this study of the Marxist novel.
Cites Dell's conversion of George Cram Cook to socialism,
his review of Harold Varney's Revolt, his relation to the
Masses, his appearance as a character in Dorothy Day's
The Eleventh Virgin, and his role in development of Marx-
ian criticism.

908 SHAFTER, TOBY. Edna St. Vincent Millay: America's Best
Loved Poet. New York: Julian Messner, p. 128.
Brief mention of Dell auditioning and hiring Millay to act
the part of Annabelle in the Provincetown Players' production
of his "The Angel Intrudes."

909 SINCLAIR, MARY CRAIG. Southern Belle. New York: Crown
Publishers, pp. 169, 330.
This is the autobiography of Upton Sinclair's wife. Dell
mentioned as one of the Village rebels at Croton-on-Hudson.
Because he was "charitable" Mary and Upton thought he was
America's best literary critic. Recounts the Sinclairs' re-
union with Dell in Los Angeles in the 1930's. Lists his
literary accomplishments. Physical description of Dell.

1958

910 CLARK, JAMES JEFFERSON. "The Theme of Success in American Literature, 1914-1929." Ph.D. dissertation. New York University, pp. 133, 134, 150, 158, 160-62, 248-50, 302, 310, 404, 490-95.

Dell's heroes are representative of a type of success that was admired during this time. Dell was "the superficial expounder of freedom according to Freud." He was ineffective as a critic of society because "of his pretense of Bohemianism." His social philosophy embraced only free love. His study of money makers in Janet March is "one of the most effective" and sympathetic in the 1920's. Financial success which destroys artistic success is not Dell's main theme.

911 DICKSINON, A. T., JR. American Historical Fiction. New York: The Scarecrow Press, p. 159.

Diana Stair included in list of historical novels dealing with abolition. Very brief summary.

912 HEINEY, DONALD. Recent American Literature. Great Neck, N.Y.: Barron's Educational Series, pp. 563, 600.

In this handbook, Dell is included among writers of psychological and psychoanalytical criticism. He was one of first to apply Freudian theory to literature. Paragraph on his "informal" influence. Listed in bibliography of recent literature.

1959: Books

913 TANSELLE, G[EORGE] THOMAS. "Faun at the Barricades; The Life and Work of Floyd Dell." Ph.D. dissertation, Northwestern University, 613 pp.

A major work on Dell. Bibliography includes all his published work through 1958. A long study of his life and work. The biographical information is based on Homecoming. Discusses Dell's fiction, nonfiction, poems, plays, and short stories. Although a minor figure, Dell is important because he was in contact with contemporary matters of intellectual concern and because of his influence and importance in his own time. His career is the embodiment of his times. Sees Dell as a utopian with a dualism of mind--a radical and a dreamer. Dell's book reviews in the Masses and the Liberator are the product more of the moon-calf than the militant, socialist, or Marxist. The novels deal with revolt against convention by a basically conservative character.

1959: Shorter Writings

914 ANON. The Greenwich Village Guide. Edited by William H.

Honan. New York: Bryan Publications, pp. 23, 100, 102.
Places Dell in milieu of the Village. Locates his residence
at Madame Branchard's boarding house, the old Liberal Club,
and Polly Holliday's restaurant where he ate. Summarizes
the Masses trial.

915 CHURCHILL, ALLEN. The Improper Bohemians; A Recreation
of Greenwich Village in its Heyday. New York: E. P. Dutton, 349 pp., passim.
Account of life in the Village from 1912 to 1930. Places
Dell in the Village milieu and articulates his contribution to
the life lived there.

916 DREISER, THEODORE. Letters of Theodore Dreiser. Edited
by Robert H. Elias. Vol. 1. Philadelphia: University of
Pennsylvania Press, pp. 123, 126, 128, 190-91, 198, 230,
232, 301-302, 307, 310, 311, 314, 347, 384.
One letter to Dell praises Moon-Calf and others comment
on the novel. Reference to Dell's review of Jennie Gerhardt.
Dreiser later claims Dell is not his friend. Mentions Dell as
good writer and recommends him as contributor to Hearst's
International.

917 MAY, HENRY F. The End of American Innocence; A Study
of the First Years of Our Own Time 1912-1917. New York:
Alfred A. Knopf, pp. 146, 205, 230, 237, 252, 253, 255,
258-59, 260, 268, 284, 285, 287, 288, 289, 291, 298, 309,
315, 396.
Treats Dell's important position in milieu of prewar thought.
"Floyd Dell was the unquestioned leader of the young."
Gives short biography. Notes his association with Sherwood
Anderson, the Liberal Club, the Provincetown Players, and
the Masses. Dell is representative of the early Chicago
rebel as well as of the pre-war creativeness of Greenwich
Village. Moon-Calf shows insight into the times. Notes
his admiration for Francis Guerson and G. B. Shaw and his
meeting with William James.

918 MOERS, ELLEN. Two Dreisers. New York: The Viking Press,
pp. 204, 261, 277, 350.
Brief mentions of Dell in this study of Sister Carrie and
An American Tragedy. Names Dell as one of Dreiser's editors. Sees Dell as a leader in the rise of intellectual interest in Freud's studies. Cites him as a realistic novelist in
quote from Dreiser.

919 RUGGLES, ELEANOR. The West-Going Heart; A Life of Vachel
Lindsay. New York: W. W. Norton, pp. 156, 227.
Quotes Dell's review of The Tramp's Excuse, "one of the
first serious appraisals" of Lindsay's poetry. Says Lindsay
later "cemented" his friendship with Dell.

920 TANNER, LOUISE. Here Today. New York: Thomas Y.
     Crowell, pp. 54, 57, 58, 59-60, 63, 69, 73.
        Short references to Dell in the chapter "Our Own Latch-
     keys; Edna St. Vincent Millay," a biography of Millay.
     Notes Dell's part in origins of Millay's poem "Recuerdo."
     Quotes from Homecoming. Describes Dell as a "hopeless
     counterrevolutionary" in attitude to marriage. Implies Dell
     is egotistical.

                              1960

921 ATHERTON, GERTRUDE. Letter to Upton Sinclair in Sinclair's
     My Lifetime in Letters. Columbia: University of Missouri
     Press, pp. 191.
        Short. Comments on Dell's biography of Sinclair, Upton
     Sinclair. Atherton finds it "the very most interesting biog-
     raphy I ever read of a contemporary."

922 HELBURN, THERESA. A Wayward Quest; The Autobiography
     of Theresa Helburn. Boston: Little, Brown, p. 50.
        Brief mention of Helburn hearing Dell argue about the re-
     lationship of propaganda to art.

923 LEONARD, WILLIAM ELLERY. Letter to Upton Sinclair in
     Sinclair's My Lifetime in Letters. Columbia: University of
     Missouri Press, p. 284.
        Brief mention of author's concurrence with Dell's note on
     Oil!

924 MENCKEN, H[ENRY] L. Letter to Upton Sinclair in Sinclair's
     My Lifetime in Letters. Columbia: University of Missouri
     Press, p. 252.
        Brief paragraph commenting on Dell's biography of Sinclair,
     Upton Sinclair. Thinks "Dell will make an excellent job."
     Promises to review the book in American Mercury.

925 PARRY, ALBERT. Garrets and Pretenders: A History of
     Bohemianism in America. Revised edition. New York:
     Dover Publications, pp. 187, 189-90, 200, 270, 277, 278,
     287-89, 293, 297, 302, 355, 361.
        Revised from no. 742. Revision consists of addition of new
     chapter at end by Harry T. Moore.

926 SINCLAIR, UPTON. My Lifetime in Letters. Columbia: Uni-
     versity of Missouri Press, p. 258, 272, 273.
        Brief comments on letters from Dell to Sinclair.

927 TANNER, L[OUISE]. "Edna St. Vincent Millay: Candle
     Burned at Both Ends." Coronet, 47 (March), 76-79 [76,
     78].

Short biography of Millay. Names Dell one of the persons
with whom she celebrated the false armistice. Notes Dell's
treatment of Millay in his autobiography, which remains unnamed. Says Dell tried to awaken Millay to revolutionary
thought.

928 THORP, WILLARD. American Writing in the Twentieth Century.
Cambridge, Mass.: Harvard University Press, p. 26.
Cites the publication of The Briary-Bush as a bohemian
landmark in the new American literary culture that was
emerging between 1912 and 1922.

1961

929 AARON, DANIEL. Writers on the Left; Episodes in American
Literary Communism. New York: Harcourt, Brace and
World, 460 pp. passim.
This book deals with left wing writers from 1912 to the
1940's. Shows Dell's important place in the group. Sum-
marizes Intellectual Vagabondage and treats Dell's fall from
grace with the Mike Gold generation of radicals. Discusses
Dell's relationship with and opinion of Mike Gold, Joseph
Freeman, Bertrand Russell, the Bolshevik Revolution, art
and politics, sex and politics, and G. K. Chesterton.
Treats Dell on the individual poet and his reponsibility to
society.

930 DREISER, THEODORE. Letter of April 26, 1915, in H. L.
Mencken's Letters of H. L. Mencken. Selected by Guy J.
Forgue. New York: Alfred A. Knopf, p. 69.
Praises Dell's poetry.

931 LIGHT, MARTIN. "A Further Word on Sinclair Lewis' Prize-
Consciousness." Western Humanities Review, 15 (Autumn),
368-71 [370].
A discussion of Lewis' maneuvers to win the Nobel Prize.
Cites his exploitation of the controversy surrounding the
portrayal of small towns in Main Street and Moon-Calf.
Lists Dell among those reviewers to whom Lewis wished to
send a "Letter to Critics" in order to draw attention to
Main Street.

932 MENCKEN, H[ENRY] L. Letters of H. L. Mencken. Selected
by Guy J. Forgue. New York: Alfred A. Knopf, pp. 27,
68, 69, 70, 211, 222.
Letters express Mencken's dislike of Dell's work. Brief
comments on Moon-Calf.

933 SCHORER, MARK. Sinclair Lewis: An American Life. New
York: McGraw-Hill, pp. 4, 176, 177, 182, 183, 200, 201,
269, 276-78, 285-86, 288, 292, 771.

Mentions Dell's place in Lewis' life. Sees Moon-Calf as
representative of typical American adolescent experience.
Notes Dell's name on list of people seen most often by Lewis
between 1915 and 1920, Dell's views of H. G. Wells in Intellectual Vagabondage, and connection between success of
Main Street and Moon-Calf. Describes astrological chart
drawn by Lewis that includes Dell.

934 SNELL, GEORGE. The Shapers of American Fiction 1798-1947.
New York: Cooper Square Publications, p. 243.
Reprinted from no. 832.

935 TANSELLE, G[EORGE] THOMAS. "Ezra Pound and a Story of
Floyd Dell's." Notes and Queries, 8 (September), 350-52.
Says Dell's short story "Jessica Screams" published in
Smart Set in 1913 is based on Ezra Pound's experience as
instructor at Wabash College in Crawfordsville, Indiana.
Documents Dell's secondhand knowledge of Pound's life there,
retells the story, and cites the similarities between the hero
and Pound.

936 TANSELLE, G[EORGE] THOMAS. "F[itzgerald] and Floyd
Dell." Fitzgerald Newsletter, no. 13 (Spring), pp. 2-3.
Takes for granted the contrast between Dell and Fitzgerald but points out that they disliked each other's work.
Quotes each man on the other's work. These two authors
illustrate the "diversity of the twenties." Reprinted in no.
1017.

937 TANSELLE, G[EORGE] THOMAS. "The Friday Literary Review and the Chicago Renaissance." Journalism Quarterly,
38 (Summer), 332-36.
Dell is mentioned throughout this article on the goals and
content of the Chicago Evening Post's literary review section. Dell's approach to literary criticism while editor cited.
Stresses importance of the Review in the Chicago Renaissance and Dell's role as editor. "It was under Dell that
the Review reached its highest point both in critical perception and in historical importance."

1962

938 GELB, ARTHUR, and BARBARA GELB. O'Neill. New York:
Harper and Row, pp. 318, 344, 356, 358, 442.
Brief mentions of Dell in connection with the Masses trial
and his position on the publication. Lists "King Arthur's
Socks" as one of the premiere plays in the Provincetown
Players' first New York season. Describes Dell as "its
panicky author." Reprinted in no. 1055.

939 GURKO, MIRIAM. Restless Spirit; The Life of Edna St.

Vincent Millay. New York: Thomas Y. Crowell, pp. 77, 85, 87, 89-90, 91-93, 96-99, 104-106, 108, 125, 126, 127, 128, 178, 240.

Biography of Millay deals with her personal relationship with Dell. Also includes brief quotes from Dell dealing with Millay. Treats their association with the Provincetown Players.

940 HART, JOHN. "Floyd Dell: Intellectual Vagabond." Western Humanities Review, 16 (Winter), 67-75.

Discusses intellectual vagabondage as exemplified in Dell's own life and in his trilogy about Felix Fay. Integrates Dell's biography with discussions of Moon-Calf, The Briary-Bush, and Souvenir. Dell's work is important partly because of its record of literary life in Chicago during the "Renaissance" and in Greenwich Village. An even more important contribution is Dell's portayal of the human "spirit of wandering."

941 LASCH, CHRISTOPHER. The American Liberals and the Russian Revolution. New York: Columbia University Press, p. 98.

Cites Dell's willingness to be drafted in World War I as evidence that socialists at that time no longer opposed the war.

942 MUNSON, GORHAM. "Greenwich Village That Was: Seedbed of the Nineteen-Twenties." Literary Review, 5, pp. 313-335 [324, 328, 329, 335].

Relates Munson's memories of the Village. Lists Dell as a member of the Liberal Club. Notes his use of Henrietta Rodman as the model for Egeria in Love in Greenwich Village and quotes a description of her. Cites his position on the editorial staff of the Masses. Quotes from Dell in determining the date of the end of the Village. Disagrees with Dell's date of 1924. The Literary Review is published by Fairleigh Dickinson University, Teaneck, New Jersey.

943 SINCLAIR, UPTON. The Autobiography of Upton Sinclair. New York: Harcourt, Brace, and World, pp. 34, 88-90, 99, 204, 261.

Incorporates and goes beyond American Outpost. Calls Dell his friend and biographer. Quotes him at length on Arthur Stirling. Mentions Dell's questioning of Sinclair in preparation for the biography. Dell is part of the "radical colony" in Croton-on-Hudson. Reports that Dell wrote him from New York of William Fox threatening to publish Upton Sinclair Presents William Fox in 1933.

944 TANSELLE, G[EORGE] THOMAS. "The First Notice of Sherwood Anderson." Notes and Queries, 207 (August), 307-309.

Locates in the Friday Literary Review of the Chicago
Evening Post the September 5, 1913, reference to Windy
McPherson's Son.

945 TANSELLE, G[EORGE] THOMAS. "The Lyric Year: A Bibliographical Study." The Papers of the Bibliographical
Society of America, 56 (Fourth Quarter), 454-71 [455].
Brief mention of Dell. Says Joseph Freeman in An American Testament was in error when attributing the phrase
"lyric year" to Dell. Quotes from a letter by Dell to Tanselle that says he did not originate the phrase, and goes on
to interpret its meaning.

946 TANSELLE, G[EORGE] THOMAS. "Two Early Letters of Ezra
Pound." American Literature, 34 (March), 114-19.
Discusses the relationship between Dell and Pound. Dell
was one of the first to admire Pound's work. Quotes and
comments on two previously unpublished letters from Pound
to Dell.

947 TURNBULL, ANDREW. Scott Fitzgerald. New York: Charles
Scribner's Sons, p. 126.
Mentions Fitzgerald's opinion that in Moon-Calf Dell reached
the "depths of banality."

1963

948 CANBY, HENRY SEIDEL. "Fiction Sums Up a Century," in
Literary History of the United States: History. Edited by
Robert E. Spiller, Willard Thorp, Thomas H. Johnson, Henry
Seidel Canby, Richard M. Ludwig. Third edition, revised.
New York: Macmillan, pp. 1208-36 [1235].
The information referring to Dell is identical to the first
edition. See nos. 834, 882, and 1052.

949 FITZGERALD, F. SCOTT. The Letters of F. Scott Fitzgerald.
Edited by Andrew Turnbull. New York: Charles Scribner's
Sons, pp. 146-47, 149, 194, 463, 464-65.
A 1921 letter to Max Perkins compares Scribner's advertising of This Side of Paradise to Knopf's of Moon-Calf. Letter to Perkins finds The Briary-Bush "another rotten novel
by Floyd Dell" "without a touch of grace or beauty or wit."
A 1925 letter to Perkins sees Dell's latest novel as "lousy."
A 1920 letter to Burton Rascoe finds Moon-Calf "a wretched
thing without a hint of glamor, utterly undistinguished,
childhood impressions." Another 1920 letter to James Branch
Cabell calls Moon-Calf a "bogus masterpiece" "without glamor,
without ideas."

950 HILFER, ANTHONY CHANNELL. "The Revolt from the Village

in American Literature: 1915-1930." Ph.D. dissertation,
University of North Carolina at Chapel Hill, p. 198.
Study of historical and critical background of the revolt
from small town America. Credits Dell with arranging for
publication of Sherwood Anderson's first novel. See no.
1012.

951 HOFFMAN, FREDERICK J. The Modern Novel in America.
Revised. A Gateway Edition. Chicago: Henry Regnery,
pp. 115, 116.
Revised from no. 851. The information on Dell is the
same.

952 KRUTCH, JOSEPH WOOD. "Eugene O'Neill," in Literary His-
tory of the United States: History. Edited by Robert E.
Spiller, Willard Thorp, Thomas H. Johnson, Henry Seidel
Canby, Richard M. Ludwig. Third edition, revised. New
York: Macmillan, pp. 1237-50 [1239].
The reference to Dell is identical to the first edition.
See nos. 838, 886, and 1057.

953 MAY, HENRY. The Discontent of the Intellectuals: A Problem of the Twenties. The Berkeley Series in American History. Edited by Charles Sellers. Chicago: Rand McNally,
p. 4.
Brief mention of Dell helping make the Masses into "the
most striking and original left-wing journal the United
States has ever seen."

954 MIZENER, ARTHUR. The Sense of Life in the Modern Novel.
Boston: Houghton Mifflin, p. 144.
Brief mention of The Briary-Bush as an attempt to inte-
grate an individual's inner life and contemporary social
history.

955 SHANNON, DAVID A. Twentieth Century America; The United
States Since the 1890s. Chicago: Rand-McNally, p. 398.
In the 1930's, Dell, who was popular in the 1920's, was
unread and forgotten. See no. 1015 for second edition.
Dell is not mentioned in a 1977 edition.

956 TANSELLE, G[EORGE] THOMAS. "Floyd Dell in the Friday
Literary Review." The Papers of the Bibliographical Society
of America, 57 (Third Quarter), 371-76.
Attempt at reevaluating Dell by looking at his contributions to the Friday Literary Review. Lists his contributions
under categories of "poems," "editorials," "essays," and
"reviews." His work here is of interest because he, "though
he has been neglected by literary historians, is as representative of the literary and intellectual concerns of the first
twenty-five years of this century as any figure one could

find." The <u>Friday Literary Review</u> is important as a champion of the new literature and as an example of excellence in a publication reviewing books.

957 TANSELLE, G[EORGE] THOMAS. "Millay, Dell, and 'Recuerdo.'" <u>Colby Library Quarterly</u>, 6 (March), 202-205.
Discusses the origin of Edna St. Vincent Millay's poem "Recuerdo." Cites Dell's part in the original ferry ride and his opinion that it was Salomón de la Selva, not Jack Reed, who was Edna's companion on the ferry. Quotes for the first time Dell's poem "Break the Spell of the Goblin Queen" which uses the "Recuerdo" stanza form to call upon Millay to give up her Republican opinions.

958 TANSELLE, G[EORGE] THOMAS. "Realist or Dreamer: Letters of Sherwood Anderson and Floyd Dell." <u>Modern Language Review</u>, 58 (October), 532-37.
History of relationship between Anderson and Dell. Reprints letters showing the attitudes of each toward "the craft of fiction." Anderson was the realist who followed poetic impulses, Dell the poet who repressed poetic tendencies.

959 ZABEL, MORTON D. "Summary in Criticism," in <u>Literary History of the United States: History</u>. Edited by Robert E. Spiller, Willard Thorp, Thomas H. Johnson, Henry Seidel Canby, Richard M. Ludwig. Third edition, revised. New York: Macmillan, pp. 1358-73 [1361].
The reference to Dell is identical to the first edition. See nos. 839, 888, and 1063.

<u>1964</u>

960 ATKINS, ELIZABETH. <u>Edna St. Vincent Millay and Her Times</u>. New York: Russell and Russell, pp. 15, 64.
Reprinted from no. 781.

961 BURBANK, REX. <u>Sherwood Anderson</u>. Twayne's United States Authors Series. Edited by Sylvia E. Bowman. New York: Twayne, pp. 35, 36.
Tells how Karl Anderson showed the manuscript of <u>Windy McPherson's Son</u> to Dell who praised it in the <u>Friday Literary Review</u>. Sherwood frequented Dell's literary gatherings and met other writers. Stresses the interest in Freudianism prevalent in the group.

962 CURTI, MERLE. <u>The Growth of American Thought</u>. Third edition. New York: Harper and Row, p. 691.
The information on Dell is identical to that in nos. 819 and 848.

963 DUNCAN, HUGH DALZIEL. The Rise of Chicago as a Literary
    Center from 1885-1920; A Sociological Essay in American Cul-
    ture. Totowa, N.J.: Bedminster Press, pp. 130, 131, 133,
    135, 140, 141, 143, 144, 148.
       This is a revision of Duncan's doctoral dissertation at the
    University of Chicago. See no. 835. Names Dell as part
    of the literary renaissance in Chicago. He was a pioneer
    in newspaper book reviewing and, as a newspaperman, de-
    nounced the conservative, moralistic, Anglo-Saxon academic
    writers.

964 EASTMAN, MAX. Love and Revolution; My Journey Through
    an Epoch. New York: Random House, pp. 17, 37, 43,
    65, 70, 73, 74, 83, 88-89, 90, 94, 97, 98, 99, 119, 121,
    140, 178, 194, 222, 223-24, 254, 266, 267, 269, 441, 491,
    533.
       Eastman's autobiography from 1917 to 1941. Numerous
    mentions of Dell place him in this era and reflect Eastman's
    opinion of him. Many mentions of Dell in context of Masses
    and Liberator editorships and Masses trial. Eastman com-
    ments on Dell's literary criticism. Believes Dell's socialism
    kept the Masses and Liberator from having rightful place in
    history of American culture. Lists Dell's faults but admires
    his wit, insight, and ability to work.

965 GERBER, PHILIP L. Theodore Dreiser. Twayne's United
    States Authors Series. Edited by Sylvia E. Bowman. New
    York: Twayne, p. 155.
       Brief mention of inclusion of Dell's name in a letter from
    Horace Liveright to Dreiser indicating the praise won by new
    writers.

966 LOVETT, ROBERT MORSS. "Sherwood Anderson," in After
    the Genteel Tradition; American Writers 1910-1930. Edited
    by Malcolm Cowley. Revised edition. Crosscurrents-Modern
    Critiques Series. Edited by Harry T. Moore. Carbondale:
    Southern Illinois University Press, pp. 74-82 [74-75].
       Reprinted from no. 794.

967 TANSELLE, G[EORGE] THOMAS. "Sinclair Lewis and Floyd
    Dell: Two Views of the Midwest." Twentiety Century Lit-
    erature, 9 (January), 175-84.
       Examines letters exchanged between Dell and Lewis com-
    paring Moon-Calf and Main Street and discusses the novels.
    Concludes that in spite of being classified together as part
    of "the revolt from the village" the two represent different
    points of view. Lewis deals specifically with the Midwest
    and its provincialism whereas Dell writes not a regional novel,
    but one concentrating on personal growth. Tanselle shows
    also that Dell and Lewis are ambivalent in their attitudes
    to the small town.

968 TANSELLE, G[EORGE] THOMAS. "Vachel Lindsay Writes to
Floyd Dell." Journal of the Illinois State Historical Society,
57 (Winter), 366-79.
Reproduces and comments on six letters from Lindsay to
Dell written between 1909 and 1912 on the subject of litera-
ture. Notes Dell's help to and influence on Lindsay.

1965

969 DUNCAN, HUGH DALZIEL. Culture and Democracy. Totowa,
N.J.: The Bedminster Press, pp. 84, 100, 111.
Brief mention of Dell and others not relating art to the
architecture of their time in Chicago. In Dell's Chicago
novels, independent women are represented in a new relationship with men. Notes Dell's presence at parties in Chicago art circles.

970 HALE, NATHAN GEORGE, JR. "The Origins and Foundation
of the Psychoanalytic Movement in America, 1909-1914."
Ph.D. dissertation. University of California at Berkeley,
pp. 335, 369.
Brief mention of Dell having written about benefits of
psychotherapy. Statement based on 1960 interview with
Dell.

971 MCMICHAEL, GEORGE. Journey to Obscurity; The Life of
Octave Thanet. Lincoln: University of Nebraska Press,
p. 181.
Brief mention of Dell in biography of Thanet. In her
diary Thanet recorded Arthur Davison Ficke's dinner conversation about Dell and George Cram Cook, two of Davenport's "'emerging literary figures.'" Thanet herself had
met Dell but only vaguely remembered him as a socialist
poet.

972 MIZENER, ARTHUR. The Far Side of Paradise; A Biography
of F. Scott Fitzgerald. Sentry Edition. Boston: Houghton
Mifflin, pp. 121-22.
Revised from no. 858. Omits letter about summer in
Antibes.

973 SWANBERG, W. A. Dreiser. New York: Charles Scribner's
Sons, pp. 93, 147, 155, 164, 166, 167, 169, 177, 180, 182,
187, 188, 189, 190, 192, 197, 203-204, 209, 223, 230, 233,
238, 249, 251, 262, 263, 297, 326, 376, 409, 424, 500.
Brief mentions of Dell throughout this exhaustive biography
of Theodore Dresier. Points out their friendship and Dell's
editing of The "Genius", the frequency with which they saw
each other, and their ultimate political disagreements. Dell
is seen as a younger "famous" writer who benefited from the
freedom of literary expression won by Dreiser.

974 TAUBMAN, HOWARD. The Making of the American Theatre. New York: Coward-McCann, p. 153.
    Includes Dell in list of persons associated with the Provincetown Players "who made a difference on the American theatrical and literary scene." Revised edition, no. 996.

975 UNTERMEYER, LOUIS. Bygones: The Recollections of Louis Untermeyer. New York: Harcourt, Brace and World, pp. 32, 33, 34, 37.
    Untermeyer's autobiography. Mentions Dell's association with the Masses, his poetic aspirations, and his job in Washington, D.C.

1966

976 EARNEST, ERNEST. "The American Ariel." South Atlantic Quarterly, 65 (Spring), 192-200 [192, 196, 198].
    Discusses the American Ariel, a literary archetype representing the compassionless artist, a rebel against his birthplace and its values. Dell and his work are used as examples. Moon-Calf represents this archetype. One paragraph is devoted to discussing Felix Fay as Ariel.

977 FLANAGAN, JOHN T. "Theodore Dreiser's Chicago." Revue des Langues Vivantes, 32, 131-44 [131].
    Briefly names Dell as a writer who includes Chicago in his subject matter.

978 KRAMER, DALE. Chicago Renaissance; The Literary Life in the Midwest 1900-1930. New York: Appleton-Century, 365 pp., passim.
    Gossipy, interesting account of the literary milieu of the Chicago area. Stresses individual achievements and interrelationships of persons involved. Good for placing Dell in the times. Discusses his relationship with Margaret Anderson, Sherwood Anderson, Theodore Dreiser, and others, his marriage, and his work on the Friday Literary Review.

979 LEHAN, RICHARD DANIEL. F. Scott Fitzgerald and the Craft of Fiction. Crosscurrents-Modern Critiques Series. Edited by Harry T. Moore. Carbondale: Southern Illinois University Press, pp. 70, 174.
    Compares attitude to youth expressed in The Briary-Bush and This Side of Paradise. Mentions Del's novels as being concerned with escape from Midwest conformity.

980 NOLTE, WILLIAM H. H. L. Mencken: Literary Critic. Middletown, Conn.: Wesleyan University Press, pp. 212, 240.
    Notes that Dell praised Jennie Gerhardt after Mencken. Lists Dell as a writer aided by Mencken.

981 O'NEILL, WILLIAM L. Echoes of Revolt; "The Masses" 1911-
1917. Edited by William L. O'Neill. Chicago: Quadrangle
Books, pp. 18, 19, 21, 22, 23-24, 49, 53, 54, 63, 67, 78,
96, 113, 179, 225, 295.
This is an anthology of articles and drawings from the
Masses arranged according to subject matter. Introductory
comments by the editor elucidate Dell's contribution to the
publication. Sees Dell as responsible for the high quality
of the literature and drama reviews and for the selection of
advanced short stories for inclusion. Notes Dell's complete
personal identification with "the radical optimism of the high
Progressive Era."

982 WATERMAN, ARTHUR E. Susan Glaspell. Twayne's United
States Authors Series. Edited by Sylvia E. Bowman. New
York: Twayne, pp. 34, 35, 48, 51, 52, 54.
Brief mentions of Dell in this biography and analysis of
Glaspell. Claims Dell is partly responsible for enriching and
expanding Glaspell's views of life and literature.

983 WILSON, GARFF B. A History of American Acting. Blooming-
ton: Indiana University Press, p. 243.
Dell is briefly listed with others who were members of the
famed Provincetown Players.

1967

984 BALDWIN, CHARLES C. "Floyd Dell," in The Men Who Make
Our Novels. Essay Index Reprint Series. Freeport, N.Y.:
Books for Libraries Press, pp. 129-33.
Reprinted from no. 364.

985 BRITTIN, NORMAN A. Edna St. Vincent Millay. Twayne's
United States Authors Series. Edited by Sylvia E. Bowman.
New York: Twayne, pp. 34, 36-37, 38, 39, 42, 43, 51,
52, 53, 75, 80, 110, 113.
Relates Dell's place in Millay's personal life and his views
of some of her work. Describes briefly their affair in winter
of 1917-1918, Millay's promise to marry him, and the end of
the relationship. Dell's opinion of Village influence on Millay's character. Says his plays are "all more or less sym-
bolic works self-consciously representing the 'advanced'
ideas of Greenwich Village." Lists the ideas.

986 BUTLER, FRANCELIA, and RICHARD H. W. DILLARD.
"Parnassus in the 1920s: Floyd Dell Contemplates His Own
Period." Tennessee Studies in Literature, 12, pp. 131-48.
Reviews Dell's accomplishments which are seen to be a
pioneering use of Freud in literature and an encouragement
of other writers. He was "a central figure in one of the
most flourishing periods of American literature" as well as

a successful writer. Records in question-answer form a conversation with Dell centering mainly on the relation of the
writer to his work, methods of composition, Dreiser, S. Lewis,
E. Millay, and Dos Passos. Summarizes Dell's views including
his idea that "contemporary criticism is unreliable."

987 HAHN, EMILY. Romantic Rebels; An Informal History of Bohemianism in America. Boston: Houghton Mifflin, pp. 176-
83.
 Dell's place in American bohemianism described. Short
biography. Notes his "surprising influence" on literary
taste in Chicago. Recounts 1964 conversation with Dell on
Bohemia. Places him in Greenwich Village milieu. Discusses
his relations with Edna Millay.

988 HORTON, ROD W., and HERBERT W. EDWARDS. Backgrounds
of American Literary Thought. Second edition. Appleton-
Century Handbooks of Literature. Edited by Albert C.
Baugh. New York: Appleton-Century-Crofts, pp. 239, 356.
 Revised from no. 867. Information on Dell is the same.
Revised in no. 1056.

989 MATTHEWS, F. H. "The Americanization of Sigmund Freud:
Adaptations of Psychoanalysis before 1917." Journal of
American Studies, 1 (April), 39-62 [51, 54-55].
 Notes importance of Homecoming to the section of this
discussion of Freudianism and young intellectuals. Names
Dell as Sherwood Anderson's mentor. Discusses Dell's personal experience with psychoanalysis. "Dell's experience
illustrates what was to become the most characteristic American use of Freudian ideas: their role as a tool for adjusting
the deviant individual to social norms, considered as part of
'objective' reality."

990 MICHAUD, REGIS. The American Novel To-day: A Social and
Psychological Study. Port Washington, N.Y.: Kennikat
Press, pp. 22, 254.
 Reprinted from no. 595. Reprinted in 1079.

991 O'CONNOR, RICHARD, and DALE L. WALKER. The Lost
Revolutionary; A Biography of John Reed. New York:
Harcourt, Brace and World, pp. 96, 128, 238, 239-40, 250.
 Brief mentions of and quotes from Dell. Says Dell took
Reed's place on the Masses. Dell's view of Reed as a new
Jack London. Mentions Dell and the Masses trials, as well
as Dell, Reed, and Edna Millay's ferry boat ride.

992 PHILLIPS, WILLIAM. "Old Flames." The New York Review
of Books, 8 (9 March), 7-8.
 Review of Echoes of Revolt (see no. 981). Critical of the
outlook of the Masses. Names Dell as one of the "famous

rebels of the time." Briefly mentions, not by name but by plot, one of his stories published in the Masses. Says the literary criticism in the Masses was unsophisticated, unaware of then-modern trends, and conservative.

993 POUND, EZRA. Pound/Joyce; The Letters of Ezra Pound to James Joyce, with Pound's Essays on Joyce. Edited by Forrest Read. New York: New Directions Books, p. 285.
In a May 1916 letter to Elkin Mathews on the subject of censorship, Pound notes that Dell was the first person to see that Pound wrote in the Latin, not the Greek, tradition.

994 SHANNON, DAVID A. The Socialist Party of America; A History. Chicago: Quadrangle Books, pp. 9, 208.
Reprinted from no. 896.

995 SKLAR, ROBERT. F. Scott Fitzgerald: The Last Laocoön. London: Oxford University Press, pp. 80-81, 108, 121, 137.
A study of the development of Fitzgerald's artistry and intellect. Quotes letters from Fitzgerald and Burton Rascoe on Moon-Calf. Fitzgerald dislikes the novel and Rascoe questions the motivation behind that dislike. Mentions Dell as a popular writer who did not surpass Fitzgerald in critical or popular success. Fitzgerald saw Dell as his competitor.

996 TAUBMAN, HOWARD. The Making of the American Theatre. Revised edition. New York: Coward-McCann, p. 153.
Unchanged from no. 974.

997 WEINSTEIN, JAMES. The Decline of Socialism in America, 1912-1925. New York: Monthly Review Press, p. 1.
Brief mention of Dell as intellectual attracted to the I.W.W. movement.

998 WILSON, EDMUND. "The All-Star Literary Vaudeville," in American Criticism 1926. Edited by William A. Drake. Freeport, N.Y.: Books for Libraries Press, pp. 337-58 [338].
Reprinted from no. 515.

1968: Books

999 HORBERG, RICHARD OSCAR. "To the Twentieth Century and Back; A Round Trip with Floyd Dell." Ph.D. dissertation, University of Minnesota, 273 pp.
Harsh assessment of Dell and his contributions to literature. Dell should not be characterized only in his bohemianism. Dell helps understand the social, political, and literary movements of pre- and post-World War I America. He "embraces so many of the paradoxes in American life

and reveals so many of the tensions of the period." Examines Dell's attitude toward feminism, nature, the machine,
socialism, education prohibition, politics, and collectivism in
light of the times. Dell's novels are interpreted as a failure
of imagination. Dell's gift was for irony, lightness, and
humor. But because of his radical principles he adopted
the mode of realism. Psychoanalysis removed the tensions
which made him an artist.

1968:   Shorter Writings

1000   CARGILL, OSCAR.   Intellectual America; Ideas on the March.
New York: Cooper Square, pp. 166, 323, 324, 330, 507,
592, 637-38, 651-60, 662, 665, 763.
Reprinted from no. 811.

1001   GILBERT, JAMES BURKHART.   Writers and Partisans; A
History of Literary Radicalism in America.   American Cultural History Series.   Edited by Loren Baritz and William R.
Taylor.   New York: John Wiley and Sons, pp. 2, 9, 18,
25, 28, 39, 51, 53, 54, 56, 58, 67, 70, 71, 72, 73, 76, 78,
82, 86, 101-102, 254.
Chronicles Dell's important place in the history of the literary left in America.   Calls him "one of the most important
of the earliest radicals."   Credits Dell's part in evolving the
literary criticism   called sociological criticism.   Sees Dell as
interpreter of Freud and as a "custodian of prewar tradition" in Greenwich Village who helped associate this tradition with communism.   Notes his loss of affinity with the
communists who went beyond his sociological criticism, his
opinions of the intellectual vagabond and America's literary
heritage.   Interprets his disassociation from politics after
the 1930s.

1002   HICKS, GRANVILLE.   John Reed: The Making of a Revolutionary.   New York: B. Blom, pp. 110, 208, 214, 219,
231, 240, 304, 308.
Reprinted from no. 784.

1003   MCALEER, JOHN J.   Theodore Dreiser; An Introduction.
American Authors and Critics Series.   Edited by John
Mahoney.   New York: Holt, Rinehart and Winston, p. 120.
Briefly mentions that Dell and Frederic Chapman cut
100,000 words when editing The "Genius".

1004   MENCKEN, H[ENRY] L.   "Fifteen Years," in H. L. Mencken's
"Smart Set" Criticism.   Edited by William H. Nolte.   Ithaca,
N.Y.:   Cornell University Press, pp. 324-34 [330].
Brief mention of Dell not living up to his artistic promise.

1005 PECK, DAVID RUSSELL. "The Development of an American
Marxist Literary Criticism: The Monthly New Masses."
Ph.D. dissertation, Temple University, pp. 22, 31, 33,
34-35, 36-37, 40, 41, 45, 47, 52, 53, 57, 82, 88, 97, 107,
108, 117.
  Numerous brief mentions of Dell in his relationship to the
Masses, the Liberator, and the New Masses. Dell's work is
important because the Marxist criticism in the New Masses
developed partly out of his sociological criticism. He tried
to describe "the relationship between literature and social
and historical forces in his own time." Discusses the importance of Intellectual Vagabondage as a link between
Masses-Liberator criticism and that of the New Masses.
It was sociological criticism but it failed because it lacked
a well defined theoretical base and it did not link criticism
with social and economic forces. Dell did not see a pattern
in the relationship between these forces and literature.
Dell exhibited "critical vagueness." By 1930, Dell was
part of an older generation of writers.

1969

1006 ANDERSON, ELIZABETH, and GERALD R. KELLY. Miss
Elizabeth; A Memoir. Boston: Little, Brown, p. 25-26.
  Memoir of second wife of Sherwood Anderson. Dell
rented the basement apartment in her building in Greenwich Village. Describes him and his activities. Dell was
visiting in her apartment when he was subpoenaed for the
Masses trial. Describes what took place.

1007 ANON. "Floyd Dell Dead; Novelist and Editor." Washington
Post (29 July), sec. C, p. 5.
  Obituary. Includes biographical details. One of few
sources to say anything about his activities after 1935.

1008 ANON. "Floyd Dell Dies at 82; 'Chicago Group' Writer."
Washington Evening Star (29 July), sec. B, p. 4.
  Obituary. Biographical facts. Details of life after 1935
identical with no. 1007.

1009 GOULD, JEAN. Poet and Her Book; A Biography of Edna
St. Vincent Millary. New York: Dodd, Mead, pp. 25,
31, 41, 47, 79-80, 82-83, 84-86, 87-90, 91-92, 93, 94,
95, 97-98, 101-103, 110, 118, 123-24, 152, 156, 157, 176.
  Several quotes from Dell on aspects of Millay's life. Discusses his relationship with the Provincetown Players. Details his romantic involvement with Millay. Focuses on his
intellectual influence on her and on his insistence on the
benefits of psychoanalysis.

1010 HERRON, IMA HONAKER. <u>The Small Town in American Drama</u>.
Dallas, Tex.: Southern Methodist University Press, p. 262.
Quotes <u>Moon-Calf</u> to express feelings of small town characters of 1920's and 1930's who act out of hatred of con-
servativism and joyless sexuality and out of ambition.

1011 HICKS, GRANVILLE. <u>The Great Tradition; An Interpretation</u>
<u>of American Literature Since the Civil War</u>. Chicago:
Quadrangle Books, p. 212.
Revised from no. 776. The only alteration is the inclusion
of a new foreword and afterword.

1012 HILFER, ANTHONY CHANNELL. <u>The Revolt from the Village</u>,
<u>1915-1930</u>. Chapel Hill: University of North Carolina Press,
pp. 175-76.
This book is derived from Hilfer's dissertation (see no.
950). Deals with American writers' attitudes toward the
small town during the years 1915 to 1930. There is a brief
mention of Dell's opinion that <u>Main Street</u> did not fairly
represent the small town and of Sinclair Lewis' response that
the town of <u>Main Street</u> was much smaller than that represented in <u>Moon-Calf</u>.

1013 LEHAN, RICHARD. <u>Theodore Dreiser; His World and His</u>
<u>Novels</u>. Carbondale: Southern Illinois University Press,
pp. 134-35, 138, 177, 264.
Discusses the dual influence on Dreiser of H. L. Mencken
and the <u>Masses</u> editors (Max Eastman, John Reed, and Floyd
Dell). Quotes a Dreiser letter to Mencken defending Dell's
radicalism. Notes Dell's disagreement with Mencken's outlook
on politics. Explains Dreiser's attraction to Dell as a common
desire to "scorn the middle class." Cites Dell's membership
in the John Reed Club. Says Dreiser took away the affec-
tions of Dell's girlfriend Kirah Markham.

1014 RICHWINE, KEITH NORTON. "The Liberal Club; Bohemia
and the Resurgence in Greenwich Village 1912-1918." Ph.D.
dissertation, University of Pennsylvania, 214 pp., passim.
Study of the Liberal Club as it was associated with the
ferment of new ideas in Greenwich Village. Dell is a "prime
mover" of the Liberal Club. Dell calls himself a poet first
and a radical second. He sees art as socially redemptive.
He tries to unify art and politics. Discusses his part in
the drama of the Liberal Club. Describes his socialism.

1015 SHANNON, DAVID A. <u>Twentieth Century America; The United</u>
<u>States Since the 1890s</u>. Second edition. Chicago: Rand-
McNally, p. 398.
Reprinted from no. 955.

1016 SMITH, PAUL JORDAN. <u>For the Love of Books; The Adven-</u>

tures of an Impecunious Collector. Essay Index Reprint
Series. Freeport, N.Y.: Books for Libraries Press, pp.
153-54, 168-69.
Reprinted from no. 770. See nos. 804 and 828.

1017 TANSELLE, G[EORGE] THOMAS. "F[itzgerald] and Floyd
Dell," in Fitzgerald Newsletter. Edited by Matthew J.
Bruccoli. New York: Microcard Editions, p. 54.
Reprinted from no. 936.

1018 WHITMAN, ALDEN. "Floyd Dell, Novelist of 1920's and 'Village' Figure, Is Dead." New York Times (30 July), p. 39.
Long obituary. Dell cited as "one of the most influential
American novelists of 50 years ago." Credits him with being an initiator of frank talk about sex in novels. As editor of the Friday Literary Review, Dell made it "a national
model of excellence." Dell's radicalism was not ideological,
but romantic and utopian.

1970: Books

1019 SMITH, JOHN THOMAS. "Feminism in the Novels of Floyd
Dell." Ph.D. dissertation, University of Texas at Austin,
166 pp.
Describes early twentieth-century feminism, then focuses
on Dell. Dell advocated freedom for women, but he became
increasingly skeptical about the New Woman. He saw tradi-
tional marriage and motherhood as the goal of women who
wished a complete life. Because his novels reflect social
changes, they are useful in understanding the women's
rights movement.

1970: Shorter Writings

1020 ANON. "Floyd Dell," in The Literary Spotlight. Essay
Index Reprint Series. Freeport, N.Y.: Books for Li-
braries Press, pp. 65-76.
Reprinted from no. 305.

1021 CLEATON, IRENE, and ALLEN CLEATON. Books and Battles; American Literature, 1920-1930. New York: Cooper
Square, pp. xvii, 67, 74, 95, 100, 110, 159, 160, 180,
202, 213.
Reprint of no. 789.

1022 DREISER, THEODORE. Letter to Horace Liveright in Walker
Gilmer's Horace Liveright; Publisher of the Twenties. New
York: David Lewis, p. 43.
Praises Dell's book which is unnamed but which must be

Moon-Calf. "It is exceedingly good." Describes Dell's
publisher's window displays for book stores. This letter
is printed in full in no. 916.

1023 ELIAS, ROBERT H. Theodore Dreiser; Apostle of Nature.
Emended edition with a survey of research and criticism.
Ithaca, N.Y.: Cornell University Press, pp. 171, 179,
182, 184.
Revised from no. 840. The information on Dell is identi-
cal.

1024 GILMER, WALKER. Horace Liveright; Publisher of the Twenties. New York: David Lewis, pp. 4, 8, 27, 43, 44, 60,
106.
Brief mentions of Dell in this biography of Liveright.
Notes Dell's efforts to have Windy McPherson's Son published. Says Dell's description of Anthony Comstock and
John Sumner in Homecoming does not malign the censors.

1025 LIVERIGHT, HORACE. Letter to Theodore Dresier in Walker
Gilmer's Horace Liveright; Publisher of the Twenties. New
York: David Lewis, p. 44.
Comments on Dreiser's description of store window dis-
plays of Floyd Dell's books by saying that Liveright is
promoting Dreiser just as well.

1026 MOORE, JACK B. Maxwell Bodenheim. Twayne's United
States Authors Series. Edited by Sylvia E. Bowman.
New York: Twayne Publishers, pp. 15, 18, 34, 159.
Includes Dell's conjectures about Bodenheim's behavior
and beliefs. Cites Joseph Freeman on Dell as a true radi-
cal.

1027 OSTRANDER, GILMAN M. American Civilization in the First
Machine Age: 1890-1940. New York: Harper and Row,
pp. 23, 24, 137, 173, 176, 178, 179, 180, 187-88, 189.
Brief mentions of Dell and quotations from him. Sees
him as part of a younger generation. Gives his opinion
of James G. Huneker. Notes his Chicago soirees and his
move to New York. Places him in Village attitudes to sex.
Cites his interest and participation in psychoanalysis.

1028 TINGLEY, DONALD F. "The 'Robin's Egg Renaissance':
Chicago and the Arts, 1910-1920." Journal of the Illinois
State Historical Society, 63 (Spring), 35-54 [37, 38, 40-
41, 49].
Unoriginal article discussing the young people and general artistic atmosphere in Chicago from 1910 to 1920.
Cites Dell's editorship of the Friday Literary Review, his
married life-style, and his and Margery Currey's central
position in a group of bohemian intellectuals and literary

people. Includes picture of Dell. Treats Margaret Anderson, the Dill Pickle Club, Ben Hecht, Emanuel Carnevali, Vachel Lindsay, Henry B. Fuller, Theodore Dreiser, and others. Draws heavily on Dell's Homecoming and the memoirs of others.

1029 WILSON, EDMUND. "The All-Star Literary Vaudeville," in The Plastic Age (1917-1930). Edited by Robert Shear. The American Culture Series. Edited by Neil Harris. New York: George Braziller, pp. 152-64 [152].
Revised from no. 514. Essentially the same, but includes the first names of four reviewers of which Dell is one.

1971: Books

1030 HART, JOHN E. Floyd Dell. Twayne's United States Authors Series. Edited by Sylvia E. Bowman. New York: Twayne Publishers, 190 pp.
Biography of Dell and analysis of his life and work. Takes point of view of Dell as an idealist adapting himself to realities of life. Sees his work as an attempt to deal with personal as well as general human frustrations involved in this adaptation. Includes short annotated bibliography of works about Dell as well as a list of works by Dell. A major work on Dell.

1971: Shorter Writings

1031 CHENEY, MARTHA ANNE. "This Door You Might Not Open: Floyd Dell," in "Millay in the Village." Ph.D. dissertation, Florida State University. pp. 57-74.
Chapter on Dell's relationship with Edna St. Vincent Millay during the time both lived in Greenwich Village. Discusses his personal, professional, artistic, and social influence on Millay. "Dell was too meddlesome and talkative to be the perfect man for Millay, although he helped her clarify her attitude toward women." Compares Dell's and Millay's abilities as literary critics. Finds Dell "verbose" and romantic.

1032 FITZGERALD, F. SCOTT. "The Credo of F. Scott Fitzgerald" in F. Scott Fitzgerald in His Own Time: A Miscellany. Edited by Matthew J. Bruccoli and Jackson R. Bryer. Kent, Ohio: The Kent State University Press, pp. 165-66 [165].
Reprinted with omissions from no. 228.

1033 FITZGERALD, F. SCOTT. Dear Scott/Dear Max; The Fitzgerald-Perkins Correspondence. Edited by John Kuehl

and Jackson R. Bryer. New York: Charles Scribner's
Sons, pp. 39, 42, 126.
Includes a 1921 letter comparing Scribners' advertising
of This Side of Paradise to Knopf's advertising of Moon-
Calf and another 1921 letter commenting unfavorably on
The Briary-Bush. There is a 1925 letter expressing dis-
dain of Dell's latest novel.

1034 FITZGERALD, F. SCOTT. "Three Soldiers," in F. Scott
Fitzgerald in His Own Time: A Miscellany. Edited by
Matthew J. Bruccoli and Jackson R. Bryer. Kent, Ohio:
The Kent State University Press, pp. 121-24 [123].
Reprinted from no. 230.

1035 GASSMAN, JANET. "Edna St. Vincent Millay: 'Nobody's
Own.'" Colby Library Quarterly, 9 (June), 297-310 [299,
300-301, 302, 303, 305, 306-307, 308].
Article on Millay's insistence on freedom to explore her
own individuality. Dell frequently mentioned as her first
lover. Discusses their estrangement due to his excessive
questioning and prying into her privacy. Notes his attitude to her after the end of the relationship. Discusses
his general attitude to marriage.

1036 HALE, NATHAN G., JR. Freud and the Americans; The
Beginning of Psychoanalysis in the United States, 1876-
1917. Vol. 1 of Freud in America. New York: Oxford
University Press, pp. 401, 403-404, 407.
Dell mentioned as a popularizer of psychoanalysis.

1037 MAYFIELD, SARA. Exiles from Paradise; Zelda and Scott
Fitzgerald. New York: Delacorte Press, p. 72.
Paraphrases Fitzgerald letter to Maxwell Perkins compar-
ing Scribner's advertising of This Side of Paradise to
Knopf's of Moon-Calf. See no. 1033 for text of letter.

1972

1038 ANDREWS, CLARENCE A. A Literary History of Iowa. Iowa
City: University of Iowa Press, pp. 124, 165, 167-69,
170-71, 172, 175, 176, 177, 182.
Chronicles Dell's place in the literary life and scene of
Davenport, Iowa, in the early 1900's. Brief biography.
His friendship with George Cram Cook cited. Speculates
on his influence upon Susan Glaspell. Comments on Dell's
first two novels. Moon-Calf differs from his actual life.
Finds "nothing at all of a period quality in his novel."
Partially reprints Arthur Davison Ficke's poem "An Out-
rageous Person to Floyd Dell."

1039 HOMBERGER, ERIC. "Introduction," in Ezra Pound: The
     Critical Heritage. The Critical Heritage Series. Edited
     by B. C. Southam. London: Routledge and Kegan Paul,
     pp. 1-32 [7-8, 30].
        Names Dell. Quotes his review of Pound's Provenca.
     Notes that Pound was pleased with the review.

1040 MIZENER, ARTHUR. Scott Fitzgerald and His World. New
     York: G. P. Putnam's Sons, p. 74.
        Brief report of Dell's presence in Antibes in 1925.

1041 SOCHEN, JUNE. The New Woman; Feminism in Greenwich
     Village, 1910-1920. New York: Quadrangle Books, 175
     pp., passim.
        Discusses Dell as a male feminist and his fiction as rep-
     resentative of bohemian feminism. Notes his writing and
     beliefs on birth control. Discusses his advocacy of alter-
     nate marriage styles, free love, and new family structure.
     Cites his work on the Masses and with the Provincetown
     Players.

1042 SUTTON, WILLIAM A. The Road to Winesburg; A Mosaic of
     the Imaginative Life of Sherwood Anderson. Metuchen, N.J.:
     Scarecrow Press, pp. 247, 258, 277, 285-90, 305, 318-19,
     334, 338, 344, 347, 350-51, 365-66, 368, 434, 452, 607-12.
        Relates the Dell-Anderson relationship in the Chicago
     years. Dell's association with the "Talbot Whittingham manu-
     script." Recounts Dell's efforts to have Windy McPherson's
     Son and Marching Men published. Anderson's bad feelings
     toward Dell as a result of the Masses not publishing all of
     the Winesburg stories. The last pages are two letters from
     Dell commenting on Sutton's manuscript.

1973

1043 DASH, JOAN. A Life of One's Own; Three Gifted Women and
     the Men They Married. New York: Harper and Row, pp.
     120, 140, 141-42, 143, 144, 159, 160, 169, 170.
        Dell mentioned in the section on the life of Edna St. Vin-
     cent Millay. Quotes on how Millay was raised. Identified
     as her lover and as an influence on her ideal of social
     justice. Discusses relationship between Dell and Millay.
     Quotes Dell on Millay's relationship with her husband.

1044 FLANAGAN, JOHN T. "A Letter from Floyd Dell." American
     Literature, 45 (November), 441-52.
        Most of the article reproduces an April 29, 1952, letter
     from Dell to Flanagan. To introduce the letter, Flanagan
     tells about Dell's appearance at the 1952 Newberry Library

Conference on American Studies. Gives short biography of
Dell. Concludes that "for a number of years he was in the
forefront of radical journalism, a role which probably weakened his impact as a creative writer."

1045 GELB, BARBARA. So Short a Time; A Biography of John
Reed and Louise Bryant. New York: W. W. Norton, pp.
53, 102, 224-25.
Brief mention of Dell as associate editor of the Masses.
Describes him physically. Indicates his ambition was to
become a novelist. Dell's play "The Game" shared with
"Bound East for Cardiff" the first bill of the Playwright
Theater. Quotes from Homecoming on relationship of Edna
Millay and John Reed.

1046 HEINEY, DONALD, and LENTHIEL H. DOWNS. Recent American Literature to 1933. Essentials of Contemporary Literature of the Western World. Vol. 3. New York: Barron's
Educational Series, pp. 338, 367.
Lists Dell among the psychological and psychoanalytical
critics. Credits Dell with being one of the first to apply
Freud to literature. As editor and critic, he criticized
literature from a Marxist viewpoint. Thus his influence
on psychological literature was informal. His most important critical work is Love in the Machine Age.

1047 JOHNS, ORRICK. Time of Our Lives; The Story of My Father
and Myself. New York: Octagon Books, pp. 215, 216,
220, 245.
Reprinted from no. 791.

1974

1048 AARON, DANIEL. "Good Morning, New York, 1919-1921,"
in The American Radical Press, 1880-1960. Vol. 2. Edited
by Joseph R. Conlin. Westport, Conn.: Greenwood Press,
pp. 585-89 [585].
This article deals with Art Young and Good Morning.
Dell's involvement with the Masses trial is briefly mentioned.

1049 ANDERSON, DAVID D. "Chicago as Metaphor." Great Lakes
Review, 1 (Summer), 3-15 [5, 6, 7, 14].
This article deals with Chicago as a symbol of America,
American ideals, and harshness of reality. Names Dell as
a writer who explored the ideal and reality of Chicago in
his work and in his life.

1050 ANON. "Bibliographies: Literature and Culture," in Literary History of the United States: Bibliography. Edited
by Robert E. Spiller, Willard Thorp, Thomas H. Johnson,

Henry Seidel Canby, Richard M. Ludwig, William M. Gibson. Fourth edition revised. New York: Macmillan, pp. 33-217 [63, 150, 168].

Homecoming is an "interesting account of literary life in Chicago and New York, dealing especially with Eastman's ten years as editor of the Masses and the Liberator." Briefly mentions the popular success of Moon-Calf.

1051 ANON. "Upton Sinclair," in Literary History of the United States: Bibliography. Edited by Robert E. Spiller, Willard Thorp, Thomas H. Johnson, Henry Seidel Canby, Richard M. Ludwig, William M. Gibson. Fourth edition revised. New York: Macmillan, pp. 723-25 [724].

Briefly mentions Upton Sinclair as an early study of that author.

1052 CANBY, HENRY SEIDEL. "Fiction Sums Up a Century," in Literary History of the United States: History. Edited by Robert E. Spiller, Willard Thorp, Thomas H. Johnson, Henry Seidel Canby, Richard M. Ludwig, William M. Gibson. Fourth edition revised. New York: Macmillan, pp. 1208-36 [1235].

The part pertaining to Dell is identical to no. 834.

1053 DRINNON, RICHARD. "Mother Earth Bulletin New York, 1906-1918," in The American Radical Press 1880-1960. Vol. 2. Edited by Joseph R. Conlin. Westport, Conn.: Greenwood Press, 392-99 [395].

This article treats Emma Goldman and the significance of Mother Earth. Brief mention of Dell's stories being published here.

1054 FITZGERALD, RICHARD. "Masses, New York, 1911-1917, Liberator, New York, 1918-1924," in The American Radical Press 1880-1960. Vol. 2. Edited by Joseph R. Conlin. Westport, Conn.: Greenwood Press, 532-38 [533, 534, 537].

Describes and discusses the two publications. Says Dell "exercised a disproportionate influence" on matter chosen for inclusion in the Masses. Notes Dell's view of the Village in his autobiography. Quotes him on the transcendentalists. Gives John Sloan's opinion of Dell's captions for drawings.

1055 GELB, ARTHUR, and BARBARA GELB. O'Neill. New York: Harper and Row, pp. 318, 344, 356, 358, 442.

Reprinted from no. 938.

1056 HORTON, ROD W., and HERBERT W. EDWARDS. Backgrounds of American Literary Thought. Third edition. Englewood Cliffs, N.J.: Prentice-Hall, pp. 247, 364.

Revised from no. 988. Information on Dell is identical.

1057 KRUTCH, JOSEPH WOOD. "Eugene O'Neill," in Literary History of the United States: History. Edited by Robert E. Spiller, Willard Thorp, Thomas H. Johnson, Henry Seidel Canby, Richard M. Ludwig, William M. Gibson. Fourth edition revised. New York: Macmillan, 1237-50 [1239].
The information referring to Dell is identical to the 1948 edition. See no. 838.

1058 LUNDQUIST, JAMES. Theodore Dreiser. Modern Literature Monographs. New York: Frederick Ungar Publishing Co., pp. 17, 23, 59.
Brief mentions of Dell. Names him as editor of the Masses and as one of those persons seen by Dreiser in Greenwich Village between 1914 and 1919. Lists Dell as a member of a committee formed by Dreiser to examine Paramount's movie version of An American Tragedy. Credits Dell with editing The "Genius".

1059 MILLETT, FRED. "Introduction to Contemporary American Literature," in John Matthews Manly and Edith Rickert's Contemporary American Literature. Revised by Fred B. Millett. New York: Haskell House, pp. 3-99 [30].
Reprinted from no. 627.

1060 MOOKERJEE, R. N. Theodore Dreiser; His Thought and Social Criticism. Delhi, India: National, p. 77.
Quotes Dell's remark to Dreiser on changing world conditions due to human effort. Source of quote is no. 973.

1061 SCHULTZ, STANLEY E. "Upton Sinclair's Pasadena, California, 1918-1919," in The American Radical Press, 1880-1960. Vol. 2. Edited by Joseph R. Conlin. Westport, Conn.: Greenwood Press, 572-84 [574, 581].
This article deals with Upton Sinclair and his magazine. Numbers Dell among the "distinguished editors" of the Masses. Sinclair urged fair treatment for Dell and others indicted and tried under the Espionage Act.

1062 STERN, MADELEINE B. "The Forerunner, New York, 1909-1916," in The American Radical Press 1880-1960. Vol. 2. Edited by Joseph R. Conlin. Westport, Conn.: Greenwood Press, 433-41 [433].
This essay deals with the life of Charlotte Perkins Gilman and with her publication The Forerunner. Brief quotation from Dell on Gilman's feminist views.

1063 ZABEL, MORTON D. "Summary in Criticism," in Literary

History of the United States: History. Edited by Robert
E. Spiller, Willard Thorp, Thomas H. Johnson, Henry
Seidel Canby, Richard M. Ludwig, William M. Gibson.
Fourth edition revised. New York: Macmillan, pp. 1358-
73 [1361].
   The information pertaining to Dell is identical to the 1948
edition. See no. 839.

1975

1064 CHENEY, ANNE. "Edna St. Vincent Millay in the Village;
      The Men in Millay's Life." Village Voice, 20 (1 Septem-
      ber), 41-43.
         Excerpted from nos. 1065 and 1066.

1065 CHENEY, ANNE. Millay in Greenwich Village. University:
      The University of Alabama Press, pp. 2-4, 30, 31, 32, 33,
      36-38, 39, 40, 83, 86, 89, 92, 94, 101, 103, 107, 119-20,
      125, 133, 136, 138.
         Psychological biography of Edna Millay concentrating on
      her lovers in the Village. Numerous references to Dell's
      place in her life. Based on no. 1066.

1066 CHENEY, ANNE. "This Door You Might Not Open: Floyd
      Dell," in Millay in Greenwich Village. University: Uni-
      versity of Alabama Press, pp. 56-70.
         Discusses the relationship between Dell and Edna Millay.
      Tells of their activities in the Provincetown Players and
      their influence on each other's poetry. Credits Dell with
      introducing Millay to Village milieu and with exposing her
      to his ideas on marriage and feminism. As her first male
      lover he helped her clarify her relationship to men and to
      love.

1067 GOIST, PARK DIXON. "Community and Self in the Midwest
      Town: Floyd Dell's Moon-Calf." Midamerica, 2, pp. 88-92.
         Although Moon-Calf is part of the Midwest "revolt from
      the village," "the image of community is evident." Com-
      pares the theme of community in Main Street and Moon-
      Calf. Concludes that the hero Felix does not flee the
      small town when he moves to Chicago, but that the move
      "is more a natural step in his pursuit of Self."

1068 HARRIS, LEON. Upton Sinclair; American Rebel. New
      York: Thomas Y. Crowell, pp. 20, 56, 221, 232-35, 238,
      245, 257, 280, 359, 362, 364, 365, 389, 397.
         Chronicles the long friendship and relationship of Floyd
      Dell and Sinclair.

1069 MARRINER, GERALD L. "Floyd Dell: Freedom or Marriage."
      Midamerica, 2, pp. 63-79.

A review of Dell's attitudes to love and marriage. Though
his behavior and theories were radical, he was inwardly conservative. Psychoanalysis enabled him to sacrifice freedom
for the stability of marriage. His marriage caused him to
be criticized for not being a true radical. His first three
novels as well as some nonfiction are mentioned as representative of his opinions or experiences.

1070 ROSENSTONE, ROBERT A. Romantic Revolutionary; A Biography of John Reed. New York: Alfred A. Knopf, pp. 4,
102, 103, 112, 142, 143, 181-82, 241, 245, 262, 266, 323,
347.
Brief references to and quotes from Dell. Several notes
of his presence and activities in Greenwich Village. Dell's
involvement with the Masses and the Masses trial. Dell's
association with the commercialization of the Village.

1071 STANBROUGH, JANE. Review of Millay in Greenwich Village.
The Denver Quarterly, 10 (Autumn) 142-45 [143].
Cheney credits Dell with introducing Millay to hetero-
sexuality and to turning her away from lesbianism. Stanbrough questions the accuracy of Dell's recollections about
Millay. Says she was already sexually experienced before
writing Renascence. See no. 1065.

1976

1072 EDMISTON, SUSAN, and LINDA D. CIRINO. Literary New
York. Boston: Houghton Mifflin, pp. 56, 57, 67, 71.
Cites Dell's involvement with the Masses and his indictment by the government. Says Dreiser "hired" Dell to help
edit The "Genius". Notes Dell's friendship with the Millay
sisters.

1073 FISHBEIN, LESLIE. "Floyd Dell: The Impact of Freud and
Marx on a Radical Mind." The Psychoanalytic Review, 63,
(Summer), 267-80.
Discusses Dell's understanding of Marxist theory which
was tempered by his view of himself as an adherent of
modernism. Dell aspired to the romanticism of Marxism,
not its claim to scientific truth. Dell's view of Freudianism focused on the freedom achieved by therapy, not on
the repression Freud felt was necessary for social behavior.
In Homecoming Dell interprets his life according to his in-
terpretations of Freud and Marx. Gives a sensitive discussion of Dell's views of his personal achievement of maturity.
Concludes that Dell provides no synthesis of Marx and
Freud.

1074 TANSELLE, G[EORGE] THOMAS. "Addenda to Dingman:

Eight Limited Signed Editions." Papers of the Bibliographical Society of America, 70 (third quarter), 419-20.

Tanselle comments on Larry Dingman's Bibliography of Limited and Signed Editions in Literature, Twentieth Century American Authors. Relevant to Dell only in that Tanselle includes Dell's Runaway among eight works not listed by Dingman. Says it had five hundred numbered and signed copies.

1977

1075 GOIST, PARK DIXON. "The Ideal Questioned but not Abandoned: Sherwood Anderson, Sinclair Lewis, and Floyd Dell," in his From Main Street to State Street; Town, City, and Community in America. National University Publications Interdisciplinary Urban Series. Edited by Raymond A. Mohl. Port Washington, N.Y.: Kennikat Press, pp. 21-34 [29-34].

Discusses Winesburg, Ohio, Main Street, and Moon-Calf in their attitudes to small towns. Moon-Calf is biographical. It "paints an essentially favorable picture of the towns and cities of mid-America." The hero has a sense of community and belonging in his small town, but he leaves for the big city. He has not been personally crushed by the town. He is neither victim nor rebel. His departure is not a flight, but a search for self.

1076 GOIST, PARK DIXON. From Main Street to State Street; Town, City, and Community in America. National University Publications Interdisciplinary Urban Series. Edited by Raymond A. Mohl. Port Washington, N.Y.: Kennikat Press, pp. 8, 46, 55, 160.

Brief mentions of Dell upholding the ideal of town as community in Moon-Calf. His work is marked by an atmosphere of "quiet egalitarianism."

1077 JOHNSON, WILLIAM C. "The Family of Love in Stuart Literature: A Chronology of Name-Crossed Lovers." The Journal of Medieval and Renaissance Studies, 7 (Spring), 95-112 [106].

Deals with seventeenth-century religious sect. Chooses Dell's and Jordan-Smith's translation of Robert Burton's Anatomy of Melancholy from which to quote. Included because it shows that after fifty years Dell's work is still current.

1078 MARRINER, GERALD L. "A Victorian in the Modern World; The 'Liberated' Male's Adjustment to the New Woman and the New Morality." The South Atlantic Quarterly, 76 (Spring), 190-203 [196].

This article details Hutchins Hapgood's efforts to free himself from Victorian notions of sexual morality. Quotes Dell on Hapgood's idea of the impossibility of knowing the basis for feelings. A footnote mentions the pains suffered by radicals who tried to excise love from marriage.

1079 MICHAUD, REGIS. The American Novel To-day; A Social and Psychological Study. Westport, Conn.: Greenwood Press, pp. 22, 254.
Reprinted from no. 595.

1080 PENKOWER, MONTY NOAM. The Federal Writers' Project; A Study in Government Patronage of the Arts. Urbana: University of Illinois Press, pp. 12, 35-36.
Lists Dell's name among those who approved of the New York based Unemployed Writers' Association proposals for government employment for its members. Identifies Dell as "the noted author and critic" who worked for the Federal Writers' Project as advisory editor. For one year Dell wrote inspiring progress reports.

1081 RIGGIO, THOMAS P. "Europe Without A. E. Baedeker: The Omitted Hanscha Jower Story--From A Traveler at Forty." Modern Fiction Studies, 23 (Autumn), 423-40 [424-25].
Quotes Dell's review of Traveler to show that the edited version appears to be a travelogue view of mid-nineteenth-century Europe. Speculates that Dell's view would have differed had he read the unexpurgated text.

1082 SARLOS, ROBERT K. "Dionysos in 1915: A Pioneer Theatre Collective." Theatre Research International, 3 (October), 33-53 [41, 47, 48, 50, 53].
Discusses the collective nature of the Provincetown Players. Concentrates on the role of George Cram Cook in the group's creativity. Quotes from Dell and comments on his opinions of Cook whom Dell knew well.

1083 SCAFIDEL, J. B. "Sexuality in Windy McPherson's Son." Twentieth Century Literature, 23 (February), 94-101 [98].
Analysis of the novel based on premise that its theme is impotence. Cites Dell's claim about altering the number of children at the end of the novel. Gives Dell credit for selling the book to John Lane Co. of London.

1084 TAYLOR, WELFORD DUNAWAY. Sherwood Anderson. Modern Literature Monographs. Edited by Lina Mainiero. New York: Frederick Ungar, pp. 8, 37.
Briefly mentions Anderson's association with Dell in Chicago and Dell's alleged charge that the Winesburg stories were formless.

1085 WILSON, EDMUND. <u>Letters on Literature and Politics 1912-</u><u>1972</u>. Edited by Elena Wilson. New York: Farrar, Straus and Giroux, pp. 54, 64, 68, 70-72, 79, 441, 509.

Includes a 1921 letter to Stanley Dell which calls <u>Moon-Calf</u> "very poor." Another 1921 letter to F. Scott Fitzgerald includes Dell among writers who owe their success to "a traditionless and half-educated public." A 1922 letter to Stanley Dell contrasts <u>Moon-Calf</u> with <u>The Triumph of the Egg</u>. Seven letters to F. Dell about Edna Millay. In a 1957 letter to John Austin, Wilson says he met Dell only once. A 1952 letter to Dell appraises "the school of Wells and Shaw."

<u>1978</u>

1086 ANDREWS, CLARENCE A. "GLR Bibliography: Literature of Place--Chicago: Part I." <u>Great Lakes Review</u>, 5 (Summer), 67-92 [77].

Lists books and films primarily set in Chicago. Includes <u>The Briary-Bush</u>. Brief plot summary.

1087 BRITTIN, NORMAN A. Review of <u>Millay in Greenwich Village</u>. <u>Southern Humanities Review</u>, 12 (Winter), 73-74 [73].

Brief mention of Dell. In Brittin's <u>Edna St. Vincent Millay</u> (no. 985) he stated, based on information provided by Dell, that Millay wrote the sonnet "Lord Archer, Death" for John Reed. Actually, it was published before Reed's death in 1920. See no. 1065.

1088 GOLDMAN, ARNOLD. "The Culture of the Provincetown Players." <u>Journal of American Studies</u>, 12 (December), 291-310 [300, 302, 308].

A history of the Provincetown Players. The group is seen as the channel for a progressive social vision which it both embodied and exemplified. Three brief references to Dell and quotes from <u>Homecoming</u>. Dell's account of the birth of the group is "cruel" and affected. Dell is "jaundiced" in his account of the relationship between Cook and O'Neill.

1089 SILET, CHARLES L. P., and KAY H. SILET. "Vincent Starrett and <u>The Wave</u>: A Little Magazine of Chicago in the 1920s." <u>Great Lakes Review</u>, 4 (Winter), 1-18 [1].

Summarizes the history of <u>The Wave</u>, its achievements and trials and Vincent Starrett's role in its creation and composition. Includes index to all eight issues. Briefly mentions Dell as a writer who moved to Chicago from a nearby rural area.

1090 SUTHERLAND, CYNTHIA. "American Women Playwrights as

Mediators of the 'Woman Problem.' " Modern Drama, 21 (September), 319-36 [333].

Footnote number seventeen refers to Homecoming. Notes that Henrietta Rodman was upset by Dell's comic treatment of woman's suffrage in "What Eight Million Women Want."

1979

1091 BERRY, EDWARD I. "Rosalynde and Rosalind." Shakespeare Quarterly, 31 (Spring), 42-52 [50].

Reference to Dell's edition of Burton's Anatomy of Melancholy. Included to show that after fifty-two years the edition is still current.

1092 WALTERS, THOMAS N. "Floyd Dell, Literary Radical: The Apple Pie Evolution." Pembroke Magazine, 11, pp. 194-203.

Tortuous examination of Dell's movement from radicalism to conservatism, a typically American "apple pie evolution." This same progress is seen in his fictional persona, Felix Fay. Reviews this change in three areas of concern to Dell and Fay: socialism, marriage, and literature. Dell "is a centrally typical figure of the twentieth-century's first radical wave."

1980

1093 ANDERSON, DAVID D. "Midwestern Writers and the Myth of the Search." The Georgia Review, 34 (Spring), 131-43 [134-35, 138-39].

This is a consideration of the American writers' search for personal fulfillment in movement and their use of experiences in their work. Dell is an important member of the group that matured before World War I. Dell's first two novels reflect Fay's "search for identity" within and beyond the Midwest. The story implies that Fay might have found what he wanted had he remained at home. Dell and his character returned to their origins in terms of values and ways of living.

1094 FITZGERALD, F. SCOTT. Correspondence of F. Scott Fitzgerald. Edited by Matthew J. Bruccoli and Margaret M. Duggan. New York: Random House, pp. 72, 73, 75, 77, 79, 88, 137.

Letters to Burton Rascoe express Fitzgerald's low opinion of Moon-Calf. Letter to H. L. Mencken suggests Dell borrowed from Fitzgerald in last two pages of Moon-Calf. Later regrets the charge. Letter to Thomas Boyd classifies Moon-Calf as part of the genre " 'history of a young man.' " Reprinted with omissions from no. 228. Letter to

Maxwell Perkins reiterates low opinion of <u>Moon-Calf</u>. Letter to Bernard Vaughan finds <u>Janet March</u> "drab, dull." "How such an intelligent, sophisticated man" can write such work is not understood. Reprinted from no. 328.

<u>1981</u>

1095 BENEDICT, STEWART. "New York and Environs," in <u>The Literary Guide to the United States</u>. Edited by Stewart Benedict. New York: Facts on File, pp. 1-51 [18, 19, 22, 30].
      Mentions <u>Masses</u> trial, Dell as <u>Masses</u> staff member, Dell's relationship with Edna Millay, and his association with the Provincetown Players.

1096 BRUCCOLI, MATTHEW J. <u>Some Sort of Epic Grandeur; The Life of F. Scott Fitzgerald</u>. New York: Harcourt Brace Jovanovich, pp. 162, 239.
      Quotes no. 230. Quotes Fitzgerald's 1925 letter to John Peale Bishop noting Dell's presence in Antibes that summer.

1097 FISHBEIN, LESLIE. "Freud and the Radicals: The Sexual Revolution Comes to Greenwich Village." <u>The Canadian Review of American Studies</u>, 12 (Fall), 173-89 [175, 176, 177, 178-79, 180-81, 182-83, 184, 185].
      Discusses the acceptance, use, and interpretation of Freudianism by pre-World War I Greenwich Village radicals and Marxists. Dell failed to reconcile Freudianism and socialism/Marxism. Discusses Dell's approach to analysis and his experience with it. Compares his experience to that of Max Eastman, Waldo Frank, and Hutchins Hapgood. In "The Angel Intrudes" and "King Arthur's Socks" Dell and the Provincetown Players were able to make fun of Freudianism in spite of the regard in which it was held.

1098 HART, JOHN. "Floyd Dell," in <u>American Novelists, 1910-1945</u>. Louis Adamic - Vardis Fisher Dictionary of Literary Biography. Vol. 9. Edited by James J. Martine. Detroit: Gale Research, pp. 192-200.
      Informal review of Dell's life and career. Focuses on each novel and most other books. "In <u>Moon-Calf</u> the writing is clear and precise; the abundant detail illumines rather than obscures. In later novels detail often becomes excessive and seems only tedious repetition." Notes Dell's prodigious output. While writing novels, "his career as editor, reviewer, essayist, playwright, and literary historian was astonishingly productive." Summarizes Dell's contribution as novelist, editor, literary historian, and literary personality.

1099 SPAYDE, JON. "The Midwest," in <u>The Literary Guide to the</u>
      <u>United States</u>. Edited by Stewart Benedict. New York:
      Facts on File, pp. 87-128 [105-108, 113-14, 120].
         Discusses the literary image of the Midwest and the his-
      torical reality. Names Dell as "the promoter and critical
      patron" of the Chicago Renaissance. Discusses the young
      group of writers which included Masters, Sandburg, Lind-
      say, Lewis, Anderson, and Dell. Tells about Dell's meet-
      ings with Arnold Bennett. In his attention to the detail
      of rural towns, Dell was an example to the writers of the
      WPA State Guides.

INDEX